Poor Richard's Rich Life:
Positive Psychology and Ben Franklin

By John J. Rooney, Ph.D.

Authors' profits will be donated to
La Salle University, Office of Development
1900 W. Olney Ave.
Phila. PA 19141

Acknowledgements

I would like to dedicate this book to my son, John, who, in many aspects of his life, reflects the entrepreneurial spirit of Ben Franklin.

I want to thank the many members of my extended family, my colleagues at La Salle University and my friends at Fort Washington Estates Retirement Community for their support and encouragement including Cathy Bolton, Jon Caroulis, Margaret Dorsey, Elaine Elezko, David Falcone, Lyman Hanson, Keith Heinly, John Keenan, Thomas McCarthy, Don McDermott, MaryAnn Miller Messana, Dolores Miller, Gerard Molyneaux, John Rossi, John Seydow, Barbara Santone, John A. Smith, Donna Tonrey. I also want to acknowledge the professional editorial assistance of David Tabatsky.

ISBN: 978-1-62249-624-2

Published by
Biblio Publishing
Columbus, Ohio
BiblioPublishing.com

Bio Margaret McManus

Author Chapter 14
Technology to Enrich Your Life

Dr. Margaret (Peg) McManus has been actively involved in the information technology field as it developed from mainframe computers to handheld smart devices. Her interest in Collaborative Learning and Technologies, Information and Instructional Technology, and IT Leadership give her a broad perspective regarding technology for Positive Psychology. Dr. McManus has served both as a faculty member and an academic administrator in her 32-year career at La Salle University. As a faculty member, she achieved the rank of Professor in the Department of Mathematics and Computer Science teaching courses in programming languages and databases. As an academic administrator, she served as the Associate Provost for Graduate Studies, the Associate Dean in the School of Arts and Sciences, the Interim Dean of Arts and Sciences, the Executive Director of Graduate Studies, and the Director of the M.S. programs in Computer Information Science and in Information Technology Leadership. She has given numerous talks and panel discussions at academic and professional conferences as well as on public television, for the Mayor's Commission on Technology, the CIO Forum, the Council of Colleges of Arts and Sciences, and the Council of Graduate Schools. She holds a Bachelor's degree in Mathematics from Immaculata University, a Master's degree in Computer Science from The Pennsylvania State University, and a Ph.D. in Computer and Information Sciences from Temple University. She also participated in the Management Development Program at the Harvard Institute for Higher Education. She is actively involved in the Philadelphia Chapter of the Society for Information Management (SIM) and its philanthropic arm, the Philadelphia Philanthropic Society for Information Management Inc. She has been honored with the IT Leadership Award from La Salle University.

Table of Contents

Chapter 1.
Introduction

Origin of the Book

When I first decided to write this book my friends asked me why? And what was I going to say? It was hard to know my own motives. It's the pleasure a teacher gets when helping a student accomplish something worthwhile. Why not draw on my long career as a psychologist and my own life experience and pass the best of it on to readers?

My Life Experience

First, some background. I never expected to attend college. None of my friends and only a handful of students from my high school would do so. I was 17 and needed to get a job. I soon found out, however, that the law said one must be 18 to take on full-time work. My parents went into a huddle and decided they could scrape up enough money for one year of college. When the year was up, I discovered that, with summer and part-time jobs, a bit of financial aid and encouragement from parents, I could continue my studies. What luck! I was undecided on a major, but selected chemistry since I was intrigued by the possibilities of science from my high school experience and visits to science exhibits at the Franklin Institute. I believed science could change the world! it has. Sometimes even for the better!

In college, my introduction to psychology opened my mind to a new world. We could utilize the methodology of science to better understand and improve ourselves and our society. But a career in psychology was out of reach. The preparation for it took too long and was too costly.

Like most of my generation, plans for the future were interrupted by WWII. I was accepted for Navy flight training and became a flight instructor after I completed it. During my time as a pilot, I saw numerous instances in which psychologists were introducing improvements and noted possibilities for many more. Research in selection and training, communication, and the design of controls and instruments were all producing valuable findings, and I was experiencing their value firsthand.

During that time, I lived and worked with college students from all over the country, and we often discussed how America should change after the war. We experienced the effects of segregation, saw women taking on new roles and argued over the place America should take in the international community.

Starting in psychology

After the war, I completed my degree in chemistry (the college did not have a major in psychology), worked for several months in a laboratory (official job classification, "junior chemical engineer"), but decided to make the move to psychology. I enrolled in a part-time graduate psychology program at Temple University and obtained a job as a counselor at a Veteran's Guidance Center-one of many that the VA had set up to assist veterans in their educational and career plans. Although the agency had serious limitations, I envisioned unlimited possibilities for such counseling as more educational opportunities opened and countless students would be seeking professional guidance in planning for satisfying careers.

I was offered a position as in Instructor at La Salle College. In addition to teaching, I developed a summer program for incoming students in which they took a one-day series of aptitude, interest and personality tests. Results were discussed with them and used as a springboard to consider possible careers and courses to look into. It may well have been the first such program in the country. Students were enthusiastic about it, and that class had a high retention rate.

During my lengthy career at La Salle (70 years), I was enthusiastically involved in teaching, counseling, administration, developing new programs, consulting, conducting research and writing. I was energized by the work I was doing, the people I worked with and the collaborative nature of the university. I found positive relationships with students, faculty, administrators, staff and alumni. I hope readers will find similar satisfaction in their work. With this in mind, I am drawing on my life experience as well as relevant research in psychology and related sciences in my recommendations.

The attraction of science

To me, the appeal of psychology is congruent with the appeal of all science. Science enhances our lives in two major ways. One is by feeding our intellectual curiosity. Filling us with wonder and providing us with a never-ending challenge. The other is by applying its discoveries for the benefit of mankind.

Astronomy, for one, is a fascinating science, opening our minds to our entire physical universe from planets and stars to galaxies and black holes so distant as to bogle the mind. Paleontology and related sciences study the history of life on earth based on fossil findings of various species including near ancestors of humans. Both exercise our intellectual muscles, neither, however, has much immediate practical value.

Biology and chemistry are equally fascinating sciences. In addition, they make a significant contribution to improving our health and longevity. Still, far too many people reject, ignore, or distrust the recommendations of medical science as we have seen all too evidently in our response to the COVID 19 pandemic.

Psychology and other behavioral sciences are also a source of progress for each of us and for our society. Here even more people discount empirical findings and depend on ideas passed from generation to generation and modified by their own limited experience in relating to people and addressing societies pressing social problems. They know a lot of psychology; some useful; some partially right or misunderstood, and some completely at odds with the evidence.

Ben Franklin As Scientist

Benjamin Franklin was a scientist who was well ahead of his time. He valued the wisdom of the past: religion, the classics and philosophy, but thought their teachings required modification based on the systematic empirical observations of science. He believed that our understanding of human behavior would especially benefit from this approach. He also emphasized the practical value of psychological research, contending its judicious application would bring about substantial improvements in our lives.

In writing this book, I draw on the life of Ben Franklin to illustrate how his embracing positive psychology enabled him to move from a member of the working class to become one of the most respected and influential man of his times.

A changing perspective

Ben Franklin used his talents to build a better world. Psychology finds that the successful life, i. e. the happiest life, comes not from outdoing others but from developing positive relationships with them. And the current Corona virus pandemic is a wakeup call to the need to work together to address societal problems. We are all interconnected. So, discrepancies between agencies in our society that impact two groups usually alert us that something more general is wrong. Police abuse, a more serious and more obvious problem for Blacks, is an outgrowth of a more general culture of abuse in the process of controlling behavior; improved education for Blacks adds more talent to meet national needs and helps reduce the number of unemployed and underemployed people. Every step of the life cycle, from prenatal health and childcare to retirement communities and nursing homes requires our attention in order to build a better community for all of us.

So, in addition to emphasizing how a knowledge of positive psychology can enrich our individual lives, I have tried to place it in the context of community and social relations.

Overview

I draw on our knowledge of our brain and related biological substructure as a major source of cognitive development including memory, problem solving and decision making, and consider how judicious use of tools and technology can enhance them. Additionally, I discuss the role of emotions, both positive and negative in our personal and social development. Throughout, I consider how psychological knowledge can influence morality in

5

our relationships with people and in building a better society.

In all of this, I draw on Ben Franklin as a striking example of someone who embraced positive psychology and used it to accomplish so much during his life.

Today, we need people like Franklin more than ever.

Chapter 2.
Benjamin Franklin-Our First Psychologist

Introduction

One way we learn is from the example of other people. You could hardly do better than to select Benjamin Franklin as a path to self-improvement.

Ben was one of the most fascinating men ever to walk this earth. Born into a working-class family; practically no formal education; yet became one of the most wealthy, influential, loved, and respected men of all time. Europeans dubbed him "the best president America never had." His excess energy made him an indefatigable worker, but it was, his enthusiasm for life and his insatiable intellectual curiosity that most distinguished him. Throughout his long and productive career, he was always observing, reading, discussing, testing, questioning.

He has been honored as a scientist, diplomat, businessman, entrepreneur, patriot, and administrator, but his contributions to psychology are so striking that he deserves to be recognized as one of the founders of this field. He counseled us, "Learn to know people, thyself, especially." His life and work reflect this advice and provide a font of psychological wisdom invaluable to anyone desiring to understand that complicated creature the human person and to enjoy a more successful, more fulfilling life.

His Approach to Life

By now, you may be thinking, "How did he accomplish so much?" In his own progress, Ben drew on three main sources: 1. the wisdom of the past through reading (especially the Bible and classic works), and by seeking advice from older, experienced successful people; 2. the ideas of his contemporaries, including leading figures in religion, science, philosophy, politics and business; and 3. his own experience, particularly his systematic observation, experimentation and reflection.

In implementing your own self-improvement program, Ben's perspective provides a valuable guide. You already have a great deal of "wisdom of the past" from your own experience. Improvement does not require discarding it but reexamining it and modifying it based on contemporary findings. Remember too, contemporary research doesn't provide final answers to life's questions. It is, instead, the best we can offer today. So, be yourself while you are becoming a better self!

His youth and development

Let's move back to Ben as a boy in Boston. He faced life with an inquisitive mind and an adventurous spirit. He wanted to accomplish something worthwhile in life but had no idea how to do so. His father, a candlemaker, introduced him to various craftsman and their work as a way of helping him find a career. He decided to serve as an indentured apprentice with his older brother, James, a printer. Ben was a voracious reader who envisioned possibilities for testing his ideas by interacting with a wide group of readers.

At age 17, he broke his indentured contact with his brother and set sail for Philadelphia in search of a successful career. Perhaps more significantly, he set out a plan for his life-to become a "virtuous and manly person". Many of us wish to improve, but most of us end up with the equivalent of broken New Year's resolutions. Ben set out a systematic procedure to implement his plan and stuck to it. He admitted he was never able to accomplish all he wanted but considered himself a better man from his attempt. Today, psychologists have rediscovered Ben's system and use it with considerable success. You can do it too!

He selected 13 virtues to work on. We can look forward to discussing them later in this chapter.

Early in his career, Ben recognized he could accomplish more, both in personal development and in improving his community, by working collectively. Consequently, he gathered together a group of tradesman, artisans and merchants who shared his goals. Calling themselves the Junto, they met regularly to discuss an informative article or book, or a pertinent presentation by a member or guest. But it was more than a stimulating discussion group. They carried out social-improvement projects and those designed to aid their own businesses. It should be no surprise that Ben's later well-recognized talent in politics and international relations was first formed by his interactions with fellow members of his Junto.

Development as a scientist

Although Ben valued and respected conventional wisdom, he realized that much of it was flawed and required questioning and testing in order to verify it, modify it or reject it. This is the methodology of science, and Franklin utilized it constantly, particularly in looking for solutions to practical problems.

Moreover, he tested his ideas by publishing them, often using humor to spice them for readers and encourage responses. One example, consistent with his "early to bed..." recommendation, was a piece he published after debating the merits of a new oil lamp compared with candlelight with a group of friends. They had argued over the cost of oil versus candle wax and the quality of light from each. In his article he writes that he went to bed that night with that question on his mind and was awakened early morning, much surprised to find, that while neither candle nor oil lamp was burning his room was filled with light. His reaction follows: *This event has given rise in my mind to several serious and important reflections. I considered that, if I had not been awakened so early in the morning, I should have Slept six hours longer by the light of the sun, and in exchange have lived six hours the following night by candle-light; and, the latter being a much more expensive light than the former, my love of economy induced me to muster up what little arithmetic I was master of, and to make some calculations, which I shall give you, after observing that utility is, in my opinion the test of value in matters of invention, and that a discovery which can be applied to no use, or is not good for something, is good for nothing.* Franklin, a former candle maker well aware of the cost of wax, then estimates (perhaps with a bit of hyperbole) that a total of 64 million pounds of wax could be saved in Paris over a six-month period if its citizens would follow his advice-"Early to bed and early to rise..."

You may be familiar with the Franklin Stove, another example of his early advocacy for conserving energy. After studying the design of a typical stove, he concluded that it was inefficient- too much heat was lost up the flue. He redesigned it so more heat would warm the room rather than be wasted. Variations of it are still in use today.

Although he is best known as a scientist, for his discovery that lightning is a form of electricity, that finding was initially rejected by most of the scientific community. Rather than become embroiled in lengthy disputes with his critics, he devoted his time to additional research. His findings were soon confirmed by scientists in Europe leading to a recognition of the importance of his work.

Ben was always investigating some phenomenon that he encountered, from how to convert his chair to a stepladder to how to extend the reach of his arm. Think of all his discoveries as a result. Have you ever used swim fins? He constructed them after musing about how to become a better swimmer. Are you aware of the influence of the Gulf Stream? In his sailings to and from Europe, Ben occupied much of his time measuring the currents. He mapped and publicized the Gulf Stream and showed how ship's captains could cut considerable time from Atlantic crossings by taking advantage of this knowledge. He also observed the Aurora Borealis or "Northern Lights" during these ocean trips and added to sciences understanding of their nature.

One of his contributions to meteorology was his discovery that storms need not travel in the direction of prevailing winds. Even today, along our East Coast, we call storms "Northeasters" when wind is whipping at us from the northeast even though they arrive from the west.

Another of his devices we use widely today is bifocal glasses. Franklin developed them because he felt limited by spectacles of his day. Ben joked about how much this helped at dinner parties in Paris, enabling him to both see his food and study expressions of others during dinner conversation.

No matter where we look, we encounter examples of his work. Your kitchen refrigerator owes its existence to principles of refrigeration discovered by Franklin in collaboration with John Hadley of England.

You probably have not heard of a musical instrument he deigned, called the glass armonica. You may, however, have experimented with producing musical notes by rubbing moist fingers against glasses filled with varying amounts of water. Ben used this phenomenon to develop a new musical instrument. He fitted a series of graduated glass disks on a spindle which could be rotated by a foot treadle. It produced a wide variety and a rich quality of tones when moistened fingers stroked the <u>disks</u>. Ben's armonica acquired considerable popularity in Europe, with Mozart and Beethoven composing music for it.

Role in the Scientific Community

In addition to his own scientific work, Ben kept informed on what others had found, speculated about future advances, and influenced ideas of other intellectuals in his own generation and those to come. Among spectators gathered in Paris to watch the first liftoff of a hot air balloon, he speculated about its significance for aviation. What marvels, he wondered, might we see in the future?

Among the most publicized phenomena of Franklin's time were demonstrations by Anton Mesmer, a doctor who claimed to cure diseases and produce amazing effects through a method he called animal magnetism. He contended that an invisible force travels between two persons just as the force of a magnet reaches a nearby metal.

Because of controversy surrounding Mesmer's widespread popularity in France, King Louis XVI convened a committed to investigate the dispute. Franklin, who served on the committee, rejected Mesmer's claims. He considered the power of suggestion as the likely cause for any improvement that occurred. This is the generally accepted position today where we see hypnotism (mesmerism) as a potentially valuable treatment, but still not sufficiently predictable.

You may not associate Franklin with the theory of evolution (one of the most influential discoveries in centuries), but his contributions are worthy of note. Piqued by the far-flung locations of fossils of fish and shellfish he wondered, "How did they get so far inland"? Two possible explanations occurred to him: either oceans had at one time covered more land, or the land had shifted considerably over time.

He noted how the human population in America was increasing rapidly and speculated about what it would mean for its future- an early contribution to demography. He also observed the wide variety of species of plants and animals, including how some flourished and others died out.

As a Psychologist

This seems like a good time to consider a main point of this book. Many of Ben's contribution to physical and biological science, like his investigation of hypnosis and his speculations on evolution, advanced our understanding of psychology as well. His recognition as a prominent physical scientist is based not on his formal education or a position in a university or laboratory, but on work he did and discoveries he made. His inquiring mind constantly saw questions to investigate and problems to solve. In a similar way, he functioned as a psychologist, reflecting on his own behavior, and working to adjust it; observing others and seeing how their behavior could be influenced. He tested these findings empirically, modified them as necessary, kept a record of his results and shared them with his contemporaries. Although he lived well before psychology emerged as a science, the reality is, Ben Franklin should be recognized as our first psychologist, particularly for his contributions to positive applied psychology.

Self-Improvement Program

At age 20, he began a program of self-improvement, realizing that it would be difficult to break habits he had already developed and replace them with more desirable, more satisfying habits. Yet, he believed he could do it. It is just as important, he held, for people to devote time and effort to themselves as to their jobs.

First, he began giving more attention to his physical health through exercise, hygiene, a nutritious diet heavy in vegetables, moderation in alcohol, a healthy environment, including plenty of fresh air, and a minimal use of medicine.

He maintained considerable interest in religion, particularly in how people might be changed by it, sometimes dramatically. He was drawn to charismatic preachers who moved congregations, including one case in which Ben was initially inclined to give a few copper coins to support his cause. As the sermon grew more and more convincing, he first decided to give some silver and finally to part with gold. In another instance, he warned a friend not to bring any money as he would surely give it away. His friend followed his advice but was so moved during the service that he begged Ben to loan him money to contribute.

Although, intellectually, Franklin seems to have been a Deist who was influenced more by reason and experience than authority and tradition, he did not reject religion. Rather he respected it and looked to it as a source of wisdom and guidance. We will elaborate on this in a later chapter.

In coming up with a list of traits that he sought to develop in himself, he labeled them "virtues" a term consistent with religious usage and with contemporary positive psychology. He also refers to psychology as "the moral science."

In his autobiography, Franklin lists thirteen virtues he wanted to cultivate: temperance, silence, order, resolution, frugality, industry, sincerity, justice, moderation, cleanliness, tranquility, chastity and humility.

Ben worked on each virtue, focusing on one per week for 13-week period. By the end of each week he felt he was well on his way and so proceeded to the following virtue.

He worked on Temperance first, because as he said, "it tends to procure that coolness and clearness of head, which is so necessary where constant vigilance was to be kept up." Thus, in the first week, he made every effort to be temperate, exercising moderation and self-restraint.

Every evening he recorded his progress.

After each week, when he saw he had improved, he moved on to the next virtue, until he had focused on all of them. After one 13-week period, he repeated this process. Upon completing his project, he commented: "And like him who, having a garden to weed, does not attempt to eradicate all bad herbs at once, … but works on one of the beds at a time, and, having accomplish'd the first, proceeds to a second."

Learning from Others

He looked for and took advantage of what others told him about his manner of interacting with them. As a case in point, he mentions an incident from a boat trip he cites in his autobiography.

At Newport we took in a number of passengers for New York, among which were two young women, companions, and a grave, sensible, matron-like Quaker woman, with her attendants. I had shown an obliging readiness to do her some little services, which impress'd her I suppose with a degree of good will toward me; therefore, when she saw a daily growing familiarity between me and the two young women, which they appear'd to encourage, she took me aside, and said: "Young man, I am concern'd for thee, as thou has no friend with thee, and seems not to know much of the world, or of the snares youth is expos'd to; depend upon it those are very bad women; I can see it in all their actions, and if thee art not upon thy guard, they will draw thee into some danger; they are strangers to thee, and I advise thee, in a friendly concern for thy welfare, to have no acquaintance with them." As I seem'd at first not to think so ill of them as she did, she mentioned some things she had observ'd and heard that had escap'd my notice, but now convinc'd me she was right. I thank'd her for her kind advice, and promis'd to follow it. When we arriv'd at New York, they told me where they liv'd, and invited me to come and see them; but I avoided it, and it was well I did; for the next day the captain miss'd a silver spoon and some other things, that had been taken out of his cabbin, and, knowing that these were a couple of strumpets, he got a warrant to search their lodgings, found the stolen goods, and had the thieves arrested.

Another way he obtained feedback from others was through his writings. Often, he tested ideas by publishing them under an assumed name and getting comment from his readers. In that way, he avoided acquiring a reputation based on some idea or approach he was experimenting with.

He recognized the value of a good reputation. Wanting others to know they could trust him and depend on him, he conducted himself accordantly. He also realized that you are judged by your associates. They influence you, and influence people's opinion of you. In the light of this, he avoided some people and their lifestyle, even when it had a strong appeal.

Becoming a Man of Influence

Although a natural leader, he learned from attempting to persuade others to join him in a cause that it was better to downplay his own role, rather than present himself as an authority. Consequently, he would first get several like-minded, influential people to agree to join in the effort and permit him to use their names. Then, when he approached others for support, he referred to himself as "representing a group of citizens who had asked him to speak for them." Using the Socratic method, he would listen to them, draw them out, get them involved and give credit for what they had done. He was well aware that a group of "movers and shakers" can accomplish far more than a most talented person working alone.

If you are at all acquainted with Benjamin Franklin, you know he considered wealth almost as important as health, and encouraged everyone to work, save and invest to improve their finances. He recognized that as wealth increases, so does influence. Moreover, he believed that money, like time, should not be wasted but should be used to produce something of value. This psychological approach to economics, emphasizes money's role as a tool to change people and their institutions. Think of how Franklin used knowledge of human psychology, wealth, and influence to get things done. From organizing a town watch, starting a fire company and paving streets, to founding a university and raising an army, Franklin was able to accomplish things. And he was able to obtain public support and money. He used a variety of methods depending on the project and who benefitted most from it: subscription, taxation, contributions, insurance, volunteerism.

Let's move next to another area of psychology that intrigued Franklin, and one that is still a major challenge today- prejudice. He saw evidence of it all around him, was aware of it in himself and attempted to understand and change it.

Prejudice

English colonists generally disliked and were suspicious of other nationalities, particularly Dutch and Germans. Although Philadelphia (the City of Brotherly Love) was relatively tolerant of religious differences, there was still considerable religious animosity, including concerted efforts to close the one Catholic church. Slavery was widely accepted, as was the indentured system and the inferior status of women.

As we might expect, the worst hostility was directed toward American Indians. Franklin tried to understand and ameliorate it. In particular, he thought it would help to try to see things from the perspective of others, as illustrated by his observations on American Indians. The following is an example of Franklin's view of such prejudice:

Savages we call them, because their Manners differ from ours, which we think the Perfection of Civility. They think the same of theirs. Perhaps if we could examine the Manners of different Nations with Impartiality, we should find no People so rude as to be without Rules of Politeness, nor any so polite as not to have some Remains of Rudeness. He goes on to mention their way of listening thoughtfully to a speaker and expressing their own ideas clearly and carefully. He contrasts this with discussion in the English Parliament and in English culture in general, in which people rudely interrupt speakers, rush to get their say and ignore most of the ideas of others.

Consider Franklin's most daunting diplomatic accomplishment- obtaining desperately needed financial and military support for the American Colonies from France. His sensitivity to complexities of French culture and awareness of the role of informal social relations in paving the way for governmental decisions provided the key to opening their minds and their treasury.

Summary and Recommendations

I think of Benjamin Franklin as a person most of us can relate to as a role model. With no inherited wealth or power, he rose to a position of prominence by deciding how he wanted to improve. His process for personal development is nothing secret or esoteric. He spelled it out clearly, including pitfalls he encountered as well as his successes. This does not imply his system is easy. It is comprehensive and complex, ranging from nutrition, exercise and sleep, to controlling emotions, overcoming prejudices, improving memory, reasoning and decision making, working effectively with individuals and groups and doing it all with the joy that comes from having a meaningful purpose in your life. I invite you to come along as we consider how to profit from his wisdom.

I admire him, not only for his personal successes, but for what he contributed to our understanding of the world of science and of human relationships, and for his role in bringing about vast societal change. Throughout his life he reached out to people including those with different customs and from other cultures, learning from them and understanding how to work effectively with them.

In contrast with some who are skillful at influencing people, he was open with what he found to be effective and freely shared this with others, believing that learning principles and skills in human relations would benefit everyone.

In your own life, when confronted with a thorny decision, you might want to ask yourself, "What would Ben Franklin do?"

Planning for the Future

And Ben's planning for the future also considered the distant future- including the times we live in today. In his will, he specified that 2,000-pound sterling be divided equally between Boston and Philadelphia and invested. Then, 100 years after his death, part of this money should be disbursed, with the remainder given out a century later, i.e. 1990. He earmarked the money to provide training for apprenticeships but allowed flexibility to accommodate changes that would occur over time. Today, what remains of Franklin's bequest is worth about $6.5 million.

Chapter 3.
Psychology in Action

My Introduction

The conditions I experienced and the challenges I faced when getting ready for life as an adult were markedly different from Franklin. In 1940, the Great Depression had been dragging on forever. As a 17-year-old high school senior faced with decisions about what to do after graduation, I was floundering.

Why not seek advice from one of our faculty, almost all priests with years of higher education? I picked one who seemed particularly astute and set up an appointment. Our conversation went like this:

Me." Father, I really don't have any idea what to do after high school, do you have any suggestions"?

Priest. Have you thought of becoming a priest"?

Me. (taken aback). No, No, I don't have a vocation to be a priest."

Priest. "Well, you've been working hard, just take it easy during the summer and something will turn up."

My disappointment at his inability to help was tapered somewhat by a lesson it taught me- someone may be a giant in theoretical knowledge but short in practical know-how.

Somehow, on the Tuesday after Labor Day, there I sat-in a college classroom, not quite sure how I got there or what to expect. It happened because one requirement for the job my family had lined up for me (and for almost all jobs at that time) was to be at least 18. My parents figured out a way they could scrape up enough money (with help from a partial scholarship) to pay tuition for one year (no one thought of taking out a loan in those days).

I had expected college to be a sequel to high school: more facts and more tests, but more difficult. Instead, it opened my eyes and started opening my mind. As one of my classmates joked: "this place isn't fair; they make you think." The place- La Salle College and "they" - its faculty. They functioned as an inclusive rather than an exclusive group, inviting students to participate in and be a part of college life. They popped up everywhere: joining in bull sessions in hallways after class, seeking our opinions, encouraging criticism, challenging us, laughing, and joking and clearly enjoying their work. They joined us in pick-up basketball and softball games, helped us obtain part-time jobs, supported our social activities and invited us to participate in opportunities Philadelphia and surroundings provided to widen our horizons.

I had made my decision to major in chemistry after a brief session with an advisor. Brother Felix, an elderly man, skinny as a greyhound, with a protruding belly, white goatee, and a cap, like ones used to cover a tonsure, perched on back of his pate, greeted me cordially. "Well now, what do you want to major in"? I admitted I really didn't have any idea. He followed up with, "what subjects did you like in high school"? After a pause for thought. I said, "well, I kinda liked chemistry." "Good!" he concluded. Chemistry it is! So much for career counseling!

While I came to appreciate science, with its empirical approach, the curriculum provided a broader menu to satisfy one's taste for knowledge. Literature, history, sociology and philosophy all stimulated my intellectual curiosity. One predominant question hung over my head, however "What good are they in a practical sense"? Chemistry prepared me for a job; none of the others did.

It may surprise you to hear that La Salle had no psychology department in those days. Like other Catholic colleges, psychology was taught in our philosophy department, typically by faculty who emphasized ideas from Aristotle, Plato and Socrates, particularly as interpreted by Thomas Aquinas.

Luckily, a philosophy professor who introduced me to psychology focused instead on contemporary findings. Emphasizing their pragmatic value, he cited numerous ways psychology could be applied to our lives and potential careers on the horizon. He opened a fascinating new world to me. I realized you could apply scientific methodology to studying human behavior.

Of his many memorable examples, one sticks to my mind. He often stressed that psychology, while effective in helping you reach your goals, cannot tell you which goals you should opt for: values also come into play. You can employ psychology for good or ill. His memorable example? You might use it to develop a healthy relationship with women or learn ways to seduce them. Inevitably, several of us learned an unintended lesson.

What then had I learned in college so far? Mainly, that the world was full of opportunities, that I had so much yet to learn and more potential than I had thought. And some kind of career in psychology might be possible.

WWII. Navy Flight Training and Psychology

Selection and classification

World War II is still the most prominent example of the widespread utilization of psychology in response to the challenges of the time. Psychologists designed much of the assessment process employed in selecting prospective pilots, as well as America's huge program of selection and classification required for such a vast military buildup-probably history's most successful mass application of psychology. I encountered a sample of this prior to acceptance into flight training and at several stages along the way. In addition to a rigid physical, I recall being checked for depth perception, balance, and ability to maintain equilibrium while spinning in a chair.

The selection process also featured an interview with a naval officer who was not a psychologist. What form it took depended on his inclination that day. One of my new friends described his unorthodox experience: Interviewer. "Tell me, what have you done to make us think we should accept you for flight training?

"Well...uh...er..I did a lot of work on model airplanes."

"What! You expect the Navy to give you a $30,000 education because you play with model airplanes?

"Well...uh... I wanna fight Japs!"

"Good! That's what we're looking for.

In addition to large scale assessment, psychologists were called on to devise ways of selecting candidates for duty requiring complex, unusual talents. Tests developed for our newly formed Office of Strategic Services (OSS), forerunner of our CIA, exemplify this. Candidates were scrutinized and rated on their skill, ingenuity and clear headedness while negotiating a three-day series of demanding tasks. In one, they are subject to interrogation after being caught rummaging through a high-ranking officer's desk. How would they handle this? Could they remain calm, think fast, and come up with a plausible story? Or did they fall apart? In another test, candidates, must supervise two assistants in completing a construction job in a limited time. Both assistants, however, are confederates of the psychologists. One has difficulty understanding directions, works at a snail's pace and repeatedly raises asinine questions. The other is an "eager beaver" making new mistakes faster than previous ones can be corrected. This task proves impossible to complete in time. It must have looked like a Jackie Gleason/Art Carney television skit! But what was the real test? How did he function in this frustrating situation? Was he able to control his emotions, retain his judgment and persist with the job? Or did he punch one of his helpers, fire them both or just quit (incidents that actually occurred!).

German military psychologist first tried this type of assessment on a large scale and British psychologists soon followed.

Training

Psychologists worked with our military to improve traditional training, modify it for the vast numbers involved, and speed up the process. In my nearly two years of flight training and several months as a primary flight instructor, I saw a variety of ways in which psychologists participated, including at least one who went through flight training with us to experience it for himself.

One welcome change began during pre-flight training at Chapel Hill where they stressed physical conditioning: calisthenics, football, basketball, soccer, boxing, wrestling, gymnastics, hand-to hand combat, swimming, and running an obstacle course. Somewhere along the way, however, Dr. Edmund Jacobsen, a pioneer in research on progressive muscle relaxation, convinced Navy officials that ability to overcome stress and tension was just as important to a pilot as physical fitness. Thus, partway through my time at Chapel Hill, relaxation sessions replaced calisthenics. Instead of working out in the gym, we relaxed on our bunks with a mantra blaring from a loud- speaker, "now your left foot is relaxing…" now your left calf is relaxing" … We joked that its main value consisted of getting us out of calisthenics. In truth, I regularly use this practice, encourage others to use it and follow subsequent developments in this important area of applied psychology. In addition to muscle relaxation, several other approaches are utilized today for stress reduction including controlled breathing, visual imagery, yoga, mindfulness, and meditation. I discuss these more fully elsewhere.

Navy psychologists made a dramatic change in introducing students to flying. Most of us had never been in an airplane before, and media reports, highlighting airplane disasters and dramatizing flight's dangers had raised our apprehension level.

Psychologists quickly wondered, why did flight instructors follow a tradition of making neophytes first flights harrowing ones, "putting them through the wringer" and "toughening them up.?" They found this practice increased anxiety, made learning more difficult and caused more students to wash out. When instructors substituted a more positive approach, students became more proficient more quickly and developed more confidence in their skills.

Human factors psychology

It made a difference! I saw a sample of their work in aviation and realized much more was entailed. Flight instruments were difficult to read and interpret with needed speed and accuracy; controls were often confusing and hard to manipulate with precision. In one phase of training, we had just completed a series of flight lessons in a plane in which you pushed a lever located by your left hand to lower your landing gear. We next moved to a plane in which a similar lever in the same location released a bomb. They called it "pilot error." It was poor design.

Redesigning an aircraft often starts with feedback from pilots. In one case psychologists asked us, "Is having only one white light on the tail of a plane responsible for mistakes in recognizing other planes and coordination with them"? At first none of us would admit making any mistakes, but eventually we conceded it was a problem. Replacing a single light with three colored lights, minimized such mistakes.

The Link Trainer made a major contribution to flight training. This device enabled students to simulate maneuvers and have them critiqued while remaining firmly grounded. Hearing an instructor say, "you just crashed into a mountain," may be discouraging, but with simulated flight, a student can walk away from his lesson, learn from his mistakes and try again.

Psychology and policy

At top levels of administration, knowledge of psychology can be crucial. One instance involved relative emphasis placed on safety and daring. At base where I served, Bunker Hill, Indiana, they maintained an excellent safety record, prompting top brass to wonder if pilots were being too cautious. Another base, Pensacola's "Bloody Barin" at Foley, Alabama had a reputation for encouraging daredevil stunts and recklessness. Its high casualty rate became a public issue when, in 1944, radio and newspaper commentator Walter Winchell took it on as a personal cause. Shortly thereafter, senior officers cracked down on unauthorized maneuvers, flying under hazardous conditions and lack of pilot discipline. Its accident rate declined to a more acceptable level.

Other roles for psychology

Psychologists' roles expanded greatly as war progressed, their expertise being applied to diverse areas, including assessing morale, producing propaganda, and conducting espionage.

World War I provided an earlier instance of psychology's use in morale and propaganda. Edward Bernays, nephew of Freud, who worked closely with President Woodrow Wilson, coined the slogan "Make America Safe for Democracy," to drum up support for American intervention. He geared his "public relations" (a term he preferred to propaganda) to the public's emotions, particularly unconscious ones, and was employed by many American corporations, government agencies, and politicians. His ideas so impressed Joseph Goebbels, Nazi minister of propaganda, that he used them extensively to build support for Hitler.

To sum all this up, in my navy days, I saw numerous ways in which psychology could be of value and began seriously considering a career in it.

Veterans Counseling and College Counseling

Immediately following World War II, America faced the task of transitioning vast numbers of returning veterans to civilian life. Learning a lesson from World War I, when veterans felt neglected and disillusioned, congress passed a law, called the G.I. Bill. It provided extensive benefits to veterans. including free tuition for college or technical training and low interest housing loans. You may recall someone in your family who benefitted from it. For it proved to be one of the most influential laws in American history, lifting a whole generation of Americans from poverty and working class to middle class and beyond. In addition, it gave a better start in life to their children and grandchildren.

A provision of the bill that influenced my life, set up veterans' guidance centers offering educational and vocational counseling. I thought, why not take advantage of it?

I completed a battery of aptitude, interest and personality tests to help in my career planning. After consulting results, my VA counselor told me I should consider engineering. I had, however, become more interested in process than results. I realized my test scores, despite their limitations, provided valuable information about my aptitudes and interests, including how they compared with members of various occupations. I was impressed by the process of career counseling and decided to prepare for a career in it. I completed my degree in chemistry, enrolled in a graduate course in counseling and obtained a position in a VA center at a local college. The VA center where I worked, suffered from inadequate facilities, counselors with little or no training and a poorly organized program; despite this, I had become convinced that career counseling, properly done could be of considerable value.

College counseling

Later, after completing my M.A. degree and beginning my doctoral training, I obtained a faculty position at La Salle College, and helped initiate a counseling program there.

One of our early innovations involved bringing all first-year students to campus during the summer before they started class. Each group spent a full day completing aptitude, interest and personality tests and inventories. A counselor then interviewed each student to discuss educational and career plans and resources we had available to assist students while they were with us. We put our emphasis on positive development during college. In a follow-up survey, students praised the process as helping them get off to a good start. Moreover, first-year classes attained a strikingly high retention rate.

From these evaluations, we also found that students who experienced problems at home did not achieve up to their potential. At this time, nearly all La Salle students were commuters, and first in their families to attend college. Hence, we began inviting parents to accompany students to their campus visit. We answered questions, clarified concerns and enabled them to be more prepared for their new experience. Most parents were happy to participate and be involved in the student's college venture. Today, it is well accepted that a positive attitude in a family has a significant influence on performance in school and at work.

I still imagine what changes might be brought about by incorporating a large-scale program of this type, into our nation's educational system. I believe it would revolutionize American education.

Moving back to our program, we had decided from day one to develop a reputation for providing services to help all students thrive in college, rather than be seen as a remedial service for those experiencing problems. Therefore, we offered programs for students preparing for law school and those competing for prestigious graduate scholarships as well as students who were undecided on a choice of career or struggling with the demands of college life.

During these years, I had worked closely with a friend and colleague, Tom McCarthy. His son and namesake, a history professor at the U.S. Naval Academy, has used our work at La Salle to exemplify the widespread changes taking place throughout the country in psychology, counseling, student affairs administration and higher education in general. His 2018 book, a biography of his father, is entitled, *Developing the Whole Person: A Practitioner's Tale of Counseling, College and the American Promise*. It provides a historical perspective to our work at that time.

Work Habits and Attitudes

While teaching and counseling students, I became convinced that their work habits and attitudes were just as important as ability in determining success in college-and in life beyond college. In the light of this, I chose to investigate this topic for my doctoral dissertation at Temple University. Working with faculty advisors, I developed a test of these traits, administered them to students and followed up to determine how work habits and attitudes affected achievement. Results were clear. Positive attitudes added a significant component to aptitude in determining student performance and persistence. We also found positive attitudes and initiative more important than specific habits of work; that is, not all high performing individuals approached their work in the same way but used a variety of styles in accomplishing it. Furthermore, some students were more motivated by how faculty taught; others had an inherent interest in the subject itself. A combination of both proved most effective.

We can see parallels in other organizations. Administrators who set clear goals and help develop positive attitudes can allow flexibility in how employees get the job done. This approach encourages initiative and ingenuity. Results also suggest that more workers than you might think are invested in their work and require little encouragement from a supervisor, whereas others benefit from attention and recognition.

Two other findings of interest to me: 1. socially active students were more likely to complete college, but no more likely than other students to receive high grades, and 2. Confident students performed a high level.

What does all this tell us? In short, research by psychologists and educators was helping us understand what make for a positive college experience and a successful outcome. I was gratified to be a part of this effort.

Teaching and Learning Positive Psychology

College teaching

In my early teaching experience, I emphasized applied psychology, using textbooks with titles like "How We Influence One Another," "Psychology Applied to Life and Work" and "The Psychology of Adjustment."

At that time, however, the application of psychology to the everyday concerns of people had been given low priority by the powers-that-be in psychology. Professional journals were loath to publish findings in this area, and academic departments in universities counted it of minor worth when evaluating faculty for promotion and tenure. As La Salle moved more into mainstream psychology, our departmental curriculum took a more theoretical direction and dropped most of these applied courses. I then included assignments which required students to use what they learned to improve themselves in some way. Can you guess projects they might select? Stopping smoking, reducing drinking, improving nutrition, developing an exercise routine, spending more time in study were frequent choices. Others decided perform volunteer work or similar helpful activities. They managed to come up with a number of ingenious ways of using their newly acquired knowledge in a positive way.

Another instance of introducing students to ways psychology can improve their lives occurred when our Business School Dean requested a member of our department to design a new course for business students. "What is the most important thing they could learn from psychology in one course," he asked. The outcome was *Psychology of Effective Communication*, a course in which students interacted with one another focusing on understanding each person's point of view. It was an immediate success. Soon sections appeared taught by psychologists or faculty with comparable background in our Management and Communications Departments. Students flocked to it. Moreover, they believed skills they learned helped them relate more confidently to other students and faculty and profit more from discussions in other courses. One class I recall as particularly memorable. An evening class of older students, who triggered a bit apprehensive when they introduced themselves and gave a sample of their background. It included: a tavern owner and a member of AA; a business manager and a union official; a Black militant and Whites with strong racial prejudice: and an ardent atheist along with more than one student with strong religious beliefs. It proved a revelation how well our discussion evolved. Being able to state their beliefs and have others listen attentively offered a positive experience for all of them.

I taught a variety of courses over time in which I included positions advanced by influential behavioral scientists. I consider them harbingers of contemporary positive psychology and want to discuss them next.

Psychoanalytic Contributions

Although the efforts of Sigmund Freud and other psychoanalysts were primarily directed at understanding and treating psychopathology, they have implications for normal functioning as well. Many psychologists contend that there is not a sharp dichotomy between normal functioning and pathology. Instead, they see variation in terms of degree of adjustment along a bell-shaped curve, with seriously maladjusted at one end, unusually well-adjusted at the other and most of us somewhere in middle range. Furthermore, any one person's level of adjustment is not fixed. We all encounter our share of setbacks, conflicts and frustrations and experience anxiety, tension, sadness, worry, moodiness and anger. Don't we see apparently successful people in all walks of life, including government officials, corporate executives, scientists and media celebrities, who experience serious psychological problems? Of course! That means, it is argued, that findings about human functioning that emerge in treating, psychopathology have significant relevance for understanding human behavior in general. Such findings include a recognition that much of our behavior is governed by unconscious motives, and that we are often concerned more with defending our self-concept than with achieving our goals.

It also reminds us that general principals and recommendations are no substitute for individual consultation. If you want to maintain your physical health, you combine healthful day to day activities and regular medical checkups. In the same way, you should supplement a psychologically sound lifestyle by periodic consultations with a mental health professional (preferably one who emphasizes positive psychology).

William James, philosopher-psychologist

One of the earliest psychologists to emphasize positive development was William James, a pragmatic philosopher, trained in medicine and art, experienced in anthropology and fascinated with human experience. His faculty position at Harvard provided a secure base that enabled him to disseminate psychology's findings, including their potential value and precautions required in applying them. His writings were widely circulated and are still of relevance today, including his "Varieties of Religious Experience," and his "Talks to Teachers." In the latter, he stresses a point worth remembering-psychology doesn't teach you how to teach. You learn it by what you already know about children: what interests and motivates them, what works best to spark and sustain their interest and how can you facilitate this. Don't discard this knowledge! "Use psychology to modify it and build on it, not to replace it! And most of all, don't start to view students as objects of psychological study-nothing would interfere more with your teaching.

Have you encountered people who demonstrate their psychological acumen by identifying symptoms they discern in you? "A bit defensive, I see1" "I think you're being somewhat paranoid here! And other such annoying observations. James's advice extends well beyond teacher-pupil relationships. People you interact with, he reminds us, are not subjects for psychological study! You have been with people all your life and have developed a natural style. Your newly-learned psychology should enhance it, not replace it!

One of his many quotable statements consistent with contemporary psychology is, "the greatest discovery of my generation is that human beings can alter their lives by altering their attitudes of mind."

Humanistic psychology

During my early years of teaching and counseling, a new movement, humanistic psychology, grabbed the attention of mental health professionals. How did it affect me? For one, it caused me to be careful not to focus too much on factual information in teaching and on aptitude and interest tests in counseling. Instead, I realized I should be more attuned to developing a positive working relationship. More generally, we all must learn to strike a balance between our task at hand and our relationships with people we are working with to accomplish the task.

But the humanistic movement influenced psychology much more broadly. It is an umbrella term for a group whose focus is on the person rather than technique. A look at three influential members of this movement should give you a sense of its contributions.

Abraham Maslow

Abraham Maslow, in the 1950's, concerned that psychology spent too much effort on pathology, proposed an account of human behavior focusing on human potential and positive development. According to Maslow, a person is always becoming, never remaining static. Moreover, he considered it unfortunate that most of us do not realize potential we possess. As he put it, "the story of the human race is the story of men and women selling themselves short."

He also formulated a hierarchy of needs (or motives). According to this theory, higher needs, including a thirst for learning and an appreciation of beauty, are relatively dormant until lower needs, such as safety, security and belongingness, are reasonably satisfied. Finally, our self-actualization needs emerge. We then direct our efforts to realizing personal potential and self-fulfillment and helping others achieve self-actualization.

This theory generated several questions. Don't people who are hungry still want respect and affection? Would people's positive motives prevail if basic needs were met? What kind of evidence would help determine the theory's validity?

Still, Maslow helped push psychology toward more concern for positive personal development.

Carl Rogers

Even more influential in this movement, and in my own orientation, was psychologist Carl Rogers. Shortly after World War 11, he became director of a veteran's guidance center at the University of Chicago. In addition to providing counseling for veterans, he organized a training program for counselors and conducted research on characteristics of effective counseling.

Rogers presented his conclusions at the 1958 convention of counseling professionals. He claimed conditions that produce effective counseling are conducive to positive relationships in a wide range of situations as well, including teaching, parenting and social work. It also should improve our relationships with friends and colleagues. His position emphasizes relationship rather than techniques. Its underlying assumption is that people possess resources within themselves to make choices, move forward and enjoy a better life. Counselors (and everyone else) who help others feel accepted, respected and understood, facilitate personal growth.

What, then, makes a person effective in relating to people? Rogers identified three characteristics: empathy, authenticity and positive regard. Empathy involves ability to see things from another person's perspective- to "walk in their shoes." An empathic person is an especially good listener, not only attending to the substance of conversations, but to attitudes and feelings. It is what psychotherapist Theodor Reik called "listening with the third ear." Awareness of tone of voice, facial expression, gestures and other bodily cues, helps us recognize how someone is feeling. Active listeners are not silent but seek clarification to be sure they understand, and the person realizes they understand. This contrasts with most conversations, in which one person is speaking, and one thinking of what to say next.

I recall giving basic instructions to a student about how to listen. She was "listening," nodding her head in agreement, smiling and repeating "I see," and "I understand." When I said "Good! Now please tell me what I just said, in your own words," her smile morphed into a look of near panic. After an embarrassing pause, she asked if I would repeat my instructions. It is easy to say, "I understand." It takes concentration to actually understand, and prolonged practice to be truly empathic.

By positive self-regard, Rogers means you respect and value people not for who they are, how they act or how they relate to you or other people, but because you believe each person merits this.

Showing empathy and positive regard for people in our interpersonal interactions may seem to be readily learned. Complicating this learning, however, and making it more challenging, is a third trait-authenticity. People intuitively sense whether you are sincere or acting. Think of how the smile you beam when you meet someone you like differs from one you manage to produce when you are pretending to be glad to see someone.

Consequently, becoming more effective in relating to people requires not only learning more facts and skills, but becoming a better person: one who likes and can relate to people of all backgrounds and all types. This is the challenge for those who want to incorporate positive psychology into their lives. A good surgeon need not be a good person; a good counselor must!

Rogers urged that his theories be tested to determine if they would be supported by empirical evidence. Subsequent studies yielded mostly positive results although they suggest several modifications. One finding shows that how best to relate to people varies with the person and your relationship. For example, confident, well-adjusted people often prefer, and benefit from a more direct, fact-focused interaction. With such achievement-oriented people, emphasize external goals and steps to take to reach them rather than affiliation. In leadership studies, such differences have been labeled task-oriented and person-oriented leadership. Effective leaders give appropriate emphasis to each.

One criticism I agree with is his assumption that people are naturally inclined to develop in a wholesome manner if they experience positive regard. I wish it were so! Positive regard (being loved and respected) is essential, but learning respect for others, self-discipline, limits of self- assertiveness and how to carry out responsibilities is crucial to a child's development. This requires direction, criticism and appropriate punishments as needed in addition to being loved.

Rogers spent many of his later years traveling throughout the world working to reduce tension and conflicts among groups. For his efforts, particularly his contributions to progress in Northern Ireland and South Africa, he was nominated in 1979, for the Nobel Peace Prize. Who received the award that year? Mother Theresa!

Viktor Frankl

Austrian psychiatrist and Holocaust survivor Viktor Frankl, is best-known for his 1946 psychological memoir *Man's Search for Meaning* (originally titled From Death Camp To Existentialism) — a meditation on what killings and degradations in a Nazi concentration camp taught him about our primary motives in life.

His previous training in psychoanalysis had emphasized past experience in determining one's present behavior. While undergoing horrors in a concentration camp however, he concluded one's view of the future mattered more. Those who had a chance to survive Auschwitz, he noticed, had found something to live for, hope for their future, some purpose or meaning in their lives; those who felt hopeless and helpless succumbed quickly. To find purpose in life, he recommended meaningful work, love and courage.

Cognitive-behavioral psychology

Cognitive Behavioral Psychology emphasizes that our thoughts, feelings and actions influence one another. A change in one, produces changes in the other two. It grew from two closely related types of therapy, Rational Emotive Therapy, originating with Albert Ellis in the 1950's and Cognitive Therapy, a product of Aaron Beck's work in the 1960's. Ellis's approach focuses on resolving emotional and behavioral problems by helping change irrational beliefs into more rational ones. Beck believed negative thoughts about the self, the world and the future were the source of depression and low self-concept.

Today, cognitive behavioral approaches are widely used in fostering change. If you want to change the way you feel, change the way you think; to change your thinking, change your behavior. It sounds easy, but it takes work and often benefits from working with a professional with appropriate training.

What do these perspectives of psychoanalysts, humanists, cognitive-behavioral psychologists and William James contribute to us today? Basically, they tell us that although contemporary positive psychology often presents itself as an entirely new movement, it is most useful in conjunction with findings of earlier applied psychologists.

Giving psychology away

In 1969, American Psychological Association president George Miller gave fresh impetus to positive psychology with his presidential address "Psychology as a Means of Promoting Human Welfare," in which he stated "I can think of nothing we could do that would be more relevant to human welfare, and nothing that could possess a greater challenge to the next generation of psychologists, than to discover how best to give psychology away." He pointed out that most urgent problems of our world are human problems whose solutions will require us to change our behavior and our social institutions. How can we do this?

Not so much by how knowledgeable psychologists are about people as by how knowledgeable people are about psychology! As Miller expressed it: "Our responsibility is less to assume the role of experts and try to apply psychology ourselves than to give it away to people who really need it — and that includes everyone."

This is a challenge that Ben Franklin would relish. He was renowned for sharing his scientific discoveries freely, for giving others credit when they had made contributions to it, for encouraging others to work on refining and applying his results and for mobilizing community leaders to utilize scientific research for the common good. Widespread dissemination of knowledge, he emphasized, benefits a whole society.

It's a challenge we face today. How can we use psychology for the common good?

Miller's presidential address spurred many psychologists to action, including founders of today's positive psychology movement.

Chapter 4.
The Positive Psychology Movement

Introduction

It is perhaps no mere coincidence that the modern positive psychology movement received much of its impetus from a professor at the University of Pennsylvania, an institution founded by Benjamin Franklin. Penn's Martin Seligman, a former American Psychology Association president, along with Mihaly Csikszentmihalyi, a professor at Claremont University, first employed the term positive psychology in 1998. These founders of the movement aimed to concentrate on human well-being and conditions that enable people to thrive. They have met with considerable success.

Themes

Here are its five major themes: 1. Focus on the positive. ("Keep your eyes on the prize" and reinforce whatever good you accomplish.) 2, Draw on empirical evidence. (We now know a lot about what enhances a person's life and what detracts from it. Why not utilize it?), 3. Learn from the wisdom of the past. (New empirical research should enhance past wisdom, not replace it!) 4. Incorporate religion's message. (Religion informs us about the nature of the good life. Psychology can help us follow it). 5. Share findings with others. (Every one of us has something to contribute as well as something to learn. Boost your positive development by participating in discussions with stimulating groups.)

Have you noticed how consistent these themes are with Benjamin Franklin's views?

At Penn, its Positive Psychology Center promotes research, training, education, and dissemination of positive psychology. After years in which little work on positive psychology appeared in professional journals, articles on well-being, happiness and mindfulness now regularly appear.

Positive psychology's mission aims to better understand and improve four aspects of human behavior: our positive emotions, our individual traits, our relationships and our institutions. Additionally, it investigates how each of these influences the other.

Positive Emotions

Psychologists studying positive emotions wonder, what makes people content with their past, happy in the present and hopeful for their future?

Most people want to know this. I recall an after-class bull session back in college when I, and a handful of fellow students, were discussing how to achieve happiness in life. A friend argued that science would one day tell us the answer. He pictured himself lounging in a scientifically contoured chair under warm artificial sunlight with temperature and humidity at optimum levels. A gentle breeze wafted over him, carrying a delightful fragrance and soft relaxing music. A lovely panoramic view stretched before him. Exotic food and drink were at hand.

What research has revealed is not even close to that scenario. It tells us you won't find happiness in a state of inertia, or in a constant search for pleasure but in vigorous pursuit of worthwhile accomplishments.

Consider our Declaration of Independence, which Benjamin Franklin had a large hand in writing. It only affirms our inalienable right to the pursuit of happiness, not its attainment!

As Victor Frankl emphasized, human beings, whatever present circumstances, are empowered more by future prospects, our hopes and dreams.

Psychological research on positive emotions enables us to identify our strengths and sustain well-being. Moreover, psychologists are not alone in putting these findings into practice: human resource managers, business consultants, executive coaches and administrators in a wide variety of organizations are using newly discovered approaches to enhance strengths and build teamwork. You can draw on this knowledge yourself. Suppose, for example, you are working for an organization and waiting and hoping for a promotion. What might you do to improve your chances? Most importantly- take charge of your life! Don't just wait and hope. Plan for success! 1. Excel in your present job, especially aspects of it that showcase your talent for higher-level positions. 2 Make higher ups aware of your successes through reports, meetings and informal contacts. 3. Support your immediate supervisor, making her or him look good helps you look good. 4. Select a skill or a subject related to your prospective position and take courses or workshops in it. 5. Cultivate positive emotions; be upbeat, confident and enthusiastic. 6. Nurture positive interactions, not only with your current work group but with those who might support your advancement. Positive on-the-job interaction (formal and informal) is of primary importance here. Even so, church services, community activities, business, fraternal and professional organizations, hobbies, golf, squash racquet ball and related opportunities for networking are worth considering. 7. Note the style of successful administrators at a higher level. How do they dress? How do they conduct themselves? How do they relate to colleagues, subordinates and those above them on the organizational chart? Start modeling after them, selecting features that are in harmony with your values and self-concept. 8. And speaking of modeling- don't forget Ben Franklin!

You will see much more about understanding and utilizing your emotions in a chapter on Positive Emotional Life.

Positive Individual Traits

Stresses focusing on your strengths 1. intellectual strengths, 2. interpersonal strengths, 3. fortitude, 4. vitality, and 5. temperance

We will discuss ways of developing such positive traits in a chapter on personal development.

Positive Relationships

We come across so many examples of partners and teams that accomplish much more working together than as individuals. That's what positive psychology looks for. Ben Franklin had that kind of gift.

Have you ever worked with someone with whom you had great teamwork? You liked one another, complemented one another's talents, encouraged one another and felt upbeat about your mutual accomplishments. I've been there, and it's an exhilarating experience.

In contrast to positive relationships, negative ones often sabotage production and generate discord. You can no doubt think of plenty of instances of it. Here are two I recall that illustrate how much they can damage an organization.

In the first, a psychologist I had worked with, told of a situation from his early years as an organizational consultant. The company's president had retained him to boost performance and morale. Immediately, he encountered a major stumbling block-two vice presidents refused to speak to one another. Their discord had spread to disrupt the entire organization. In discussions with them, he came to understand and appreciate each of their viewpoints and managed to help them resolve their conflict.

The second hit closer to home. My brother, after many years of administrative experience in several locations and a variety of situations with an organization, got caught up in a major policy battle. His firm's chief financial officer embarked on a crusade to cut costs by ruthlessly cutting jobs, an approach you may have encountered dubbed 'slash and burn."

Gerry, a human resource manager who specialized in wage and salary administration, countered by suppling evidence of profits each job produced. Their conflict escalated, consuming more and more of their time and effort, including considerable overtime (the CFO even brought a cot into his office and began to spend his nights there). That kind of dissention can tear an organization apart.

After a time, Gerry considered leaving the company, and I encouraged him to do so. With the benefit of a "headhunter" he found an opening for someone with his qualifications. In his job interview, he asked how much overtime they usually worked. The reply, "Overtime?

What's overtime? We don't know the meaning of that word here!

He started with a higher salary at a more responsible position. More importantly, company environment differed dramatically. People enjoyed their jobs, worked well with one another and took pride in their departments' progress and their company's reputation. Afterward he wondered, "Why did I wait so long to change jobs?

We will cover such issues more fully in a chapter on Interpersonal Relationship, but one valuable habit is worth mentioning here. Reinforce positive relationships! Don't take family, friends and colleagues for granted; make it a point of letting them know you care for and appreciate them. Write thank you notes, share humor, plan celebrations! Keeping positive relationships alive keeps you alive and upbeat.

Positive institutions and societies.

As we see from this last example, some companies create a positive atmosphere. Its members are part of a culture that support personal development and positive relationships. This typified my many years at La Salle (with occasional exceptions), and I hope you are fortunate enough to be employed in "A Great Place to Work," a term that has become popular in describing such places in numerous books and articles. Research on organizations has tried to discover why some organizations are so successful and why employees consider such organizations a great place to work.

Robert Levering, Co-Founder of Great Place to Work writes "A great place to work is one in which you trust the people you work for, have pride in what you do, and enjoy the people you work with."

He adds: "building a great place to work is building relationships people have with their leaders, their work, and their co-workers."   '

Today, companies are often publicly recognized for obtaining high rankings as desirable places to work. Fortune magazine, for instance, rated Google number one for its program of amenities provided to employees. Philadelphia's Inquirer regularly publishes lists of organizations who score high as "great places to work." I always look to find out if one headed by a former student still tops its category. It always does.

Finally, in countries where people are working and are able to both earn a decent living and feel good about their work, we almost invariably find a satisfied society.

A large part of The International Positive Psychology Association's mission is, to "further the science of positive psychology across the globe...". It is an organization with several thousand members from 80 countries.

In a subsequent chapter, *A Healthy Society*, we will elaborate on how countries and their institutions vary in degree of satisfaction and what positive psychology is doing to benefit them.

Several positive psychology interventions have demonstrated activities that work. These typically involve positive thoughts or actions such as thinking of (or keeping a record of) your progress.

Some successful people just naturally operate that way. My favorite example is President George Bush, Sr. He and his wife, Barbara, made it a practice to review at the end of each day, whatever worthwhile things they had been able to accomplish.

A number of studies have participants perform acts of kindness or think of things they are grateful for. The Boy

Scouts have built something like this into its program by requiring members to "do a good deed every day." I remember my early experience which, after a bit of trepidation in the first few days, soon gave a daily boost to my morale as I found opportunities to perform a good deed. Although, I also remember a now classic New Yorker cartoon, which featured a boy scout trying to assist an elderly woman across the street. She is hitting him with her umbrella and complaining "but I don't want to cross the street." Don't be discouraged if your attempts at helping others are sometimes met with the equivalent of getting slapped with an umbrella. It takes practice to combine good intentions with good judgment.

Positive attitudes

Positive experience gives us a little spring in our step; we have always realized our mood can affect how we walk -- slump-shouldered if we are sad, bouncing along if we are happy. Now researchers have shown it works the other way as well - imitating a happy or sad style of walking affects our mood.

A positive attitude at work (or anywhere else) gives you a head start in progressing. Approach each project with the idea that you will do your best to make it a successful experience for everyone involved.

Positive Psychology supports organizational change.

Schools that allow children to flourish, workplaces that foster satisfaction and high productivity and communities that encourage civic engagement are all goals of positive psychology and are all consistent with Ben Franklin's efforts.

The more people, particularly leaders, know about findings of positive psychology the more effective they will be in implementing positive change.

Historically, this positive emphasis has also been characteristic of counseling psychology as exemplified in educational and career counseling) and in organizational psychology. It emphasized positive qualities of students and workers and fostered achievement and satisfaction. It still does. Today, however, a rapid rise in mental health needs and increased financial resources for addressing them have stimulated these professionals to emphasize mental health counseling. Even in college counseling centers, where tradition has been to offer a wide range of services intended to foster positive student development, the treatment of psychopathology now predominates.

Criticisms and Cautions

Although positive psychology has achieved widespread acceptance and influence, the movement has more than its share of critics. I will join their ranks and offer some cautions for readers to consider.

Keep in mind that we are not talking about a monolithic movement, but one with considerable diversity. Consequently, several objections apply to claims and practices of certain practitioners of positive psychology not necessarily the whole movement.

Commonly held claims of concern to me are: 1. That, until now, psychology has largely ignored studying positive or healthy behavior. Even a cursory look at divisions of APA or at content of courses offered in typical undergraduate psychology departments reveals that this is an inaccurate portrayal of reality. I agree, nonetheless, that devoting more of our resources to helping every person thrive is a target worth setting. 2. That positive psychology is more objective, and more scientific than previous methods used in studying healthy functioning, a position that is open to question. It is, however, certainly a desirable focus. 3.That the movement is new and revolutionary. Admittedly, revolutions occasionally occur in science. They offer a completely new perspective to its practitioners, and over time, to all of us. More typically, science (and its applications) evolves step by step, building on previous research and practice. Positive psychology has shifted the emphasis a bit, but it seems quite a stretch to call it revolutionary. 4. The three previous points are used in support of a fourth-that positive psychology provides a valuable contribution to our society and therefore deserves societal support. In making this case, advocates tend to use terms that grab attention (like revolutionary) and make striking claims even where caution is called for. Clearly, psychological research is capable of contributing mightily to improving individual, group and organizational functioning. On the other hand, caution is required in accepting recommendations based on recent empirical findings. Such results are usually, tentative and limited in their applicability, so judgment is required in utilizing them. 5. That psychology has been absorbed with psychopathology. Now the pendulum seems to be swinging in the other direction. Psychologists' efforts (and financial support) are in danger of being diverted from deviant behavior. And this at a time when society is confronting pressing problems with mental illness, addiction, suicide, hate crimes, violence (particularly gun violence), terrorism, racism, and their cumulative effect on society's inability to work together toward positive goals. 6. That positive psychology will be used for societal improvement. Knowledge is power, and we hope psychology will empower people to lead better lives and improve our society. This is what's behind the message, "Give Psychology Away." But what does experience tell us? That people with power, influence and money will use whatever works (including findings of positive psychology) to support their own interests; to gain your support, siphon off your money, and sway your vote.

We have seen how the work of Edward Bernays, "the father of public opinion," was used to support an unpopular war, overthrow the government of a neutral country and help Hitler gain a fanatic following. More recently, prominent psychologists have been employed to study interrogation methods (which many allege are forms of torture) used on suspected terrorists at Guantanamo Bay. 7. Applying psychology improves morality. You will recall a basic tenet of positive psychology- that it will incorporate what religion tells us about leading a good life. Often, psychologists give this crucial (and frequently controversial) issue short shrift. In a subsequent chapter we will explore more fully the relationship between psychology and morality.

Recommendations,

At this stage in our knowledge, I can recommend the following for your consideration:

1. Have meaningful goals and meaningful work. Whether a paid job, a volunteer activity or a hobby about which you are passionate, it means a lot to be able to utilize your talents and satisfy your interests. You can enjoy the

rainbow while soaring toward that pot of gold at its end - in a state of flow.

2. Examine your belief system. A set of beliefs gives purpose to life and serves as a guide to your actions.

3. Develop social connections. Good friends are not only a joy to be with; they have a positive influence on your development by their example, and by feedback they provide about your behavior. Groups are a source of support and a force that can accomplish much more than one person working alone. Ben Franklin and his Junto, and other groups he participated in, are noted instances of how he valued and utilized social connections.

4.Value a rich interior life. Imagination and phantasy are as much a part of life as external reality. People we get to know through biographies and fiction extend our knowledge of people well beyond the limited number we get to know in person.

John Updike contends that we learn more about others and ourselves from vicarious experience of fictional characters than we do from what we actually know about "well-known people."

In addition, imagination and creativity are essential in planning worthwhile endeavors. Albert Einstein has emphasized this in the following quote. "When I examine myself and my methods of thought, I come to the conclusion that the gift of fantasy has meant more to me than any talent for abstract, positive thinking."

5. Cultivate a positive environment. It pays to arrange your home and workplace, so they are attractive and appealing.

Surround yourself with beauty- art, flowers, furnishings, lighting, and a pleasant décor. Learn to look for and appreciate beauty. Frankl, amid horrors of a Nazi death camp, tells of an inmate turning to him and saying "Victor, have you ever seen such a beautiful sunset?"

6. Exercise. Developing a routine of regular exercise makes you feel better and accomplish more. It brings more oxygen to our brain and releases GABA, a neurotransmitter that makes you feel relaxed and in control. It is fine to exercise on your own, but it is better with a friend, your dog, your kids, or a group. It's great if you enjoy it and look forward to it, but most of all -do it!

Ben Franklin was an early proponent of physical fitness. At a time when few people knew how to swim, he learned how on his own and swam all his life. He is a member of the Swimming Hall of Fame.

7. Enjoy the outdoors. If your exercise is typically done indoors, find time to get outside too. Whether on a beach, by a stream or outside your home or workplace, you can benefit from some fresh air, blue skies and sunshine.

8. Eat well. Enjoy nutritious meals and snacks that boost your energy and give you more gusto. Avoid excessive sugary foods that spike your sugar level but leave you tired and irritable shortly thereafter. Eating something that provides a slow, steady lift for your body, such as whole grain food is a better choice. Check ingredients shown on labels when you shop to avoid unhealthy selections. Planning your menu and participating in food preparation adds to its enjoyment. Everyone should have a basic cookbook and benefit from it, but even if you merely toss

a salad, prepare a simple omelet or fix Sunday breakfast it's uplifting to be involved.

9. Sleep. Getting enough sleep maintains your social and emotional intelligence, your focus and your self-control. Sleep deprivation raises stress hormone levels. Don't sacrifice sleep because you have a lot to accomplish. Sleep deprivation diminishes your productivity so much throughout the day that you are better off spending enough time sleeping. A brief nap or period of quite relaxation can be rejuvenating. The main culprit contributing to sleep deprivation is staying up late rather than sticking to a regular, sensible bedtime. One of Ben Franklin's most quoted and least followed maxims begins with "Early to bed…"

10. Relaxation. Constant and excessive stress is a major cause of both poor performance and health problems. You can learn to perform well in stressful situations if you train yourself to relax. Athletes learn how valuable it is to be able to relax under pressure. Religious activities, such as repetitive prayer, hymns and chanting have a calming influence on many people (and some sermons likewise put the entire congregation to sleep). Relaxation reduces sleep problems too. Yoga, Tai Chi, progressive muscle relaxation, mindfulness, and meditation are some of many techniques that support relaxation. Meditation, for one, trains your brain to become more self-controlled.as you focus on your breathing and your senses; moreover, it improves your self-awareness and your ability to resist impulsive behavior. We will elaborate on relaxation methods in a later chapter.

11. Health Checkups and Prevention Regular physical and mental health checkups with an emphasis on maintaining excellent health and a positive outlook are invaluable, as is obtaining early treatment when needed.

12. Know When to Say No (And How) Are you reluctant to say no to your own impulses? To demands of others. Being unable to say no to urges that you feel, takes time away from progress on projects you have planned. Like a child running an errand to bring home ice cream for the family who is sidetracked by a playground, candy store, and a friendly dog, you start off with an enthusiasm that melts away before you finish, because something else pops up to district you. Persistence pays off! Being able to say no to other people is also a sign of maturity and self-confidence. I recall a college student remarking that in his first-year he was inclined to go along with whatever his friends were doing; whereas as a senior he was able to set his own priorities and turn down invitations and entreaties that would be a distraction from his plans. You can say no to others, and still maintain good relationships with them, if you mention a reason, and perhaps add "I would like to do it, but…To say no to a supervisor requires tact. You might mention projects and deadlines you are currently working with and ask if s/he wants you to drop or postpone any. Just remind yourself that saying no is an act of self-control that will increase your progress toward positive goals by preventing negative effects from over-commitment. Even more important- know when and how to say, Yes!

13. Don't Plan on Perfection. Do not set perfection as your target because human beings, by our very nature, are

fallible. When perfection is your goal, you are always under pressure and always have a sense of failure. You spend time regretting what you failed to accomplish and what you should have done differently instead of feeling good about what you have achieved and looking forward to future accomplishments. A sense of humor enabling you to laugh at your foibles and fallibility goes a long way. You can take your work seriously, without taking yourself too seriously.

14. Cultivate a Positive Mindset. Discouragement and depression arise from negative thinking. Often these thoughts lie beneath the surface in our mind. If we stop and realize what is happening, we are able be more clear-headed in evaluating their accuracy. Positive thinking does not mean being overly optimistic or ignoring real obstacles. It involves enjoying activities you must do as much as seeking something you would enjoy. It is being fully involved in the moment you are now living rather than mired in your past or worried about your future. It means having reasonable goals and confidence that you have talent and resources to reach them. As an old proverb reminds us, "It's good to look on the bright side, but it's wiser to look at both sides.

Summary and Conclusion

Starting with the belief of more than a few psychologists that psychology is of value to everyone; that it can enrich our lives, enhance our relationships, invigorate our organizations and improve our societies, a positive psychology movement has spread like a tide beyond the psychology profession to capture national attention. The complex process of applying and evaluating its findings continues, but so far, practitioners are optimistic. Critics usually concur with the ideals of the movement while disagreeing with claims or practices of a goodly number of its adherents.

But here comes the difficult part. When we tout psychology as a guide to finding a better life is that not the province of religion? Are findings from empirical science meant to replace or minimize traditional beliefs and practices? We will attempt to cope with that complex and often contentious issue in our next chapter.

Chapter 5.
The Good Life:
Morality, Religion, and Psychology

"Science without religion is lame, religion without science is blind. – Albert Einstein

Positive psychology, like Benjamin Franklin, has incorporated "virtue" from philosophical and religious teaching, to emphasize that it is not only intended to help us be more effective and more successful, but also to build a stronger character. Since many of us look to our Church for moral guidance, not to psychology, some see such emphasis as a threat to religion.

Conflicts Between Science and Religion.

Throughout history, misunderstandings and conflicts between traditional religious beliefs and scientific finding have cropped up.

Two notable such conflicts involved the Heliocentric Theory and Theory of Evolution. The first, that we are not at the center of our universe as we once believed, is now universally accepted; a second, that our species came about through evolution, is accepted by most people and most religions.

Additionally, traditional religions promulgated many ideas that, while not based on doctrine, were intended to motivate us to stay on the path to righteousness. You will recall the widespread notion that lightning, coming down from heaven accompanied by thunderbolts and destroying, homes, barns and other property signified the hand of a righteous God punishing sinners and warning everyone else. When Franklin reached up and pulled lightning down from the sky and employed it to serve mankind, much of the public at first saw his contribution to science as a threat to religion.

Psychology and Religion.

Psychology and religion have had their share of disagreements and misunderstandings over time, several of which remain sources of contention today. For not only does religion present a view of our place in the universe, our origin, purpose and destiny, but it endeavors to help us lead better lives. It offers a guide to becoming honorable and virtuous.

Over the years, psychologists have often criticized certain recommendations of traditional religions as retarding personal development rather than fostering it. In turn, religious leaders have decried materialistic philosophy underpinning scientific psychology. This controversy played out in pulpits, in halls of Academe and on radio and television.

For instance, the most popular TV program of its time (1950's and 60's), *Life is Worth Living* featured charismatic Catholic clergyman, Monsignor (later Bishop and Archbishop) Fulton Sheen. His witty, articulate and upbeat presentations depicted religious teaching as a road to a life worth living. His insights, advice and anecdotes also included more than a few pot shots at psychologists, whose views, he warned, would take one down the wrong path. Tempting targets were set up for him by psychologists who espoused ideas such as Freud's infantile sexuality or B.F. Skinner's belief that our behavior is determined by our environment not our own efforts.

Reruns of his TV series and his book based on them still have considerable appeal today.

As we will discuss shortly, another charismatic clergyman, Norman Vincent Peale, achieved even more widespread public recognition combining religion with popular psychology.

Psychology and Catholic Teaching

As a Catholic, teaching in a Psychology Department of a Catholic college since 1948, I was particularly aware of mistrust and misunderstanding common between religion and psychology during that time. Many Catholic colleges did not have psychology departments until years later. Relatively few Catholics took graduate work in psychology (I was the first graduate of my high school and only the second from my college to do so, as well as the first Catholic to earn a Ph. D. in psychology from Temple University).

Mainstream psychology, in turn, had its prejudices against Catholics. I experienced a sample of this myself. At one large public university, its department chairman, in inquiring if I might be interested in a faculty opening, said "I wouldn't mind having a Catholic in our department." In another case, at a similar university, I had been offered a position directing their counseling program. When I checked with its psychology chairman about also teaching a psychology course, his opening comment was: "you're a Catholic, do you think you'll fit in." I figured I would not.

Professional Associations.

In 1948, as one attempt to bridge this gap, a group of psychologists formed the American Catholic Psychological Association. Its intent was to work within both the American Psychological Association and Catholic institutions of higher learning to improve communication and understanding. I joined and played an active role in this organization. One of my colleagues at La Salle, Thomas McCarthy, served as its president for a time. By 1970, we were pleased to see it evolve into Psychologists Interested in Religious Issues, in a move to broaden its scope to all members without regard to religious affiliation. It is now a division of APA (American Psychological Association) entitled Society for the Psychology of Religion and Spirituality.

Other professional organizations have divisions or interest groups devoted to religious or spiritual issues.

Another organization working toward a rapprochement between psychology and religion was the Academy of Religion and Mental Health (ARMH). Founded in 1947 in New York through efforts of Episcopal clergyman George Christian Anderson and other interested parties and designed to foster understanding and cooperation between religious leaders and mental health professionals. Again, McCarthy and I joined, working with George Anderson for a number of years. In 1972, it merged with the American Foundation of Religion and Psychiatry, which had begun in 1951 through combined efforts of dynamic pastor Norman Vincent Peale and psychiatrist Smiley Blanton, to form an Institute of Religion and Health.

Norman Vincent Peale

For it was Peale himself not his organization that captured attention. Peale combined religious fervor and a message of positive thinking in his preaching, writings, and radio and television programs, to become one of America's most popular and influential figures. He was also one of its most controversial.

Most people know him best from *The Power of Positive Thinking,* his most widely read work. First published in 1952, it stayed on the New York Times bestseller list for month after month and sold an estimated 5 million copies. In it, he emphasizes developing the habit of cultivating positive thoughts and avoiding negative ones. Readers are guided with mantras to repeat, such as "Every day in every way I'm getting better and better."

A sample of his style appears in his inspirational quotes: "Formulate and stamp indelibly on your mind a mental picture of yourself as succeeding. Hold this picture tenaciously. Never permit it to fade. Your mind will seek to develop the picture... Do not build up obstacles in your imagination.

It is of practical value to learn to like yourself. Since you must spend so much time with yourself you might as well get some satisfaction out of the relationship."

His book generated considerable criticism, including that from many mental health professionals and religious leaders. Dr. Blanton, a psychiatrist who had previously collaborated with him, refused to endorse it.

Critics of *The Power of Positive Thinking* voiced numerous objections including

1. that it included anecdotes that were unsubstantiated; testimony from "experts" who were unidentified; and case histories that were uncorroborated.

2. that Peale attempted to persuade readers to follow his beliefs through a combination of self-hypnosis and false evidence

3. that he pictured negative forces in life as so strong that we should avoid thinking about them, rather than learning to address them, and that he held that we could not overcome our problems, even with God's help, without his auto-suggestive techniques.

4. that his book emphasized using religion to achieve material success rather than a more spiritual life.

5. that, while mental health specialists vary treatment depending on the person and their problem, Peale claimed that techniques he recommended would help everyone.

In my own view, his basic stress on a positive attitude is on target, but he missed it completely because he oversimplified, exaggerated, and distorted.

Despite his critics, he continued to enjoy widespread popularity and influence,

In 1960, as spokesman for a group of Protestant clergy, Peale opposed John F. Kennedy during his campaign for president arguing that Kennedy would serve his Church's interests before that of his country. This charge sparked considerable controversy, including a rejection of that position by a number of prominent Protestant leaders.

Former presidential candidate Adlai Stevenson, noted for his witticisms, contrasted Peale with Apostle Paul saying: "I find Paul appealing and Peale appalling."

Peale was politically and personally close to President Richard Nixon's family. A frequent White House guest during his administration, he officiated at the wedding of Julie Nixon and David Eisenhower in 1968.

Contemporary Disagreements

We find numerous examples of traditional beliefs and practices that people believe to be in accord with religious teaching, including the Bible, but which psychologists see as detrimental. The following examples, some ubiquitous and current; one (exorcism) relatively rare but striking, illustrate the range of issues in our lives where dialogue between religion and psychology is ongoing and sometimes contentious.

The Devil.

First, the devil as an agent in our lives. When tempted to violate our principles and do something wrong, is this a devil striving to lead us astray? A living creature, an omnipresent spirit, and a constant source of temptation? Or is this term used more as an illustration that evil exists, and that we have within us self-serving inclinations that entice us to deviate from the direction our moral compass leads? Psychology tells us we are better able to follow our conscience if we understand ourselves well and use this understanding to improve. Various religious teaching holds that we are helpless before the snares and wiles of the devil, and prayer is our only hope.

A recent (2019) widely circulated pamphlet, *Letter to a Suffering Church* by Bishop Robert Barron, exemplifies this dichotomy. Reflecting on the Catholic Church's horrific sex abuse scandal, he can only conclude it to be a "diabolical masterpiece." He acknowledges today's common view of the devil as "a symbol for evil in the world, a sort of colorful literary device," but can't help his conviction that the devil is real. In contrast to a host of clergy who share this conviction, however, he advocates changes in the Church, its hierarchy, seminary selection and training, and other pragmatic approaches as well.

Unfortunately, a focus on a demonic cause often distracts us from taking responsibility for our actions and working out a way to change them.

Clericalism and Authoritarianism.

As far as I can see, for instance, American bishops have failed to address two closely related issues that a host of critics believe crucial to reforming the Church - clericalism and authoritarianism. When priests, and those studying to become priests, become more interested in the power and prestige of their position, than in performing the work of their office, this is clericalism. Pope Francis has called it "the worst sin" but to date has not publicly emphasized its role in the sex abuse scandal.

When priests must obey bishops, and laity are expected to defer to priests even when their judgment or behavior is seriously flawed, it opens the door to abuse of power.

Exorcism

Are demons real and capable of possessing human beings? One of our oldest and most widely held religious beliefs is that humans can be taken over by demonic spirits and that some form of exorcism is required to cast them out. Since earliest times, people suffering from mental illness (and certain types of physical illness) were deemed possessed by a devil. To a goodly number of patients, even today, struggling in vain to control their thoughts, feelings, and behavior, it seems like struggling with demons, and requiring exorcism as its cure. My own firm belief is that there is no such individual as a devil. It is a belief akin to thinking that lightning is God's way of warning us to repent. Still, since many people think they are influenced by such an evil spirit, or wonder if they might be, it helps to understand their thinking.

By mid-20th century this esoteric ritual had moved close to obscurity in the United States, until a 1973 horror film, and best-selling novel, *The Exorcist,* based on the last known Catholic-sanctioned exorcism in the United States, changed all that. It rejuvenated fascination with this ritual and resulted in thousands claiming demonic possession and requesting help with their demons. Without official sanction, maverick priests, clergy of all denominations and self-proclaimed lay exorcists responded to their call for help.

This upsurge in exorcism prompted the Catholic Church to amend its official guidelines established in 1614. New 1999 revisions include a requirement that an individuals must be evaluated by a medical professional to be sure they are not suffering from mental illness before deciding to perform this ritual. Additionally, anyone requesting an exorcism would be encouraged to seek help from a mental health professional when deemed appropriate.

In addition, since demonic possession is considered rare, and mental illness commonly confused with it, Vatican guidelines now require each diocese to have a specially trained priest to diagnose it. Avoiding performing an exorcism on a mentally ill person is crucial since it may well exacerbate their condition and be considered abuse.

Although this revision was intended to ensure greater control over those performing exorcisms, bishops in about 200 dioceses, including quite a few who saw no need for an exorcist, now faced the task of finding and supervising one.

And so, American bishops, concerned about implementing this process, convened a conference in Baltimore in 2010. Some fifty bishops and sixty priests who attended, including quite a few who voiced skepticism, discussed issues related to exorcism, but it seemed to have been more an exchange of ideas, and an airing of concerns than a policy-making body.

Catholicism is far from the only religion facing concerns about exorcism. Although doctrine and practice vary widely, almost all Christian religions have taken a position on it, and almost all encounter self-appointed practitioners who deviate from their official stance.

Although most of us think of exorcism as a relic of the past rarely used today, consider this: Deliverance Ministry, a religion committed to exorcism, stresses that life involves a constant struggle with Satan. They feature about 500 ministries in the U.S. specializing in exorcisms and Christian counseling.

Punishment.
A widely different but much more common example of a practice a host of folks consider part of their religious upbringing is corporal punishment. "Spare the rod and spoil the child," an oft-quoted refrain justified spanking, slapping, and beating, perhaps with the intent of "beating the devil out of him."

Based on psychological research and experience showing corporal punishment to be more harmful than beneficial, we have seen a gradual but significant decrease in it use.

A case in point was our Pennsylvania Psychology Association joining with other groups in 1988 pushing a bill to abolish corporal punishment in public schools. It finally passed in 2005. While it was under review, we encountered vehement objections. Critics accused psychologists of urging schools to do away with all punishment and all discipline. Although this is a complete misrepresentation of our recommendations, I believe we were remiss in not sufficiently disseminating the value of discipline and examples of more effective methods of punishment, such as "time out" and withholding privileges.

Cooperative Progress.

Despite such ways in which contemporary psychology and traditional religions ostensibly clash, I believe the two are making progress in working together. And in realizing both provide resources to enrich our lives. Religion encourages us to "Love one another." Psychology, by its contributions to understanding others (and ourselves), helps us to express that love in our actions.

Churches and other organizations have put together lists of virtues and vices- positive traits to develop and negative ones to overcome. Being a member of such an organization supports and encourages efforts at self-improvement. In my own youth, I endeavored to follow the Boy Scout Law: a scout is trustworthy, loyal, helpful, friendly, courteous, kind, obedient, cheerful, thrifty, brave, clean and reverend (I can still rattle them off, as can most former scouts). Troop leaders, publications from national headquarters and friends in scouting reinforced my efforts. I still value this experience.

In parochial school, I learned, and tried to develop "Fruits of the Holy Spirit": charity, joy, peace, patience, kindness, goodness,

These lists can provide goals, but how to you turn them into action? First, construct your own list. Start with whatever characteristic would get you off on the right track. Once you reach your desired level of improvement, move onto your next trait, again recording your progress until you reach your next goal.

Fortunately, we are not lone passengers on our journey through life, but members of various supportive groups. What do empirical studies tell us about the effects of being part of a religious body? Several have found that people who are more religious show better emotional well-being and fewer social problems. Religion seems related to well-being because of six separate factors: (1) it includes communal support, (2) it fosters healthy lifestyles, (3) it promotes personality integration, (4) it encourages generativity and altruism, (5) it provides unique coping strategies, and (6) religion supplies a sense of purpose.

One study reported that religious people (those who prayed every day and attended services at least once a week) to be happier and more responsible citizens (in terms of voting, volunteering and similar activities) than those without a religious base. Another study found such positive results primarily for religions that emphasize love and respect for one another not for those stressing fighting evils and rejecting unbelievers.

Living a Moral Life.
But here comes the difficult part. How do we integrate morality into everyday life? We have a job to occupy our time and effort, rivals to compete with, a family to care for

and a need to save for our future. Religious teaching seems to tell us not to be concerned with money. What do psychological studies tell us? Actually, they show it can contribute to happiness. Learning to earn, save, invest and spend money wisely makes a major difference in a person's satisfaction with life.

Franklin exemplified this. He extolled the value of finding the right kind of work, being thrifty, developing sound work habits and acquiring a reputation as a person of integrity. He believed it made a better society when everyone enjoyed a decent income. He used his wealth to improve his community and encouraged others to do likewise.

Today, quite a few wealthy people get their greatest satisfaction from investing in educational or charitable causes and seeing the benefit it yields. Even those with limited income get a lift of spirit from helping those in need. Research evidence is consistent with Franklin's belief- using money to help accomplish something worthwhile does enhance happiness.

Like most of us, you surely spend a major part of your time and effort on your job. Are you making a living or making a difference? Is it a job, a career or a vocation? Is it congruent with the meaning and purpose of life?

For work matters. In their book *Good Work,* psychologists Gardner, Csikszentmihalyi and Damon conclude: "if the fundamentals of good work, excellence and ethics are in harmony, we lead a personally fulfilling and socially rewarding life."

In today's complex world making for an often-hectic life, where should we concentrate our efforts?

For one, do not spend so much time worrying about your future or living in your past that you neglect opportunities for a better life in the present? It's a common mistake. Wherever you are, be there! Positive psychology emphasizes that we are happiest when we are fully involved in something we care about in the present and feeling confident about our future.

Social Action. Edmund Burke's "All that is necessary for the triumph of evil is that good men do nothing" makes that point. Activism is difficult. Most of the Letters of St. Paul advocating for Christianity were penned from a Roman prison. We recall Gandhi and Martin Luther King as a few of the multitude demanding reform who suffered similar incarceration.

Reformers typically provoke hostile resistance. Ben Franklin experienced this when he divulged information from letters written by British officials containing plans to repress freedom in American Colonies. When his identity as the source of the leaks was uncovered, British officials attacked him harshly, attempting to destroy his reputation. Their action, in turn, moved Franklin to forego compromising with Britain and throw his support to Colonists demanding independence.

Just as individual habits are powerful, organizational customs are often deeply entrenched. Some people see the way things are now, or have always been done, as right and natural; others resist change for more selfish reasons.

Desegregation of schools is a striking example, requiring years of advocacy and coalition building to accomplish. Psychological findings played a significant role in this movement including providing a bit of key testimony before the Supreme Court. Police culture has recently come under strong criticism because of widely-publicized instances of abuse.

Regrettably, those with talent and resources for influencing our society often ignore Franklin's example of using it for the common welfare. Instead they employ their skill and power in getting us to buy a product or a politician, including ones that are worthless or harmful. A striking example is found in marketing techniques our tobacco industry has used, and in governmental financial backing they have obtained. The 2006 film "Thank You for Smoking," based on a William Buckley, Jr. book, is an astute satire of this industry's work, and it takes its share of swipes at alcohol and firearms industries as well.

Policy makers also benefit from knowledge of empirical psychology. The campaign against smoking is a case in point. Initially, as some of you will remember, it had little impact, but as organizers experimented with a varied of approaches, they created more effective ones. Today, the percentage of people who smoke, although not inconsiderable, is far lower than when this campaign began. Tobacco companies, continuing to push their product, spent $8.7 billion on cigarette advertising and promotion in 2016, an increase from $8.3 billion in 2015. Companies are also touting electronic cigarettes and related products for vaping. Today. more high school students are vaping than smoking even though a growing body of evidence indicates it may be dangerous.

What have we learned from this consideration of living a moral life guided by religious principals and utilizing our knowledge of human behavior? Basically, that we can incorporate them into our own lives. Here are a group of people who briefly state how they do it.

When I do good, I feel good. When I do bad, I feel bad. That's my religion. – Abraham Lincoln.

However many holy words you read, however many you speak, what good will they do you if you do not act upon them? – Buddha

Not all of us can do great things. But we can do small things with great love- Mother Theresa

When I admire the wonders of a sunset or the beauty of the moon, my soul expands in the worship of the creator. – Mahatma Gandhi

This is my simple religion. There is no need for temples, no need for complicated philosophy. Our own brain, our own heart is our temple; the philosophy is kindness. – Dalai Lama

Man's ethical behavior should be effectively grounded on compassion, nurture and social bonds. -Albert Einstein

We learn many virtues in our Christian families. Above all, we learn to love, asking nothing in return. – Pope Francis

"Each day brings another chance for us to make change. If we are unhappy with our lives, we can wake up and choose to change our perspective and strive to make a better, happier life for ourselves." -Eleanor Roosevelt

"I've always been an optimist and I suppose that is rooted in the belief that the power of creativity and intelligence can make the world a better place." -Bill Gates

"By faith I mean a vision of good one cherishes and enthusiasm that pushes us on to seek its fulfillment." – Helen Keller

"I have believed that the means to real happiness and the true worth of a person is by how faithfully we serve a cause greater than our self-interest." -Sen. John Mc Cain.

Examining Your Beliefs

At this point, I would like to include for your consideration a review that I wrote for the Philadelphia of a book that made an impression on me. I hope you like it too.

This I Believe: the personal philosophies of remarkable men and women Edited by Jay Allison and Dan Gediman; with John Gregory and Viki Merrick. Henry Holt.

A welcome change from the sloganeering, political mudslinging and products of spin- doctors, this volume presents people stating briefly, and often eloquently, what they truly believe. Among the eighty participants who have opened their minds and hearts to us are luminaries like: Albert Einstein, Eleanor Roosevelt, Colin Powell, Thomas Mann, Helen Hayes and Leonard Bernstein. Included also, are a number of lesser known, but equally remarkable, individuals.

The essays were originally broadcast on National Public Radio. The idea for it goes back to 1949 when a group of radio executives, unhappy with the excess of violence, negative news and partisan bickering, were seeking a positive and uplifting program for listeners. From their discussion This I Believe was born. It was an immediate success from the time it first aired over WCAU in Philadelphia. Featuring Edward R. Murrow, it soon attracted national and international audiences, and led to the publication, in 1952, of the first volume of This I Believe essays. The book sold over 300,000 copies and made the bestseller list for several years.

*Fifty years passed before it was **reviv**ed, and this latest collection of essays published.*

Even a cynical reader spending a few moments browsing through this work is bound to encounter moving or inspiring messages. Topics range from the profound to the mundane: fascination with the mystery and joy of life: the awe of a spiritual experience; the power of love and empathy; the feeling of community with humanity and the world of nature; the appeal of democracy, the challenge of the constant quest, rather than the arrival at a final answer and a recognition that food shared with a group can be an occasion for feeding our soul- that all food, shared in the right spirit, can be soul food.

Alan Lightman, an astrophysicist at M.I.T., describes his childhood fascination with the unknown in The Power of Mysteries. As a child staring out his bedroom window at the night sky, he was struck by the mysteries of the physical universe. And gazing at family photos of grandparents and great grandparents, he visualized ancestors extending back in time ad infinitum or to some unknown point of origin.

Jason Sheehan, a chef and restaurant critic, shares a more basic human experience in There Is No Such Thing as Too Much Barbecue. His description of an authentic barbecue experience with the succulent beef exuding a mouth-watering aroma and the sauce dripping down your chin and sticking under your fingernails would tempt a vegetarian to sink his teeth into a healthy chunk of this food for the soul. And the sides, he reminds us, are as important to a barbecue as rhythm is to blues.

Several contributors emphasize the wonder of American democracy, including a number of immigrants from around the globe who contrast their American experience with conditions in their countries of origin. And a tongue-in-cheek take on democracy at work cited by

*political analyst Mark Shields quoting a concession
statement of a losing candidate in a California state senate
primary: "the people have spoken...the bastards."*

*Authors hope readers will not only find
enjoyment and inspiration in these essays but will be
moved to share their own personal philosophies.*

*I, for one, live by a set of beliefs I would have
difficulty articulating or holding. Yet, like
contributors to this and previous volumes and those
posted on the web, I am now motivated to take that
first step. "This I Believe..."*

Learning About the Good Life

I believe we live and learn. Life is a journey
fueled by faith in a future and rooted in values passed
down through our ancestors. Our earliest experience
of love in a caring family forms the foundation for
our character and our basic ideas of morality-we
learn to respect and support one another.

As we mature and our world expands beyond our
family, we encounter new complexities and
unforeseen challenges in living a moral purposeful
life.

One step along the way is starting school. Robert
Fulghum, bestselling author of "All I Really Need to
Know I Learned in Kindergarten, reminds us of lessons we
learn there: "be nice." "don't fight," "don't make a mess,"
"clean up your own mess."

Throughout our school years we go on learning more
about morality through our interactions with other
students, and, if fortunate, through the example and
teaching of faculty. A major part of our responsibility is to
take full advantage of these opportunities.

In our careers we face a need to accomplish something worthwhile, to continually upgrade out knowledge and skill set, and to contribute to positive interactions supporting effective, enthusiastic teamwork.

In our families, we share a love based on our own childhood experience and moral values enhanced by our learning over time.

Religion and Everyday Life

Throughout our life, religion provides a stable supportive guide fostering morality.

In my own Catholic upbringing, I learned from my parents to respect and admire "good religious people" whatever creed they embraced. I also learned to be skeptical of certain beliefs and practices common in Catholicism that were not actually part of Church doctrine. Nonetheless, it afforded a powerful social-support system helping me throughout life. It offers a big tent with room to explore options. It is a vital part of Christianity, sharing roots in Judaism and having much in common with all major religions worldwide.

I believe our society in general, and our churches in particular, have, so far, failed to work out ways of supporting moral teaching religions emphasize. Support for educational institutions sponsored by religious denominations (or for students to have the choice to attend them) is one widely debated current example. Another, within Catholicism, is one I was a first-hand witness to.

The Church Attempting to Adapt to Change

In the 1950's I began serving as a consultant with religious communities (mostly women's communities), conducting psychological assessments of candidates to help determine whether they possessed personal characteristics needed for that life of prayer and service. In doing so, I found a small number unsuited and others for whom I recommended a delay in acceptance until they became more mature socially or emotionally. The vast majority of young women, however, impressed me with their ability, stability, and desire to live a life of service in areas such as teaching, nursing, social work and missionary work. Frequently, in discussing their calling to this vocation, they would mention their mother as a model. How she had served her family and community so well. And yet, they wanted to serve more broadly, and believed they could do it best as one of a community of dedicated women.

For most of them, their life did not pan out as planned. Sweeping cultural changes occurring in our society and attempts within the Church to adapt to a modern world, particularly through Vatican II, made it difficult for them to serve the life they had envisioned. The Church lost a large pool of dedicated and talented women who had entered religious communities to provide vital services to society.

Psychology and Morality

To conclude this consideration of psychology and morality, here are a couple of points to remember: 1. Morality is an essential part of our life, guiding us and providing purpose to it. 2. Learning is lifelong. Good intentions are a tiny step in the right direction but carrying them out requires constantly reinvigorating ourselves with new skills and new developments. 3. We don't function in a vacuum, and we are not traveling alone. We support one another through organizations and institutions including our religious institutions.4. Knowledge is power. Psychology provides power to help us change ourselves and our society; morality serves as our guide. 5. Doing good helps us feel good. Religion and positive psychology both add joy and contentment to our lives.

In our next chapter we change directions from our spiritual side to our physical, particularly our brain and how understanding its basics aids our development.

Chapter 6.
Our Brain:
An Owner's Manual Introduction

The human brain has 100 billion neurons, each neuron connected to 10 thousand other neurons. Sitting on your shoulders is the most complicated object in the known universe. Michio Kaku

Yes, one of the most remarkable and intriguing objects in the world is our human brain. Such a small bit of our anatomy. So complex and able to accomplish so much, yet so little understood. Most of us know more about our face and our feet than our brain.

For centuries, scientists and philosophers have been fascinated by our brain-such a massive puzzle. Now it is beginning to surrender its secrets. You may remember the 1990s being designated as "decade of the brain": a time in which scientists of varied specialties worldwide were enjoined to step up brain research. This effort jump-started exploration that has continued and expanded over subsequent years. Think about it! Our accelerated pace of research in neurological and behavioral science has produced more knowledge about our brain in recent years than in all previous centuries. Knowing our brain helps us know ourselves: what we might accomplish, how we can utilize its enormous potential and overcome its limitations.

What are some implications of this brain research for personal development? Quite a few. Since our brain plays an essential role in perception, problem solving, memory, habit formation, emotions, social interaction and other areas of positive psychology.

Going back for a minute to my experience as a boy, I loved science, and was fortunate to be able to explore one of Philadelphia's treasures, our Franklin Institute. I returned frequently to see and manipulate its wealth of scientific exhibits, and particularly to climb through their featured exhibit a model of a human heart that visitors could walk through and observe its parts. I remember wishing they also had a model of a brain to explore. Now, my wish has come true. They introduced an exhibit, "Your Brain," in 2014. What does this exhibit offer? Well, you get to climb through tubes of metallic mesh as you negotiate a maze of pathways. You are wending your way through a neural network. You are immersed within a huge human brain.

Neurological and Behavioral Approaches
     This might be a good time to ask, "How do researchers go about studying such a complex part of our make up? To help unlock mysteries of our brain and its role in determining our behavior, they have two main avenues of investigation: neurological and psychological.
     You are no doubt aware of studies of neural impulses, and interconnections using instrumentation such as brain scans, ultrasound, PET Scans, EEGs, and MRIs
     You may be less familiar with psychological assessment which observes our behavior under controlled conditions and draws inferences about brain functioning. It is unlikely you have ever taken an individually administered intelligence test. Such tests require a person to answer questions, manipulate objects and solve puzzles of varying degrees of difficulty. From this, we estimate level of intelligence (IQ). We assume differences in IQ reflect differences in brain functioning, but, so far, we

have not been able to identify most neurological correlates for these disparities.

Psychologists also administer neuropsychological tests (roughly like intelligence tests). It is even less likely you have ever taken one of these. They yield valuable data about functioning in different areas of our brain. Certain patterns of performance are typical of patients with a given type of disorder or level of functioning. Sometimes neuropsychological tests are more informative than neurological evaluations. I remember when my daughter, doing a n internship in neuropsychology, tested a patient who had been diagnosed as mentally retarded. Neuropsychological tests disagreed. They revealed a relatively high I.Q. and suggested damage in a given area of the brain. Further neurological studies confirmed this diagnosis.

Usually, a combination of neurological and psychological approaches works best, since we understand a phenomenon better when we examine it from more than one perspective. Thus, we may see an orange, feel it and smell it, but when we taste it, we add a completely new dimension to our knowledge of an orange. In the same way, neuropsychology adds another perspective to neurological diagnosis. Weaving both together produces a clearer picture of what goes on in the brain.

Ben Franklin was intrigued with understanding brain function. He even experimented with passing electricity through his own head and that of some of his friends. He, and others who tried it, experienced a temporary sense of elation, but on finding it also diminished memory, he abandoned this practice.

Following in Franklin's footsteps, a few physicians used clinical trials of brain stimulation with patients suffering from serious depression. Centuries later, electroconvulsive therapy became widely employed in treating depression, but physicians were blissfully unaware of the extent of accompanying memory loss. Only after thorough psychological assessment was its full impact on memory revealed.

Today, do-it-yourself electrical brain stimulation kits are being marketed for home use. (I didn't add one to my Santa Clause wish list!).

Artificial intelligence (AI)

Like most people, you have probably been intrigued by progress in artificial intelligence. So many things that we thought a machine could never do, like defeating a chess master, have now been done. What next? At present, machines calculate much faster than the brain and store far more information; the race is about even in close-coordinated movement, visual perception, language production, comprehension and basic problem solving; and our human brain's ability to control autonomic functions and emotions, experience consciousness, anticipate, plan ahead and be creative has not yet been duplicated (neither have we yet encountered robots who fall in love!). Also, our brain is always on even during sleep. It has no off button.

Research in artificial intelligence is contributing to progress in two main ways: 1. Planning how to organize available resources to accomplish goals. We learn which functions to performed by specialized technology and when we should use our brain (or the brain of experts). 2. Helping us better understand our brain and what an amazing variety of complicated things it can do.

85

To follow our discussion of the brain, you need not know complexities of neuroscience. Rudimentary knowledge is helpful background, but if you prefer to skip details of brain structure, you should still be able to follow material without difficulty.

Neural corelates of perception, thought and action

Neurotransmitters

If you could watch neural pathways in the brain, you would see a series of electrical impulses moving about between higher and lower brain centers to and from our spinal column and interacting with our peripheral nervous system. Millions of brain cells called neurons transmit signals to one another. And they do so at trillions of connections called synapses (more interconnections than in all the telephone systems on earth). Brain chemicals, called neurotransmitters, cross tiny gaps into other brain cells like soap bubbles bouncing into one) another. It is the basis of everything the brain does.

Particularly exciting is the role of four of these transmitters, – endorphin, oxytocin, serotonin, and dopamine, known as "feel good chemicals." When we engage in activities that produce these chemicals, we feel upbeat and confident. Vigorous physical activity can do this, producing a "runners high" whether you get it from running, swimming, basketball, tennis or pickleball.

We also find good news in psychological studies that ask what happens when you help someone? They find these same transmitters are activated. Doing something good makes you feel good.

Here's one example. A teacher in a suburban Philadelphia high school, looking for a way of putting her recently deceased sister's sparse amount of money to a good cause, decided to use it for a positive class project. She gave 20 dollars to each student in her class and asked them to use it for some "random act of kindness". One student gave a waitress a tip that "made her day:" another made care packages for soldiers; another bought sanitary pads for a homeless woman. All of them reported how great it felt to be able to help others. Many vowed to continue to look for chances to repeat such acts of kindness.

The four transmitters above are of most popular interest, but dozens of others have been identified, and more are being discovered every year. Other major neurotransmitters, dancing around in our brain, include:

GABA, which calms neurons and aids relaxation.

Glutamate, important in learning and memory

Oxytocin

One neurotransmitter, oxytocin has been called the "love hormone." Studies of eye contact show that it helps us create social bonds and influences feeling of belonging and connection. So, when you gaze into someone's eyes and they gaze into yours, it creates an emotional attraction. Song writers have chanted that message since the beginning of time-even though they didn't know oxytocin was at work.! Keep eye contact with people and you will generate more oxytocin. In turn, you will be more confident, calm and happy.

Although knowing how each neurotransmitter works has value, more important for most of us is realizing that our brain, and therefore our behavior, is influenced by anything chemical entering our brain: the air we breathe, chemicals in our food and drink, hormones released by our glands, medication and drugs. That's why advocates of a healthy living style recommend you: 1. exercise regularly 2. maintain a healthful diet 3. get adequate sleep. 4. use medicine Judiciously under supervision of your health care provider. 5. engage in work (paid or volunteer) in which you are doing something worthwhile; 6. stay social; participate in activities with friends; be part of a support group; 7. stretch your mind; learn new tasks; play games that challenge your thinking strategies; develop exercises to keep your memory sharp; 8. keep a positive, optimistic outlook. We will discuss this more fully in our next chapter.

Our Nervous System

This might be a good time to have a brief overview of our nervous system.

It can be organized in a number of ways, one common division breaks it down into three main parts, central, peripheral and autonomic.

You will recall that our central nervous system (CNS) is made up of our brain and spinal cord. Our brain, composed of higher and lower centers, contains roughly 100 billion neurons orchestrating that activity.

Higher Brain Centers

Our brain controls all functions of our body, including accessing and interpreting information from our external environment. It is responsible not only for our cognitive abilities, including problem solving, memory, creativity, judgment and decision making, but also for our actions and emotions.

This brain of ours receives stimuli from our senses: sight, smell, hearing, touch and taste, as well as a number of inner senses, such as balance. It organizes this input in a meaningful way and stores it in our memory. It is responsible for our inner thoughts, our outward actions and operations of organs throughout our body.

Our higher brain centers serve as command centers for our brain. Activities that require considerable thought, utilize our cerebrum and cerebellum, which are located there. Coating the surface of each is a vital layer of tissue about as thick as a linen napkin called the neocortex. It accounts for about 75% of our brain and has been called its "executive center." Most information processing takes place there. Arranged in hierarchical fashion, it receives inputs in parallel from senses and lower brain centers and stores them as patterns. These patterns form a basis for intelligence, which involves remembering and predicting patterns in our world. When we talk about "gray matter" in our brain, we are talking about this thin gray rind. Folds in the brain add to its surface area and increase gray matter.

Our lower brain centers are mainly responsible for controlling balance, movement, and reflexes. They connect with our spinal cord which runs throughout our body and controls activity in our peripheral system.

. Our peripheral nervous system includes our sense organs, sensory (afferent) nerves and motor(efferent) nerves. Sensory nerves connect our sense organs with other parts of the network. They inform us about conditions in our external world that higher brain centers organize into meaningful perceptions. They also provide considerable information about our own body's state (our internal world) much of it below conscious awareness. Motor (efferent) nerves carry signals from higher nerve centers to our muscles, telling them how to respond to a situation, and to our glands, which affect our internal functioning, including emotional centers of our brain.

Let us imagine you are walking leisurely along a familiar street. You spot someone and think you recognize her. You focus your attention on her and, sure enough, you were right. You wave, get her attention, and she responds. You cross the street, working your way through slow-moving traffic and exchange pleasantries. You sense that she is in a hurry, so, you smile, say, "have a nice day," and move on. In this brief encounter, you used sensory input, primarily visual, carried to your brain (higher centers when you thought about what you were doing, lower centers when you acted without thinking). Your brain then sent directions to your muscles controlling waving, walking, and talking.

Reflex responses

The simplest neural connection between stimulus and response is the reflex. Here sensory nerves connect with motor nerves at peripheral parts of our nervous system rather than higher centers, and activity occurs automatically. In the patellar reflex, for example, a tap on your knee produces a knee jerk without any intention on your part or control by higher brain centers.

Habits

When we examine complex material or face difficult decisions, our neocortex becomes actively involved, whereas we handle routine, habitual situations without much thought, by utilizing our lower brain centers-we get things done automatically. We thus see the value of developing desirable habits-doing what we should automatically. Positive psychology emphasizes this. So did Ben Franklin. As he put it, "Your net worth to the world is usually determined by what remains after your bad habits are subtracted from your good ones".

Neural inhibition

Keep in mind too that sensory input does not act on a static brain. Rather, its ongoing activity determines what influence new input has on our behavior. For instance, certain neural activity inhibits other neural activity.

You can experience one of my favorite examples of this with a simple tachistoscope, provided one of your eyes is dominant (a common occurrence). I first came across this surprising phenomenon, inadvertently, while looking through a tachistoscope for its more common purpose—to combine images from both eyes. In this case, with one eye you see a circus horse, with the other a circus rider. With both eyes open (provided neither eye is dominant), you see rider standing atop horse. In my case, I saw each figure clearly while using one eye. With both eyes open, however, I saw only the horse; the stimulus coming to my dominant right eye. Neural activity activated by my right eye inhibited that coming from my left, preventing it from reaching brain centers where our experience of sight takes place. By trying different stimuli, I hit upon an even more striking experience. By replacing the horse with a blank card, I could still see its rider clearly with my right eye closed, but as soon as I opened it, the rider would disappear. No matter how hard I looked, all I could see with both eyes open was a blank screen. When I closed my right eye, the rider reappeared.

Evolution of Our Brain

Origin and Implications

To help understand our brain it is worth having an idea of how it evolved over time. Charles Darwin in The Origin of Species, published in 1859, first propounded his theory of evolution. He drew on observations and writings of others who had gone before him, including, at least indirectly, Benjamin Franklin.

The brain we are born with was not built from scratch. It evolved over countless centuries from simpler brains of pre-humanoid species to a complex organ each of us comes equipped with today.

Primitive organisms can only adjust to their environment through evolution of species; mammals, such as the rat and can learn by trial and error; humans can solve problems through cognitive processes, enabling us to anticipate consequences of our actions before we act. These differences are reflected in differences in our brain.

Where, you may wonder, are habits learned or are they innate? Most are based on modules of neural connections formed in everyone's brain by thousands of hours of practice. Other modules, however, have developed in the brain of our species over millions of years of evolution. Ever so gradually, changes that enabled our ancestors to better adapt to and survive in their environment were preserved. Many of those proclivities we still retain. Therefore, we jump when something is slithering in nearby grass, even those of us who have never seen a snake; moreover, we share this innate response with other primates on the same basis. Several of our other emotional reactions, such as fear of height, and bursts of rage when threatened, seem to have an innate basis as well.

Comparative psychology studies what a given species is capable of, for example, what kinds of material they can learn, what type of problems they can solve and what emotions they display and relates this to structures present in their brain. Of course, problems can be solved in different ways. Thus, a horse, known as Clever Hans, was once renowned for its ability to solve mathematical problems and perform other intellectual tasks. It demonstrated this talent in exhibitions throughout the country to much acclaim. Upon close investigation, however, it turned out Hans used subtle cues from its trainer to nod its head when its owner called out the correct answer.

Dog lovers are often pleasantly surprised at their seeming ability to comprehend complex instructions and wonder how much they understand and what goes on in their brain. An old comedy skit involves an American couple in Paris who come across a woman talking to her dog. Her husband says: "Isn't it amazing that we have so much trouble understanding French and that little dog knows it so well."

Innate Basis of Emotions

In his book *Emotions in Man and Animals*, Darwin sought to extend his theory of natural selection beyond evolution of physical structures and into mind and behavior by exploring how emotions might have evolved. He supported his argument by pointing out how emotions are expressed similarly in people throughout the world. This observation held true, even in isolated areas where there had been little opportunity for emotional expressions to have been learned and culturally transmitted. This suggests a strong heritable component to emotions. Also pertinent to his belief is that emotions are expressed similarly across species. Dogs, cats and horses are not closely related to us, but have you seen dogs sad? horses frightened? cats angry? Their brains are sufficiently like ours to produce similar emotional responses.

At one time, our heart was considered the center of our emotions, particularly amatory ones (perhaps because we feel our heart race under strong emotions). We still see this in many expressions related to romantic love and other emotions: heartbroken, touched my heart, heart to heart, I feel it in my heart, my foolish heart. How many more come to mind? On one day of the year, the heart as symbolic of romance is evident everywhere (Valentine's Day of course).

In reality, emotional responses are the work of our brain, particularly our autonomic nervous system.

Let's move then to consider this powerful branch of our nervous system.

Our **autonomic nervous system**, controlled by the hypothalamus, connects our brain to our internal organs and glands thus regulating them. It acts largely unconsciously, controlling heart rate, digestion, respiration and sexual activity. It is composed of two main parts, sympathetic and parasympathetic.

The first is responsible for changes that occur when we are emotionally aroused: angry, fearful, worried- our "flight or fight response." The second is active when we are calm and relaxed, our "rest and relax" or "feed and breed" response. Learning to stay calm, confident, and relaxed benefits our physical and mental health (something to be discussed more fully in the chapter on Positive Emotions).

Brain Stimulation Research

In the 1950s, James Olds and Peter Milner discovered certain areas of the brain that gave rats a high. They would repeatedly press a lever to receive stimulation there, particularly in the septal area.

These experiments led us to a realize the importance of dopamine in reward. Additional research in this area concluded the brain registers all pleasures in the same way, whether they come from a drug, a financial bonus, or a sexual experience. Thus, we say our brain has a pleasure center.

Summary and transition

Keep in mind that much of what have described about the makeup of our brain and the diverse activities it can perform comes from research in neurology, biochemistry, and related branches of physical science. Research in psychology, behavior biology and related behavioral sciences also provides us with significant knowledge of the brain. Some of this research involves the effects of drugs and other substances on the brain. We next move to that. Stop

Chapter 7.
Care and Feeding of Our Brain

By now, we realize that our brain we are born which is complex, different from everyone else, and capable of learning so much that its potential seems almost unlimited. We also know that cognitive limitations that impede learning and memory are common. Aside from hereditary origins, what are the main sources of mental deficits, and how can they be avoided?

Brain development and damage

Trauma from various external and internal forces affects our brain in both obvious and hardly noticeable ways. In our early years (and in old age) our brain is particularly vulnerable. We all know that pregnant women are warned against using alcohol and other drugs. Why? Because in the prenatal stage these products and many kinds of medication (alone or in combination) can be toxic. If all women were to follow their doctor's advice during pregnancy, children in our nation would be healthier and brighter, and our educational system would be given a substantial and much-needed boost.

In recent years, we have been making concerted efforts to reduce brain damage at all ages. You might not think of maternity wards as a source of harm. Yet, one of their main problems has been the incidence of dropped infants. Hospitals currently have a campaign under way to reduce (or eliminate) this source of early brain trauma. At home, infants are still at risk, not only from accidental injury, but from mistreatment by parents or other caregivers. Shaking an infant or smacking a child in the head is now recognized as child abuse and is subject to prosecution; health providers are required to report evidence of such incidents.

Other common sources of accidental brain damage include falls, motor vehicle, bicycle and skateboard accidents, contact sports and diving into shallow water. Some head trauma is not immediately obvious but becomes so over time.

Consider contact sports. In boxing, for example, we have seen some of its most successful combatants, including some who have never been knocked out, demonstrating clear evidence of deterioration in mental competence. "Punch drunk" to describe this condition has been around for a long time. Concussions are common in other sports, particularly ice hockey and football. It was not surprising that a group of former National Football League players successfully sued the NFL citing memory loss and other difficulties in mental functioning from pounding their head took during their playing days. Youth football is a more widespread problem. About 3 million of our youth between age 6 and 18 who play football compared with about 100,000 in college and a few thousand in the NFL. Parents wonder, "should we allow our son to participate"? And with good reason. Children's brains are still forming and are susceptible to damage, including much that is not obvious.

Head injury is but one source of brain trauma. Most of us know of some people whose life has been radically changed by brain cancer, stroke, or brain infection. I remember, as a child, my shock to see the sudden deterioration of a neighbor who had a syphilitic infection from the distant past (one he thought had been cured) when it reached his brain, producing a psychotic condition known as General Paresis.

Our brain is also affected by chemicals in our blood stream. Oxygen we get from exercise, nutrition from a sensible diet and some medicines, such as those to control blood pressure or prevent blood clots, help it to function well.

Drugs aimed at enhancing mental performance have recently become available, but, so far, their benefits and potential harm are unclear.

Research, including laboratory research and personal experimentation, continues. It is clear, however, that alcohol, marijuana, nicotine, lead and many other substances have deleterious effects on our brain over time, especially for heavy users. Adding to the potential danger is the adverse reactions some individuals experience and the frequency with which prescription, over the counter and recreational drugs (legal and illegal) are combined. The more you take, the greater the risk.

Benjamin Franklin was alert to dangers to our brain posed by a variety of substances, including exposure to lead. In his work as a printer, he observed mental deterioration in workers over time, and related it to lead trays they carried. Lead rubbed off on their hands and was ingested from food held in their hands. Fellow workers generally ignored his emphasis on washing their hands thoroughly before eating. You may wonder "Why was lead paint tolerated into our present day if its toxic effects were known back in Franklin's time? It is only one of many instances (tobacco is another that comes to mind) of known harmful effects being widely ignored.

Marijuana and derivatives

Next to alcohol, marijuana is the most widely used recreational drug even though it is still illegal in most states (at this writing).

Effects

A marijuana high is relatively unpredictable. A person's response is strongly affected by factors aside from drug strength, such as: circumstances under which it is used, mood of the user and social group participating all of which contribute to the experience. As in alcohol intoxication, inhibitions are reduced, and commonplace situations may appear funny and ludicrous, or frightening and upsetting. Commonly reported experiences include spacing out, distortion of perception of time and place, increased sensory awareness, feelings of relaxation, euphoria and freedom and bursts of energy. Under its influence, many users see colors as brighter, and people and object in their world as more beautiful. They often experience an enhanced appreciation of music and may spend long hours absorbed in is effects.

Medical issues

Marijuana also produces lethargy, neglect of responsibilities, and a decline in cognitive functioning. Decision making, concentration, and memory may suffer for days after use, especially in regular users. Long-term, regular use of marijuana may impair brain development.

Value

Research on chemicals found in marijuana, called *cannabinoids*, has led to two FDA-approved medications that contain such chemicals in pill form or as a cream. Benefits include relief from pain and muscle spasm, and nausea associated with chemotherapy. Other potential benefits might include immune function, neuroplasticity, emotional and mood regulation, vascular health and digestive function. Continued research may lead to more medical use for marijuana ingredients.

Because of such promising results, many people argue that marijuana itself should be legalized, and many states have done so. Others have approved it only for medical use.

Concerns
Aside from the negative effects mentioned above, marijuana's similarity to tobacco raises concern that long-term smoking may also cause cancer and other diseases. Many years passed, and millions of people died before the link between tobacco and disease was conclusively established. While waiting for the results for marijuana, I recommend you avoid smoking it.

Legal issues
Distribution of illegal drugs supports a powerful criminal enterprise, and law enforcement agencies are determined to destroy it. Consequently, many people are, or have been, incarcerated for possession or distribution of marijuana. Back in the 1960's a college student I knew used marijuana regularly with friends. They asked him to pick up some when he was in Philadelphia, which he did. He was arrested and sentenced to five to ten years in prison although it was his first offense, and numerous character witnesses testified in his behalf. Even today, when we are more tolerant and decriminalization more

prevalent, penalties vary widely from state to state and country to country.

Driving under the influence of marijuana remains illegal, and with decriminalization, we can expect an increase in offenses.

DUI penalties for marijuana can be severe. In Pennsylvania, for example, for a first offense the listed penalty is, "Mandatory minimum of 72 hours in jail, $1,000 to $5,000 fine, must attend an alcohol highway safety school, and comply with all drug and alcohol treatment requirements; driver's license revocation for at least 18 months, may be required to complete 150 hours of community service." For a second offense, punishment increases dramatically.

Hallucinogens

Effects

These psychoactive substances cause hallucinations, perceptual distortions and related changes in thoughts and feelings.

Types and sources

LSD (acid) is one of the most powerful mind-altering drugs. It is made from lysergic acid, which is found in a fungus that grows on certain grains.

Psilocybin (magic mushrooms) comes from mushrooms found in tropical and subtropical regions of Central and South America, and the United States.

Peyote (buttons) is a small, spineless cactus with mescaline as its chief ingredient.

Experimenting With Drugs

Hallucinogens are of interest to me, in part because of the role several psychologists played in studying it and in stimulating its widespread use, including one I knew.

Timothy Leary and Frank Barron were graduate students at Berkeley in the 1950's when they undertook research on the mind-altering effects of LSD. Leary's motivation is seen in his quote, "my obsession has been to objectify inner experiences, to demystify the software of human existence. How? By relating changes in external behavior, systematically and lawfully, to changes in the brain."
Frank Barron, who had been a student at La Salle two years ahead of me, made noteworthy contributions to our understanding of personality and creativity, believed research on hallucinogens should only be conducted in laboratories under carefully controlled conditions.

Leary became a leading advocate for the widespread use of LSD. "Turn on, tune in, stop out," became his slogan and
a vast number of students and other young people took it up. Starting in the summer of 1967 in San Francisco, it spread rapidly across the country, creating a hippie subculture believing in inner transformation and liberation through the mind-altering effects of marijuana and LSD.

Coinciding with growing opposition to the war in Vietnam- "make love, not war" they chanted- and an upsurge in demonstrations associated with Civil Rights, the movements fueled one another and added to the uproar.

Addiction and tolerance

Marijuana and hallucinogens are but two of many recreational drugs people use to obtain a high that is reinforcing by stimulating pleasure centers in the brain. Habitual use produces an addiction. in which users develop a craving for the drug, and often a tolerance, in which they need ever-higher doses to obtain the same effect. Such drug use is widespread with American's spending over $100 billion per year on illicit drugs.

Opioids

At this writing, alarm bells are sounding throughout our nation as rapid growth in abuse of one of these drugs wreaks havoc in communities. It is rightly being called "our opioid crisis."

More than 2.5 million people are addicted to opioids and another 12 million are misusing them. Over 40,000 Americans have died annually in recent years from opioid overdoses. And the problem is worsening. Our communities and our health system are strained from this challenge.

Stimulants

A client came to a therapist I know because he was upset, jittery and had trouble getting to sleep. Early in his discussion, he mentioned his typical evening activity: sitting watching TV while drinking liter after liter of caffeinated soda. Case solved! Well, at least the problem was obvious. In another instance, a student showed up for his final exam trembling from head to toe. He confessed he had used a stimulant drug to cram for the exam but was clearly in no condition to take it.

By far, the most widely used stimulant is caffeine. It causes problems for some people, but more powerful stimulants including prescription drugs and illegal ones, are much more problematic. Since they reinforce users by creating a sense of well-being, increased energy, attention, and alertness, they are commonly used to obtain a high. They are also frequently employed by students and athletes to gain an edge on competitors and in occupations that require alertness over long hours.

Years ago, before the NFL acquired the prominence and wealth it enjoys today, a physician I knew was working with one of the football teams. When I asked him what he did, he said his main function was to give some players pills to calm them down before a game and others something to fire them up. Today, monitoring drug use among athletes plays a major role in athletic organizations at all levels. Every season finds several players penalized for infractions involving use of illegal substances.

Common Stimulants

Adderall, anabolic steroids, cocaine, crack cocaine, Dexedrine, ecstasy, Methamphetamine.

Harmful effects of stimulants.

Unfortunately, stimulants are a common source of both physical and psychological damage. Although the nature and extent of damage varies with type of drug, its strength, length of use and how it interacts with other substances in a person's system, stimulants, even in small amounts, present a risk.

Prevalence

Stimulant overdoses have increased dramatically in recent years, almost doubling between 2015 and 2017. Amphetamine prescription usage is responsible for much of this increase, and those taking them are typically unaware of risks involved.

Physical risks

Headaches, excessive weight loss, cardiovascular problems, digestive difficulties, lung functioning, extreme fatigue, sexual performance, seizures, stroke, brain damage.

Psychological risks

Anxiety, paranoid thinking, delusions and hallucinations.

Withdrawal symptoms, including fatigue and depression.

Prescription and over-the-counter drugs

Benefits from these products are extensively promoted, but they also present hazards, particularly when misused or taken in combination with other drugs.

The records reveal that United States does in fact have a drug problem-one with legal drugs. Spending on prescription drugs has risen from $40 billion in 1990 to a record $329 billion in 2016 (and we have spent even more on over-the-counter drugs) as people have come to believe there is a pill for every problem. Not only for pain but to help you sleep or stay awake, relax or energize you, to treat indigestion, constipation, nausea, anxiety, depression, hyperactivity and more.

Pharmaceutical companies have fueled this belief by bombarding the public with advertising touting the benefits of their products.

Medication for Mental Illness.

For me, medications prescribed for mental illness are particularly problematic. Currently 44 million American adults, or over 22 per cent of the population, are treated for mental illness annually.

The classification, based on the current edition of the Diagnostic and Statistical Manual of Mental Disorders of the American Psychiatric Association (DSM), is used in diagnosing, reporting and treating these disorders and in being reimbursed for the treatment

A group of prominent psychologists have expressed a major concern about this classification. They fear that it fosters the view that all mental disorders have a biological basis, and that medication is the preferred treatment. They also fear that too many problems people struggle with are being attributed to mental disorders rather than conditions under which they function.

Certainly, for some disorders, appropriate medication, alone or combined with psychotherapy, is most helpful; for other conditions, evidence shows counseling or psychotherapy alone to be equally or more effective without the danger of drug dependence, side effects or adverse reactions. In psychotherapy, the person typically learns better ways to deal with anxiety or depression or sources of stress and confusion. It usually involves changing habitual ways of responding to life's challenges and frustrations. It involves work, and it takes time, but those who opt for this approach are usually pleased with the outcome. Ideally, the treatment utilized for a given disorder is one that research has shown to be effective. One factor that consistently shows up as beneficial in research studies is the relationship between client and therapist. Unfortunately, pressure by insurance providers to push for a quick diagnosis using the DSM, hampers development of a therapeutic relationship.

Today's newspapers (June 1, 2019) report a new medical diagnosis added to the International Classification of Diseases by the World Health Organization- "work-related burnout"- raises concern. Why? Because, some argue, the problem often stems from intolerable working conditions. It's these that need adjustment, not the workers. Often, however, it seems less expensive to require workers to adapt to highly stressful conditions.

The bottom line often rules. Unfortunately, some members of mental health professions, pharmaceutical firms, health insurance companies and government agencies are more interested in increasing profit than improving treatment. A whale-sized bundle of money is floating in this sea of mental illness, and the financial sharks are circling it in a feeding frenzy.

Pharmaceutical companies, in their drive to increase sales, have now become the leading offenders under the False Claim Act, accounting for 25% of all federal FCA settlements over the past decade. States have also sued pharmaceutical giants for advertising drugs for conditions or populations for which they have not been approved (marketing drugs for use with children and for mental disorders for which it had not proven effective), and for paying mental health officials, doctors and university professors to promote their products. These firms have paid billions to settle claims out of court. Still they say they have done nothing wrong.

Consequently, mental health professionals and consumers do have reason to fear that inappropriate classifications may well lead to more people considered mentally ill and more and more treated with drugs.

Our Aging Brain

You remember we began this chapter noting how vulnerable our brain is early in our lives. Let's look now at our later years. Psychologists have long studied changes in cognitive functioning over the life span, in general, revealing a rapid improvement through early adulthood, a leveling off in middle years and a decline in old age. But the general principle requires considerable qualification. For one, some important mental functions (vocabulary for one) hold up well. Another consideration is that individuals differ widely from the average with many older persons functioning well throughout their lives, and others (especially those with disorders affecting the brain) demonstrating major deficits.

With a growing percent of our population living 25 to 30 years after traditional retirement age, we have become increasingly aware of the value of keeping them healthy and functioning well. We recognize that a healthy lifestyle, including physical and mental exercise, a sense of being engaged in worthwhile activities and being a part of a social support system contribute to healthy aging. We have also made considerable progress in adapting to decline that occurs, slowing memory loss and compensating for it and in rehabilitating individuals who experience setbacks.

In summary, what we have seen in this chapter is how our brain is affected by what happens to it over our lifetime, and that we have control over many of these factors. We have focused on neurological studies to support this.

Next, we will look at psychological findings, including neuropsychological research that contributes to improving our lives.

Chapter 8.
Internal Mind and External World

Introduction

Neurological research, including that with drugs, provides valuable information for us about the power, limitations, and peculiarities of our brain. Psychological studies directed at understanding what our behavior tell us about our brain may provide even more. We have previously discussed neuropsychological assessment which reveals information about brain function. Let's move next to what studies of perception tell us.

If you can imagine yourself in Philadelphia strolling through the Franklin Institute's section on the brain you might notice a display consisting of a set of letters:

"I cdnut blv tht I cld actly undrstnd wht I ws rdng,"

Even though this makes no sense, strictly speaking, I'll bet you are able to understand it. For our brain needs only a close approximation of words (or other symbols) to make sense from them. We have an inborn tendency to group and give meaning to what we perceive.

Piecing together bits of input and deriving meaning from them is the way our brain operates. We see what it can accomplish in scientific research as findings from several studies come together to provide a new perspective on a topic; we see it dramatized in crime fiction where a series of clues are pieced together to identify who did it. But the process is more commonly operating in a mundane manner every day. Thus, I look at the tiles in my bathroom and wonder why the designer included vague dancing figures. But then I realize they are more likely a series of curved lines I have organized into meaningful figures.

Perceptual defense. In addition to input from our senses, other neural activity, including that stemming from our emotions, also has an impact on our perception. Consequently, material that is a threat to our self-concept may be blocked from consciousness or distorted. This phenomenon is known as perceptual defense. I saw a vivid demonstration of this while sitting in on another instructor's class in which he described perceptual defense. One student rejected the concept vociferously, becoming more and more strident as the discussion progressed. Finally, the instructor turned and wrote the following message on the blackboard.

yur bhvr is obnxus

"What does that say"? He asked. The room grew hushed and tense. We were anxious to see how the student reacted. To our surprise he seemed neither angry nor embarrassed, just genuinely puzzled. "It doesn't say anything" he replied. "It's just a bunch of letters."

Perceptual defense is a specific instance of a more general principle that our view of the world colors our interpretation of new information. It is difficult to be objective. At this writing, impeachment proceedings for President Trump are under way. Testimony of witnesses and related evidence is interpreted quite differently by those who have a negative view of Trump and those whose opinion is positive. To the first, it seems crystal clear that he is guilty. To the second, it is added evidence that his opponents will stop at nothing to destroy him;

they, in turn, are moved to exert more effort to protect him and attack his detractors.

Attention

Making sense of our world and our life is a major project for all of us. We will discuss how psychology can help us do that throughout the book. For now, a discussion of attention helps lay a foundation.

Although sight, sounds, smells, touch and other stimuli from our environment constantly bombard our sense organs, we are unable to process all incoming material simultaneously. Instead, we focus on what attracts our attention and ignore the rest. Why, however, do we attend to one thing rather than another? And why is it often so difficult to keep our mind on things we should and ignore distractions? Our ability to concentrate depends partly on changes in our surroundings. A display of colorful, cascading fireworks or a sudden screech of brakes will automatically attract our attention. In part, what we attend to also depends on characteristics within us. On passing a young woman on the street, whether we notice her depends on both our relatively stable characteristics, such as our age, gender and sexual orientation, and on our present state of mind. Are we lonely, rushing to an important meeting, rehearsing a speech; are we late; famished and thinking only of food?

And what three men walking in a field perceive will vary with their interests. One may be enjoying watching birds, one examining the field as a possible building site and the third wondering if it might make a nice golf course.

Multitasking

Although we often want to concentrate on one task and block out distractions, many situations require us to perform two tasks simultaneously. How can we do this? Dividing attentional resources, is an essential skill we need in order to master such situations.

Multitasking can be accomplished in two quite different ways, each with advantages and problems. For one, we can master a task so well that it becomes a habit, not requiring thought or attention leaving higher brain centers available to attend to something else. A skilled typist, for example, can carry on a thoughtful conversation while rapidly turning out copy. For another, we can multitask by shifting our attention back and forth from one object to another. If we talk on the telephone while watching TV, we are alternating our attention, no doubt missing parts, but able to get the gist of each. In driving a car, we must be aware of other vehicles, pedestrians, road conditions, traffic signs, our speed, warning lights and more. We also must utilize this information in adjusting our steering wheel, brakes, accelerator and other controls. Some of this is habitual for an experienced driver, but typically requires a rapid shifting of attention from right to left, from rear view mirrors to dashboard instruments. In changing to a different car, we may get some surprises because of differences in its instrumentation and controls.

Attention and distractions

Distractions are omnipresent for drivers. One time my daughter, while riding in a car with a young man, wondered why he had gone off the road and went driving across a field. As it turned out, he had been watching a colorful bird, flying ahead of him along the road. When the road turned, the bird continued straight ahead and so did he.

Unfortunately, focusing on one thing and missing other information may be tragic. In one well-documented airplane accident, its crew were fixating on one of its warning lights that seemed to be malfunctioning. They were tapping it twisting it, discussing many possible causes of the problem when one of them interrupted with "say, the automatic pilot is on isn't it?" Those were the last words investigators heard on the black box they recovered!

Personal Factors Affecting Attention (variability)

Have you noticed times when your attention wandered because of fatigue, illness, stress, emotions, alcohol, medication or other drugs? Most of us have experienced it or have seen it in others.

Or do you frequently find yourself wrapped up in daydreams? For a high level of performance, you need a high level of focus. If you are reminiscing about past events or worried about your future, you will have difficulty accomplishing things and enjoying the present where you are living.

Broad or Narrow Focus

Often a broad focus is more effective than a narrow one. If you concentrate on one aspect of your surroundings, you miss others-perhaps crucial ones. In football, a linebacker, awaiting a play, does not direct all his attention to the quarterback. Rather, he scans the offense looking for tips from any opponent that might help him anticipate an upcoming play. A quarterback also must have broad vision, sweeping the defense to decide in a few seconds which of his receivers to target.

Similarly, when driving, you cannot simply stare at the car in front of you. You need a broad focus. In flying a plane, you must attend to what is below you and above you as well as ahead behind and, on either side (that's why pilots are said to need a swivel neck).

Effect of Maturation

Our brain changes over time, and these changes affect our attention. In childhood, adolescence and early adulthood, our brain is still maturing, consequently, hyperactivity and difficulty concentrating are common. In the elderly, brain functions are declining (sometimes gradually, sometimes precipitously) reducing our capacity for selective attention and ability to resist distractions.

Nature vs Nurture

A long-standing controversy has been the nature-nurture debate. It asks whether we are influenced more by the kind of brain we have inherited or experiences we have undergone? Are our genes more important or our learning?

Philosopher John Locke, regarded as one of the most influential contributors to the Enlightenment Movement, considered our brain as a tabula rasa, "a blank slate on which anything could be writ" This view influenced philosophy, psychology and education for years.

During much of the last century, for example, psychologist B. F. Skinner and other members of the Behaviorist school of psychology, argued that we should ignore our brain and its mental processes. Instead, he held that learning, and our environment in which we learn, is all-important. At one time, his position had many adherents, but support declined considerably as evidence against the all-importance of learning accumulated. One well-publicized instance of this took place in a debate with linguist Noam Chomsky. Chomsky's research on language acquisition in children provided convincing evidence for innate factors influencing language development. A child is ripe for acquiring a language at a certain age. Wait until later and it becomes more of a challenge.

It is now clear that our brain is anything but a "blank slate." For though, it is a learning machine that enables us to accumulate knowledge and skills with amazing rapidity, it comes equipped with a multitude of modules primed to learn connections and patterns that enhance survival of individuals and species.

In many other species, the role of innate proclivities, called instincts, is more obvious. Birds do not learn to build a nest from watching other birds. Birds raised in a laboratory where they have never seen a nest, will build ones of the same construction as other members of their species.,

Maturation in Humans

In humans, our level of maturation, particularly maturation of our brain, determines what we can learn. In fact, many things that young children "learn" do not involve much, if any, learning. You may have noticed that children will crawl, stand, and babble without any instruction or encouragement once they reach a certain level of development. And babies naturally smile when you smile at them. Since maturation is not confined to early childhood, but continues throughout our lives, it has important implications for child rearing, education, law enforcement and several other aspects of the socialization process.

In teaching a child (or someone of any age) new skills or knowledge we need to remember three related facts: 1.new learning depends on prior learning as well as maturation level; 2. students of the same chronological age vary in level of maturation; and 3. children are more mature in certain facets of development and less mature in others.

Parents and educators face challenges and see opportunities based on this knowledge. Should children in early grades be instructed to sit at a desk and listen to their teacher or should they be encouraged to roam around the classroom, examining material and asking questions? Should children be in the same classroom as others their age? Or should we be flexible in grouping children, so they are with those of the same level of readiness for a given kind of subject?

Children are ripe for certain kinds of learning (art, music, languages) at a given age. Therefore, we don't want them to miss these opportunities. I remember a PTA meeting where parents were urging the school to add a foreign language to early grades when children learn it so readily. The principal dismissed this saying "It's not practical" even though other schools did it successfully.

Nor does it make sense to force a child to learn something at an early age (with all the time, effort and frustration involved) when they can readily learn it a bit later and will do so with more interest and enthusiasm. I think back to my own struggle with handwriting. Now I realize our educational system was wrong, not me!

In some subjects, such as mathematics, new learning is highly dependent on previous learning. It thus also makes no sense, to try to teach students a higher level of mathematics without checking to see if they have a foundation for it.

Youngsters who are more talented in a given area usually get more attention than those with less ability. We see that in most sports where more athletic children at a given stage also getting more practice. The outcome is a widening gap in performance with age. Success breeds success, and "failure" discourages participation. We can understand that children with more talent in any area will be encouraged to develop that talent. Yet, children with no special proclivity for an activity should be able to participate and benefit from that experience. Art, dramatics, music and athletics, are not just for professionals; they add to every person's growth and enjoyment.

What we know about maturation has wide implications for our society. We have known for some time that adolescents lack the judgment and impulse control present in adults, therefore most criminal justice professionals treat juvenile offenders differently than adults. We also place restrictions on driving a motor vehicle, purchasing alcoholic beverages, signing contracts and many other activities based on age. Recent brain research finds evidence of significant development still occurring in young adults up to about age twenty-five. How these findings relate to behavior in that age group is still unclear.

Unconscious Behavior

In our discussion of drugs of all types, we have frequently mentioned their role in bringing unconscious mental processes to the surface.

Now, let's look a bit more at how our behavior is influenced by these processes.

Do you often do things without knowing why you are doing them? Psychologists and others who study human nature have long realized we do this constantly. Cognitive neuroscience has revealed unconscious motivation to be far more pervasive than we had thought. Its discoveries have considerable potential, not only for improved self-understanding but also for understanding and influencing individuals and groups. Such utilization requires both accurate knowledge and sound judgment.

You will remember that Sigmund Freud made the unconscious a keystone of his theory of human nature. In his clinical work, he based his treatment on digging into and uncovering material in a patient's unconscious, particularly incidents that were traumatic and which had been repressed.

He was surprised to find that many of his patients uncovered memories of earlier sex abuse. Freud believed these to be false memories, but today this question is being reexamined.

When I first met my wife, she had an appeal that I had never felt before. I soon stopped seeing other young women and directed my attention to her. Much later, after our engagement, my mother happened to remark, "doesn't Marion remind you of Helen Kane"? Helen had been my mother's best friend. As a young boy, I would often accompany my mother on visits to see her. What a good feeling to be there when they were laughing and talking and having fun. I had never realized any connection between my immediate attraction to Marion and my boyhood feelings toward Helen until my mother's comment. Such connections are common, although we do not usually become aware of them.

Sometimes we experience dissonance between conscious and unconscious muses. A frequent dilemma involves "falling madly in love" with someone that your judgment (as well as family and friends) tells you is a mistake. Do you listen to your heart or your head? Or, more technically, which parts of your brain do you follow? Are you acting on conscious motives or unconscious ones?

Hypnosis

Hypnotism provides another method to see our unconscious at work Hypnosis demonstrations show dramatically how powerful our unconscious can be. Subjects given suggestions while under hypnosis will carry them out after they have come out of their hypnotic state, without realizing why. This is called posthypnotic suggestion.

On at least one occasion, Franklin employed suggestibility to help someone, in this case a Polish prince's wife suffering from depression. Franklin spoke to her sympathetically and helped her relax by playing soothing music on the armonica (one of his inventions, you will recall). Tears trickled down her cheeks, and she began to feel better. Franklin whispered, "Madam, you are cured." He visited her several times thereafter and taught her to play the armonica. Unfortunately, after several years of improvement, she had a fatal relapse.

Carl Jung, one of Freud's contemporaries, held that we not only have a personal unconscious, based on our early repressed or forgotten experience, but a collective unconscious passed down from our primitive ancestors. In his book, *Totem and Taboo* he proposed a collective unconscious containing material common to all humanity. As evidence, he cites common symbols present in art, ceremonies, religions and music of cultures isolated from one another, and their similarity of proscriptions. At the time, Jung's beliefs seemed inconsistent with our knowledge of the brain and memory. Today, with our increased recognition of the role of genetics in our behavior, they are not so easily dismissed.

Intuition and reasoning (Systems 1 and 2)

Do you believe in intuition? Until recently, the notion that people have intuition as well as logical reasoning and that our intuitive judgment is often correct, was considered unscientific. Today, research lends considerable credence to this view.

What this suggests are two distinct cognitive systems underlying thinking and reasoning both products of evolution. They are often referred to as System 1 and System 2. The first governing intuitive impressions is implicit, automatic, rapid, nonverbal, emotional and unconscious. It is also difficult to alter. The second, evolutionarily more recent and present only in humans, takes responsibility for logical reasoning. It is explicit, controlled, rational, slow, abstract and rule based. It utilizes conscious processes and is usually altered by convincing evidence.

Our initial reaction to a new experience is intuitive, utilizing System 1. These feelings and ideas are monitored, however, by System 2, which usually confirms our first impressions and guides our actions.

System 1 is called into action where swift judgment and rapid decision-making are required. When we do not have time for deliberation, we act on impulse and hope our impulses are right. It is also responsible for our tendency to seek immediate gratification rather than plan for the future.

Evidence for the existence of these two systems rests more on behavioral research than neurological investigation, but some researchers contend brain modules oversee each of them. In this view, our brain has built-in inclinations for us to think in certain ways: to group objects into categories, build coalitions, make moral judgments and detect deception (sometimes called a "bullshit detector") and, no doubt, many more.

We have all experienced times when our intuition disagrees with our rational judgment. How to know which is right? I remember a meeting of a small professional group listening to a proposal to purchase a new service. After the presenter left the room, we sat for a time mulling over our decision. What should I say? A well-spoken man who made a nice impression, his ideas seemed to make sense. And yet, something did not sit right with me. I did not trust the man. Reluctant to say this since I had no rational basis for my feeling, I said nothing. After a time, someone finally spoke up, "You know what. I don't trust that guy." Others muttered agreement. This illustrates one way of determining whether your instincts are on target, or stem from unconscious prejudice. That is, do others get the same impression? Unfortunately, some groups share common prejudices, so this criterion is far from perfect.

Mental conflicts (conscious and unconscious)

In our chapter on morality, we discussed conflicts from a religious perspective as a struggle between good and evil. One well-known alternative to this view is one offered by Sigmund Freud. In his psychoanalytic theory, he concluded that mental conflicts involved both a battle between forces in the unconscious mind and tension between conscious and unconscious motives.

My preference varies considerably from Freud. I lean toward an underlying genetic basis for our internal conflicts. I believe we are born with a mixture of self-centered (or selfish) genes and group-centered (or altruistic) ones, with innate tendencies for each as part of our nature. The former fosters self-development, initiative, assertiveness and competitiveness; the latter, compassion, cooperation, love and social consciousness. They can also lead to egocentrism, aggressiveness and hostility in the first case and dependence and subservience in the second. Most of us have a balance between the two set of genes-we "look out for Number One" but are also concerned for the welfare of others. Some people, however, are born with more of one or the other (thus, in sociopaths, self-centered genes predominate, and altruistic ones are sparse or absent). Both tendencies can be modified by learning but our learning builds on our inherited predispositions.

One implication of this perspective is in child development. Children with altruistic inclinations tend toward respect for others, but often benefit from learning to be appropriately assertive and competitive, while those who are naturally self-centered and even abusive (as in bullying) must learn social limits, self-control and respect for the rights of others.

Drugs and the unconscious

Hypnosis and psychoanalysis (including dream interpretation and free association) offer two approaches to exploring the unconscious. Another way, as we have mentioned, is to investigate our response to drugs. Some wags have noted that, "The Superego is soluble in alcohol" because one obvious effect of alcohol is to reduce our inhibitions. Thus, our behavior reveals information about our innate, unconscious self. We have all seen a "fighting drunk", a "crying drunk" a "babbling drunk", and so on. All are revealing underlying emotions that are normally inhibited.

Have you ever interviewed for a position and been invited to have lunch (and a few drinks) with the interviewer? This approach to "seeing what a person is like beneath the façade" has had its advocates over the years, but it has its hazards and is often misleading.

One old mantra for authors is that "you should write drunk and revise sober" as a way of escaping your inhibitions. In fact, many authors draw on unconscious resources in other ways such as writing late into the night when inhibitions are reduced by fatigue and revising when rested in the light of day. In this way hoping to touch readers' unconscious emotions too.

Cognitive dissonance and brainwashing

Another phenomenon illustrating the influence of unconscious processes in a somewhat different way is cognitive dissonance. An incident Ben Franklin narrates, offers a good example. When he ran for office as a clerk, one of his colleagues delivered a fiery speech criticizing him and sullying his reputation. Although elected, he was irate with his critic. Aware that this man might one day hold considerable power, Franklin looked for a way to avoid future frictions with him.

He wanted to turn the man into an ally but to do it without being subservient. Franklin's status as a book collector gave him a reputation as a man of discriminating literary tastes, so when he wrote the man asking to borrow a relatively rare selection from his library, his rival was flattered and sent it at once. Franklin returned it shortly with a thank-you note. After the next legislature meeting, he approached Franklin and spoke to him for the first time. They soon became fast friends, a friendship that lasted until the man's death.

This illustrates that not only do our beliefs and feelings affect our actions, but our actions also shape our beliefs and feelings. You do favors for people you like. Since Franklin had asked for a favor, and his critic granted it, he naturally asks himself why he did so. The most acceptable explanation is that he must like him. This has been called the Benjamin Franklin Effect and is a well-known illustration of cognitive dissonance. Of course, this does not imply that if you want people to like you, you should go around asking everyone for favors. Rather, the kind of favor you ask and the way you ask should reflect a respect for the person, as should your way of giving thanks. It is an interaction that builds a relationship.

A most remarkable and disturbing examples of using cognitive dissonance on a wide scale was "brainwashing", introduced by Chinese during the Korean War. American officials were taken by surprise, and our troops were unprepared for it. Rather than using threats or abuse, the Chinese sought cooperation from prisoners of war by more subtle techniques. They would first get a prisoner to agree on some minor issue, such as that, for the good of all, individuals should not waste soap. Then he would be asked to read a statement to that effect to fellow captives.

He may feel uneasy about it, but since he has agreed with this statement, why should he not read it to others? Using this technique, prisoners were gradually induced to become more cooperative. Many of them changed their beliefs as well as their actions. Few attempted to escape, and to the shock of the American people, 21 of our men opted to remain in China rather than return to their own country.

Although this brainwashing generally worked, analysis revealed many mistakes. in carrying it out. A most serious one involved separating African American prisoners, believing they would be more dissatisfied with America and more subject to brainwashing. These troops saw it as both a throwback to segregation and a challenge to their ability to resist. Many prisoners also came up with subtle ways to resist, such as reading a statement in such a way that other Americans would know they disagreed with it, but their captors would not.

A more recent controversy involved interrogation of suspected terrorists held at Guantanamo Bay. American authorities employed several prominent psychologists, including a few officers of APA (American Psychological Association), in interrogating prisoners. Accusations of assisting in torture followed and generated a major scandal for APA. The association voted to prohibit its members from participating in such interrogation, asserting that it tortured detainees. Advocates of participation claim they were protecting the rights of detainees as well as aiding national security.

Ironically, the brainwashing used by the Chinese during the Korean War did not use torture (although prisoners may have seen it as a threat).

Cognitive Behavioral Therapy

Therapists, particularly cognitive behavioral therapists, apply cognitive dissonance insights in their work. Exercises assigned between therapy sessions (homework) require clients to engage in appropriate positive behavior as a way of facilitating change in their thinking and moods as well. What would happen, for example, if you saw such a therapist because you felt ill-at-ease when first meeting someone new? No doubt you would discuss those uncomfortable feelings, situations that produce them and thoughts that come to you at those first meetings. In cognitive-behavioral therapy, however, action is emphasized more than discussion.

You would be assigned tasks to perform before the next meeting, such as introducing yourself to ten people and noting your thoughts and feelings on each occasion. You will soon discover certain situations in which you are more confident and gradually take on more challenging situations. Your behavior changes: your thoughts and feelings follow. In some situations (fear of flying or driving across a bridge) you might use virtual reality initially before moving to real-life situations.

We can apply these findings in our everyday life. It has sometimes been called, "Fake it 'til you make it," but I prefer to emphasize improving how you feel, by doing something positive.

We have looked at a number of ways in which our unconscious affects us. Next, we move to the role of unconscious influences on prejudice, an issue so crucial to personal development and social change.

Prejudice, Racism and Discrimination

Ben Franklin pondered over prejudice and made recommendations to reduce it. He started with his own prejudices, which he admitted and sought to change. He mentions his dislike of Dutch and Germans (whom he saw as a threat). We have previously seen his discussion of prejudice prevalent in Colonial America against American Indians. His major recommendation: try to see things from their point of view. He saw numerous practices among Indians that puzzled and irritated colonists, but which made perfect sense if one understood their culture.

Fortunately, we are now learning more about how to overcome prejudices, starting, as Franklin did, with examining our own, and utilizing positive psychology to overcome it throughout our society. In doing so, it helps to keep in mind the difference between discrimination and prejudice even though they usually go together and influence one another. Discrimination, such as in housing, employment and educational opportunities are actions that can be changed through convincing people that these practices are wrong. Demonstrations that call them to public attention and rational arguments are an effective platform for this, Differences may exist over which programs are fairest and most effective, but people agree-discrimination is wrong.

Rational arguments are less effective in changing prejudice since it has an emotional basis. What can be done to change feelings, likes and dislikes, initial irrational reactions? Here, unfortunately, argument, criticism and demonstrations generally intensify prejudice. People dig in and refuse to budge. "Why should I change" they say. "let them change." Instead, we are more likely to change our prejudices through positive emotional experiences, often through one-on –one interaction but also vicariously through media presentation that evoke understanding and sympathy for oppressed groups. And, although rational arguments are usually ineffective, when coming from someone you like and respect, they often help.

Summary

We have considered how new research on the brain, both neurological and psychological, helps us understand others and ourselves. We have seen how much our behavior is dependent on maturation in our brain as well as on prior learning. Looking at basic brain structure, we have noted the role of higher brain centers, specifically our cerebral cortex, on rational behavior, and that of lower brain centers on habits and unconscious influences. These unconscious influences, we have concluded, are responsible for intuitive and emotional behavior. We have highlighted some of significant applications of our knowledge of unconscious factors, including cognitive dissonance, in influencing individuals and groups.

With this background we should be ready to look at what we know about memory, problem solving and decision making including how to bolster them.

Chapter 9.
Remembering What You Want To Know

"Tell me and I forget, teach me and I remember, involve me and I learn."

Benjamin Franklin

Cognitive Functioning

After looking at the brain from a neurological and psychological perspective, we are ready to see how we can improve our cognitive functioning in problem solving and decision making, including what memory contributes.

Short term memory

You probably have heard of short-term and long-term memory. Let's look at them. Material in short term memory lasts only from a few seconds to a minute without rehearsal. Some material, however, moves from it to long-term memory where it is stored and organized. Short-term memory has a capacity of about seven items, but we can increase this through chunking. In remembering a new ten-digit telephone number you use your short-term memory between looking it up and completing your call. Dividing a number into three chunks, will make it easier to remember. Remembering 2159511282 is more difficult than 215-951-1282.

Or you could jot it down.

After we have used a number frequently, we have no need to consult our directory. It is now in our long-term memory.

Why is it common to have trouble recalling names of people we meet? Just a few days after being introduced to someone, we can't come up with their name. Three main possibilities in such a situation are: 1. we didn't attend to the name when we were introduced, so we never learned it (much "forgetting" is actually "not learning"); 2. we knew it briefly (was in our short term memory), but quickly forget it, or 3. we learned it (is in our long term memory) but cannot recall it at the moment. It may pop into our head a few hours later.

Working memory is often used as synonymous with short-term memory. I prefer to employ it for information we have readily available to work with, including material from short-term memory and what we can quickly access from long term-memory.

Long-term memory can hold large quantities of information for an unlimited duration. Utilizing memory involves three steps: 1. acquisition: acquiring and storing new information; 2. consolidation: processing and incorporating it into previous memory; and 3. retrieval: accessing or recalling stored information. Each step holds possibilities for improvement.

During acquisition, **meaningful material** is easier to remember than meaningless. This list of words: *Go my swim I sometimes friends a for and*, is harder to learn than if they were arranged so they meant something: Sometimes my friends and I go for a swim.

This is worth noting because much of what we want to learn seems without much meaning, and we believe we are faced with the chore of memorizing it. Instead, it pays to approach it with an eye toward making sense of it. Finding meaning beats learning isolated facts every time.

It is not surprising then that if new learning can be related to what you already know, acquisition and retrieval are much easier. I tried a brief demonstration of this. During the 2009 baseball season, I read the following material to my class: *Leading off, Jimmy Rollins ran the count to one and one before bunting down the third base line for a single. Shane Victorino followed with a walk on four straight balls. Chase Utley was hit by the first pitch to load the bases. Ryan Howard went to a full count before hitting a grand slam to give the Phils a four-run lead.*

The results were striking. Students who knew little about baseball could recall next to nothing and were surprised to hear Phillies fans rattle it off, often word for word.

It shouldn't be any surprise to find new learning building on previous learning especially on things we know well. Our brain does not have a limited storage capacity, although it was once argued it did. The tale of an ichthyologist who refused to learn the names of his students for fear he would forget names of fish, illustrates what some people assume. In fact, the more you know about a topic the easier it is to learn more. And new learning does not cause us to forget previous material.

Relevance

Moreover, personally relevant or emotionally exciting material is more memorable. What moves you, relates to your interest and aspirations or stirs your emotions is more likely to be retained. Good teachers get students involved, stir their feelings and relate the topic to their lives; advertisers make their pitch by emphasizing their product's relevance to consumers and by attempting to make it enticing; and politicians emphasize issues that appeal to voters, such as jobs, taxes and health care (unfortunately, they often arouse our fear, anger and prejudice too).

Rehearsal

At times, new material does not seem related to anything we already know. Here we have to resort to rote learning. We must practice, practice, practice until we remember it. But whether learning meaningful material or learning by rote, some approaches are more effective. For example, you may ask," Is it better to stick with material for a long period or break it into frequent shorter segments?" The answer? Short frequent rehearsal. This is better in general, and especially helpful for rote learning. It beats cramming as a method, particularly for content you want to retain. Cramming may be necessary at times, but if you want to remember it, you better review it. In learning a foreign language, mathematical formulas, the names of bones in the body, frequent review, even for brief periods, is essential. I once faced the challenge of learning a new language when working on my doctorate. I needed to pass a difficult exam in German, a task demanding massive rote learning. Knowing the value of frequent rehearsal, even for brief periods, I carried a handful of vocabulary cue cards in my pocket and reviewed them whenever I had a few minutes free. At first, I kept forgetting what I had learned, but with frequent rehearsal I gradually made progress until I could read German fluently. Conquering this obstacle gave my confidence a boost in tackling tough tasks in the future. (In case you are wondering, I did pass the exam).

Type of rehearsal

It is particularly helpful to rehearse in the same format in which you will be required to perform, For a multiple choice test, focus on facts and making distinctions among them; for an essay, consider how you can best organize and integrate material; for an oral exam, practice by having someone ask you relevant questions and critique your answers. Want to learn your topic well? Use all three methods!

Feedback

We often find people reading and rereading material they want to learn. Is this approach. a good idea? Not really. A much better way is to test yourself often about what you study. Try asking yourself questions (or relying on a friend to ask them), writing an essay, giving a presentation or engaging in a discussion on the material. Study groups can facilitate this. One of my favorite groups of students was a half dozen members of a class in our counseling program who formed their own study group. Every Saturday or Sunday, they would get together, each with questions and ideas about subjects they were studying. They set an example for others to follow and raised the level of discourse for the entire program. It illustrates the adage previously mentioned, "give answers to students and they learn facts; ask questions and they learn to think."

Motor and interpersonal skills

Motor and interpersonal skills have something in common, you learn little more than the basics by reading or discussing- periods of practice and critique are required. Most people have more experience practicing motor skills like riding a bike or hitting a baseball than working on interpersonal skills. That's why I like to look at the way we learn the former in teaching the latter. In the 1956 movie Trapeze, featuring Burt Lancaster and Tony Curtis (and Gina Lollobrigida) as circus acrobats, Curtis practices diligently under the watchful eye of Lancaster. They work together, student and instructor, with Curtis accepting criticism, making sure he understands it, trying again and asking for more feedback. It exemplifies the kind of relationship we look for in teaching counseling or other skills involved in working effectively with people-practice, feedback, more practice, more feedback. A sure road to improvement.

Continuing in this vein, let's look at public speaking. You won't learn much by reading a book. Yet most inexperienced speakers are anxious (or should I say terrified) at the thought of practicing in front of a group. A way that works is to videotape yourself as you deliver a prepared speech. Review it, note things you want to change and try again. Gradually, you will stop looking at the ceiling, scratching your head. speaking too fast or whatever you decide needs changing. Pairing up with a friend, and/or having a sympathetic instructor critique you, facilitates progress. I should mention Toastmasters International too. They have a track record for developing communication skills, including public speaking, and they have branches in most communities.

Overlearning

Often, we make the mistake of studying material until we just barely know it. We then quickly forget it. By learning material thoroughly. i.e. "overlearning," (which does not mean spending too much time studying-as some students believe), you can retain content you have studied and skills you have practiced, for years. Consider poems, songs and such you memorized in early childhood and still remember. Of course, you don't have time to learn everything so thoroughly; you must be selective. Be on the alert to identify important facts, relationships, terminology, controversies and learn those thoroughly.

In addition, you can retain well-learned motor skills like riding a bicycle or hitting a baseball for years.

Memory retrieval

Is the process of retrieving material stored in long-term memory? Here we make a distinction between recall and recognition.

In recall, information is retrieved without obviously relevant cues. Thus for an essay exam the only cues you have to help are those you have used in memorizing material. In recognition, presenting some previously learned external material provides a cue for retrieving what you are trying to remember. A true false or multiple-choice question requires recognition. So does identifying a suspect from a picture or in a lineup. If you've ever said, "I'd know it if I saw it," you know what is meant by recognition.

Relearning

Although we gradually forget what we have learned, we usually retain the gist of it. Consequently, relearning is much faster and easier. Thus, the value of review. Studying for an examination by concentrating on new subject matter often means forgetting previously known material. It is better to spend time reviewing what you have learned until you know it well before tackling something new.

As I previously mentioned, after several years of struggle, I had learned to read German well. Following many years of disuse however, I could recall very little. In planning a trip to Switzerland, my wife and I agreed she would review French and I would review German. I was pleasantly surprised to find a month of occasional review brought much of it back. Relearning was so much easier than initial learning.

Retrieval

The process of recalling something from memory is known as retrieval, and aids to retrieval are called cues. In learning a topic, it is not only helpful to make it meaningful, personally relevant, exciting, and organized, but also to pick out cues that will assist you in recalling it.

Even if you have not thought about using cues during initial learning, anything associated with the experience may bring back memories of an event. Hearing a song you danced to when you first met your spouse will bring back memories of other happenings then. Seeing a photo of a movie actor will make you remember movies in which he appeared. Visualizing yourself in a situation from the past will bring back memories, sometimes vivid memories, you had forgotten. Just the other day, for instance, I heard a song from the past, Moonlight Becomes You and it struck me how many romantic songs feature the moon. I thought of a dozen or so before moving away from it, or I should say I thought I did. For the next few days, the moon and various songs about it kept popping into my head.

A related phenomenon is Déjà vu, a strong sense you have been through a present experience sometime in the past. Seemingly, it results from cues in the present evoking feelings connected with a previous event, but not the event itself.

Mnemonics

Another useful aid to memory is mnemonics, a term derived from the Greek word for memory. It refers to rules and devices developed to help us remember, enabling us to utilize something we can readily recall as an aid to accessing more difficult material.

Some common such devices include: "30 days has September, April, June and November…," and "ROY G BIV for the order of colors in the spectrum. To remember the number Pi to eight places, math students have used, "How I want a drink, alcoholic of course" in which the number of letters in each word is used to remember 3.1415926. More words can be added to the sentence if needed. This mnemonic comes in handy if you want to impress your friends on Pi Day (March 14, or 3-14-_ _ _ _).

Method of Loci

Another aid to memorizing a list, for example a shopping list, is known as the Method of Loci. In using it, we visualize each item on a list we want to learn and mentally place it in a familiar place in a sequence. If our list begins with milk, bread, coffee and eggs, we might visualize a stroll through our house, picturing a milk bottle on the mantel piece of our living room, then seeing a large loaf of bread propped up on a table in the dining room and then a steaming cup of coffee and a poached egg waiting in the kitchen. We can remember a long list using this technique, using any route we can visualize.

Using Pegs

Instead of using familiar places (loci) as a memory aid we might associate items on our list with familiar objects, i.e. "peg" them. A common technique is to remember "one is a bun, two is a shoe, three is a tree, four is a door, five is a hive, six is sticks, seven is heaven, eight is a gate, nine is a vine and ten is a hen," which gives us ten items to use as pegs. In this approach, we think of our first item, a bottle of milk with a bun on it, next we visualize a large shoe with a loaf of bread sticking out of it, then a cup of coffee hanging from a tree, followed by an egg perched in front of a beehive.

Using your ABC's

Another technique I and many other people find helpful in recalling a name is to go through the alphabet until you come to a letter that serves as a cue for recalling it. You ask yourself, "What was the name of the new administrator I met last week"? You then start in, "Anthony, Al, Aaron, Bill, Bert, Brett, Charles, Curtis, Claude, Dwight, Don-Yes, Don Reed! Try it. See if it works for you

Passwords

Remembering passwords, pin numbers and such, is a challenge for many of us. In selecting them, you are looking for a series of numbers or combination of numbers, words and symbols, that is easy for you to remember, but difficult for others to crack. You might draw on an address, phone number or I.D, from the past, that you would know, but potential hackers would not. Mixing letters, numbers and symbols in a systematic way (one easy to remember) and you are set.

For me, JJR031923 (my initials and date of birth) is not very secure. Much safer is 1726Whuntington (grandparents address). More secure yet, is 1&2^W.hUn*tin#gTon (scrambled address.

We have covered several aids to improving memory. From all of these suggestions, chose those that work best for you. Your memory should improve.

Components of memory

Furthermore our long-term memory involves a semantic component (semantic memory) consisting of verbal content that has been organized and classified, sensory components (primarily visual and auditory memories), an episodic component (a collection of past personal experiences and the circumstances in which they occurred, and a procedural or motor component responsible for knowing how to perform activities such as walking, shaving and playing tennis.

For most activities we draw on several parts of our memory. In attempting to retrieve the name of someone you know, you may recognize the name but not recall the face or visualize the person's face but not be able to recall their name. Most of us have a limited visual memory. Some people, however, have unusually vivid visual memories such as artists who are able to recall a scene from the past and replicate it, and scientists who can mentally compare a series of slides from "pictures they have in their heads." A few people even have a photographic memory (or eidetic imagery), enabling them to read a page from a book after closing it; they are still able to see it word for word in memory. In the same vein, musicians often possess a vivid auditory memory.

Irving Berlin, in his 1919 classic reminisces about how auditory and visual memories often go together:

A pretty girl is like a melody
That haunts you night and day
Just like the strain
Of a haunting refrain
She'll start upon a marathon and run around your brain
You can't escape she's in your memory
By morning, night and noon
She will leave you and then
Come back again
A pretty girl is just like a pretty tune.

Limitations of memory.

One way in which visual memory has been tested and found wanting is in eyewitness testimony. Juries usually weigh eyewitness testimony heavily in deciding on guilt or innocence. Research studies, conversely, find it to be mostly inaccurate and undependable. Furthermore, accuracy is unrelated to how confident witnesses are or how vividly they claim to recall an incident.

I experienced a taste of this firsthand as a victim of a robbery.

After stopping to help a young couple start their car, the man suddenly grabbed my wife's pocketbook, jumped in their car and sped away. During questioning by police, we both agreed their car was a Volkswagen, but my wife thought it was red, while I thought it was black. Such discrepancies are common, especially in emotionally charged incidents.

False memories

By this time, we know we forget or distort much of our past experience. Harder to believe is why we remember things even though they never happened. President Ronald Reagan provides a striking example of this. In reminiscing about his past, he would, from time to time, talk about incidents from old movies and believe they had actually happened. Reagan is far from alone in this kind of mistake. Recollections from the past are suspect, particularly those of older people. Fact-checking will often reveal huge discrepancies between memories and reality.

The egocentric nature of memories provides another basis for distortion. We often remember our role in an incident as more significant (and contributions of others as minimal or nonexistent) rather than as they actually were. A recently published biography of a colleague with whom I worked closely for many years brought this home to me. In it, author, Thomas McCarthy, a history professor at the U. S. Naval Academy, examined changes in higher education, psychology, counseling. and student personnel services during the years following WWII. As a concrete example he focused on LaSalle College and transformations being made in these areas during that time. In the initial draft the author drew heavily on recollections of his father, Thomas N. McCarthy, Emeritus Professor of Psychology and former Vice President of Student Affairs at La Salle. As I reviewed his account of what to me were memorable years, I found myself, at more than one section saying, "What! He wasn't the main one responsible for that. I was! Upon further review, as we exchanged recollections, and his father checked documents and other sources, it turned out I was right (well sometimes). Just as often I gave myself more credit for an accomplishment than I deserved (and at times we were both off base).

Suggestion and false memories

Of even greater concern, than the usual distortion of the past, false memories, especially memories from childhood, may be planted through suggestion (intentionally or inadvertently). This process often occurs whenever a person is in a highly suggestible state such as during hypnosis or deep psychotherapy. Intensive police interrogation too can produce false memories including memories of committing a crime. Most of us are amazed when a suspect, who confesses to a crime, is later proven beyond a doubt, to be completely innocent.

For some time, many psychotherapists believed a patient's psychiatric problems originated with repressed memories of childhood sex abuse. In attempting to uncover it, they frequently created false memories of abuse. Patients began to remember abuse that never happened or agonized over whether it happened or not. I must confess, my own interest in this is far from purely academic. I am upset and angry whenever I think of my wife's experience in therapy with a psychiatrist who believed in repressed memories. Back in the mid1980s, she was suffering from a disorder in which blood seeping from her capillaries into her muscles was causing considerable pain. In an attempt to relieve it, her hematologist suggested hypnosis. He referred her to a psychiatrist considered one of the foremost authorities in the country on hypnosis. After a few sessions, she began to believe she had been sexually molested as a child. Was it true? Who knows? Did it matter? Well, to her it did.

After a long struggle over memories true or false, she decided to forget the pursuit of the past and move on. Many others, unfortunately, had similar experiences during those years. It was far from the finest hour for the mental health professions.

Meantime, an increasing number of clinicians, researchers and criminal justice specialists had been raising questions about repressed memory and opposing its use in therapy. One of the leading figures among its critics was Elizabeth Loftus, a cognitive psychologist with a doctorate from Stanford University, who is internationally recognized for her research in memory, particularly false memories.

Her own experience triggered her concern. When she was 14, her mother had accidentally drowned in a swimming pool. In discussing it several years later, her uncle told her she had been the one who discovered her mother's body. Although she had thought little about the incident prior to the time. she now began remembering it in considerable detail. Shortly thereafter, however, she discovered her uncle had been wrong. It was her aunt who had found the body. If a false memory could be created so easily, she wondered, how often did it happen in therapy or police interrogations? In her subsequent career she specialized in research on false memories and recovered memories and helped clarify many misconceptions about them.

We see from all of this, the complexity of memory, and, despite our dependence on it, how imperfect it is. Additionally, we have discussed common errors we make and how to avoid or minimize them. We move now to other ways of improving memory.

Motivation and emotions play a significant role in initial learning and consolidation and in accessing it from long-term memory. As Benjamin Franklin noted, "creditors have better memories than debtors."

We tend to forget distasteful incidents or those reflecting poorly on our self-concept. Sometimes such forgetting is conscious (suppression), sometimes unconscious (repression). Sometimes, in addition, our memory is inaccurate because it is distorted by our motives rather than completely forgotten.

Emotions may aid memory or interfere with it. Sensational events, such as the terrorist attacks on 9-11-2001, are remembered vividly, partly because of emotions involved and partly because they have been rerun on television, in conversation and in our thoughts. Some incidents, by contrast, are so traumatic, we block them from ever becoming part of our memory, or, after initial learning, we repress them.

I recall an incident in which two training planes collided while taxiing. The student pilot in the rear seat of one plane was killed instantly as the propeller from the other plane sliced through his head. At the subsequent hearing, the instructor, who had lost consciousness during the accident, was asked what he had done at the time the collision occurred. His answer was, "I looked in the mirror to see if the student was OK." Asked what he had seen he replied, "I didn't see anything." It is clear he saw something in the mirror causing him to faint and block the horror from his mind.

Assuming initial material is learned rather than blocked, stress may interfere with its consolidation in memory, making it less accessible.

Emotions also influence our ability to retrieve material from memory. We see this frequently in test anxiety and other forms of performance anxiety. Although mild or moderate stress will usually strengthen our focus and our performance, high levels of stress interfere with our ability to recall information. We find this especially when information has been just barely learned rather than mastered well, but even well learned material can be affected. I recall a student who sat in my office a few days before a test and answered everything I asked her on the topic. It was obvious she knew the subject thoroughly. Yet, on the test, she blocked and obtained a low score on it. Other common examples of performance anxiety include writer's block and stage fright. Some athlete's, including star professional athletes, also experience such anxiety under pressure they miss games or perform far below their ability.

Stage fright

You may be familiar with P. G. Wodehouse's delightful example of stage fright in one of his short stories. His main character is a man who agrees to tour with a friend who has a bit part in a play. He sits in the audience, night after night, and watches as his companion steps on stage and speaks his only line: "pardon me sir, but there is a small conflagration in the living room." Surely, he thinks, this line could be delivered more effectively with different word emphasis, pacing, articulation, and gestures. He practices in private until one night a touch of laryngitis prompts his friend to ask him to take on his role. Here is his chance to star! As he waits in the wings for his cue, he is elated, anticipating how his performance will move the audience. Coming on stage, however, he is struck by the spotlight shining on him and conscious of an audience out there beyond the lights, waiting for him to speak out. But what is he supposed to say? He blocks. He stammers and stumbles until something finally comes to him. "Fire! Fire! he shouts and empties the theater as the crowd surges for the exits.

Summary

It is difficult to summarize all we know about memory. We know it is complex, powerful, and flawed. The better we understand it the better we can benefit from its power and minimize its weaknesses. It is, nevertheless, just one part of our intellect. Other cognitive functions are equally valuable. We can use them all in solving problems we invariably face. Which brings us to our next chapter, problem solving.

Chapter 10.
Solving Problems

Introduction

The most significant difference between humans and other species is the greater complexity of our human brain and resultant capacity to better understand our world and ourselves. We can plan ahead, solve complex problems, accomplish goals, and learn from our experience and that of others. Our rational abilities have led to remarkable achievements, including advances that have helped conquer diseases, and explore outer space. What, however, have we learned about our inner self? Our cognitive capacity should enable us to understand others and lead to more satisfying and productive lives. Yet, most of us use only a limited percentage of our brainpower. In addition, the brain we have is far from perfect. We fail to notice crucial incidents, forget valuable information, classify what we observe, in erroneous ways, have trouble identifying what is relevant, miss significant relationships and see nonexistent ones. Worse yet, some of us use their talents to exploit others or sabotage themselves.

Ben Franklin is a striking illustration of a person who used his intelligence wisely.

His discovery that lightning is electricity and his numerous valuable inventions are obvious evidence of genius. Less obvious, and even more remarkable, is the way he used his mind to better himself.

He made it a lifelong project, setting positive goals, and working assiduously toward them. One major goal was to develop his interpersonal and intergroup skills. Although not naturally gifted at relationships, his efforts paid off. Can we think of anyone who exerted more influence on the intellectual and political world of his time?

We too can use our brains to enrich our lives, by following Ben Franklin's example and using our cognitive abilities more effectively. In addition, we can learn from extensive research conducted by psychologists, cognitive scientists, neurologists, behavioral biologists and other researchers whose findings should be invaluable to those interested in improving their problem solving and decision-making skills. How to draw on their conclusions and incorporate them into our own life, is a daunting, but exhilarating challenge.

In other chapters we emphasize how motives and emotions (including those we are unaware of) affect our actions more than we usually realize

Here, in contrast, we will focus on how this conscious, cognitive, rational, logical, intellectual part of ourselves (what we previously referred to as System II in the brain) develops and functions, how it can be enhanced and what common roadblocks impede its development. For these aspects of our brain are crucial to problem solving.

Types of Problems

We encounter several kinds of problems: those with one correct solution and those with several equally acceptable ones. We will look at physical problems, quantitative problems and social problems and those in specific disciplines such as engineering, business, government, education, medicine and computer science. Most of all, we will focus on how understanding, developing and utilizing our rational, intellectual abilities can enrich our lives.

Often considered the most complex of all cognitive functions, problem solving involves a combination of skills we utilize to accomplish something of value. Throughout life, we have both short-term and long-term goals we want to reach, and obstacles we face in reaching them. Benjamin Franklin rarely met a problem he would hesitate to tackle. A look at his experience and subsequent findings from positive psychology can help us cultivate our own problem- solving abilities.

Role of Attention and Perception

We have previously considered challenges we face in multitasking. In doing so, we either alternate our attention from one task to another, give only partial attention to one or perform a task that is so automatic it really does not require attention. To experience for yourself some mindboggling demonstrations, google selective attention and watch some of the videos available.

I tried one where I attempted to attend to a plastic cup which had a piece of chocolate under it as the experimenter moved several such cups around the table. I felt pride in being able to get it right until I found a few things I hadn't noticed: a yellow chick mixed in with the cups; cups changing colors; and an extra arm manipulating the cups.

The Gorilla Study

To me, the most amazing one is a classic from 1999, based on a study Daniel Simons and Christopher Chablis. In it, volunteers observing a video in which two groups of students — some dressed in white, some in black — are passing basketballs around. Observers were to count passes among players in white. About half of them failed to notice a person in a gorilla suit walking in and out of the scene thumping its chest. Follow up studies found that even people who are told to be on the lookout for a surprising event are no better at spotting it.

Magicians have long known to use selective attention to fool and entertain. While our attention is diverted by the red silk scarf waving in his right hand, we fail to notice the coin he is palming in his left.

Setting Priorities

Since we are unable to attend to everything, we set priorities. Not only in what we notice in our physical environment but in what we attend to in our social world.

Ben Franklin indicated one of his priorities: "pay extra attention to the feelings and thoughts of the important people in your life." This is wise advice.

Courses and workshops on interpersonal communications are designed to help participants attend to more than the content of a conversation. They learn to ask, "How is this person feeling"? as well as "What are they saying'? An occasion on which I missed this basic lesson still sticks in my mind. One of my students informed me a few weeks before the end of the fall semester that he was dropping out of college and going into military service. What should I say? Since he was doing well in class, I recommended he finish the term and obtain a grade in case he later decided to return to college. He thanked me, continued to attend class, but never showed up for the final exam. A few months later, he stopped in to see me. He had had a "mental breakdown," obtained treatment and was returning to college. I had given advice without enough attention to the nature of his problem.

Even simple problems are often missed when we ignore readily available information. Try this one. Johnny's mother has three children. The first one she named April, the second she named May. What name did she give the third child? If "Johnny" comes to you immediately, and you don't see how anyone could miss it, try it on some of your friends. Most of mine couldn't find the answer even though it was right in front of them. (All right, I admit, I missed it too). Another oldie that still has us scratching out head is "Brothers and sisters have I none but this man's father is my father's son." Check it out!

In unravelling problems, we should focus our attention on relevant information and ignore that which is extraneous and misleading. In some cases, we have so much information it is difficult to tease out what is relevant. Computers can magnify this problem. They can grind out volumes of data in a few minutes, but we then often find ourselves swamped with information that is useless for our purpose (this doesn't discourage some people from using it anyhow!).

Our Perception of the Problem

Often, we must revise our perception-our initial impression proves wrong with further input.

The well-circulated story of the captain of a battleship's efforts to avoid a collision during nighttime maneuvers illustrates this well.

Signalman: "Captain there's a light from a ship ahead, and we're on a collision course with it."

Captain: "Quick, tell them to change course."

Signalman (following a quick exchange): "Captain, they say we should change course".

Captain: "What! I'll handle this!" "This is Captain Montgomery and I'm on a battleship. I order you to change course immediately!"

Reply: "This is seaman second class Kelly, and I'm on a lighthouse. You better change course."

Let's hope the captain's perception of the situation underwent a radical change.

In more complex problems facing individuals, organizations, and nations, separating significant from trivial information (often called signal and noise) can be exceedingly difficult. Yet it can be crucial.

Discerning relevance amidst information overload.
The Japanese attack on Pearl Harbor has been studied extensively to see why we were unprepared for it. In hindsight, we see a good bit of information suggesting such an attack was coming. Observers agreed Japan was planning war at any moment, probably with a surprise attack. Moreover, they concluded they might target a stronghold we would not anticipate. A number of signs, we now realize, should have pointed to Pearl Harbor: the Japanese military had recently changed their code; their carrier fleet had been maintaining strict radio silence for several weeks and a Japanese "tourist" had been apprehended photographing our battleships lined up at Pearl Harbor. Even one of our ambassadors had been told by his American counterpart that his Japanese cook had warned him Japan was ready to attack Pearl Harbor. These and other signs of impending attack, however, were buried within a mountain of accumulated information. Much of this pointed to Southeast Asia, including the Philippines,

as the likely point of attack. When naval officials pondered over an intercepted message that the Japanese ambassador was to deliver z notice to Washington at exactly 1:00 pm that they were breaking off negotiations, they immediately focused on its significance for Southeast Asia. It would be a few hours before dawn there, a logical time for an assault. Someone mentioned that it would be 7:30 a.m. on a Sunday morning at Pearl Harbor.

Army and Naval commanders at every Pacific base had been warned repetitively to be alert for an attack. At Pearl Harbor, however. their assumption was it referred to sabotage, not an aerial attack.

Similarly, before the September 11, 2001 terrorist attacks on the World Trade Center and Pentagon, The FBI and the CIA had gathered considerable information about possible terrorist action. One report from a flight instructor expressed concern about a foreign national with very little flight experience who had requested lessons on a simulator for a large passenger plane-the type terrorist used in the attacks. In retrospect, we see we had enough information to alert us to the danger, including intended targets and method of attacks. Unfortunately, selecting relevant information from the mass of data, and, coordinating and interpreting it proved exceedingly difficult.

Finding relevant information

We are stymied in solving problems if needed information is missing; if it is inaccurate, irrelevant, or misleading; or if we have accurate information but misinterpret it. At times, we recognize what we need and know how to get it. In other instances, we must use our ingenuity. In the Battle of Midway, the turning point in the Pacific War, our Navy had uncovered information about an impending major attack on an American base. But which base? The Japanese encoded their target as "AF" but, while the navy suspected it referred to Midway, they were far from certain. To find out, codebreakers sent orders to Midway to broadcast a radio message indicating its desalinization plant had broken down. As intended, the radio message was intercepted by the Japanese. In forwarding it, they identified the base as AF, confirming its location as Midway.

In addition to obtaining accurate and relevant information, we need to interpret it correctly. Let's look next at some common sources of being misled in drawing accurate conclusions from our observations:

Unwarranted assumptions:

1. A woman, who does not have her driver's license with her, turns the wrong way on a one-way street. A police officer stops her and questions her but does not give her a ticket. Why not?

2, Big hunter and little hunter are moving through the woods. Little hunter is big hunter's son, but big hunter is not little hunter's father. Explain this.

People who have difficulty in these instances are making unwarranted assumptions, in the first case assuming the woman is driving a car, and in the second that big hunter is a man.

On a different note, imagine you are looking up at the moon. Might astronauts who had landed there be looking down at you? Most of us now realize they too would be looking up toward earth. (And we thought we knew up from down!). If we move outside earth's gravitational pull, however, we must change our assumptions about up and down and see the world from a new perspective.

Sometimes unwarranted assumptions have unfortunate consequences. In another chapter, we mention a tragedy in which a plane crashed while its crew was focusing on checking a defective light bulb. They made the unfortunate assumption that the plane was on automatic pilot.

Still another instance occurred in 2012 when a major contributor to the Great Recession was assuming housing would continue to increase in value. Mortgages were granted based on this false assumption, and the housing market collapsed.

Confirmation bias is another barrier to accurate problem solving. This term is used when information we collect and the way we interpret it is influenced by our preconceived notion (or hope) of what our results will be.

As an example: A faculty member grading an essay examination from someone whom she considers an excellent student, would be inclined to give more weight to points in the examination confirming her view and less to those inconsistent with it. To avoid bias, most faculty members grade such papers without knowing names.

Another example of confirmation bias is research studies interpreting data in such a way as to confirm expectations of investigators. Research on efficacy of a new drug, for instance, is more likely to show positive results if a pharmaceutical company sponsors it than if it is conducted without such support. Scientific organizations and pharmaceutical companies have guidelines to guard against financial support influencing research results, but they are not always interpreted with scientific objectivity.

Mental set, a tendency to approach problems in a way that has been successful previously, is another common barrier to solving problems. If you read the following three names aloud one letter at a time and ask someone to pronounce each name, the third one is likely to be pronounced Mac Hinery rather than machinery because of a mental set induced by the first two Scottish names.

M-A-C-G-R-E-G-O-R, M-A-C-T-A-V-I-C-H, M-A-C-H-I–N-E-R-Y

In the classic 1954 movie the Caine Mutiny, Captain Queeg (played by Humphrey Bogart) mistakenly insists an apparent theft was the work of someone with a duplicate key, basing his assumption on a previous incident in which the culprit used a duplicate. Nothing supports this belief, but he persists in holding it.

Although we learn a great deal from previous experience, sometimes experience is misleading when we confront a new situation.

Influence of past experience

I recall an occasion when a recently- hired engineer wanted to try solving a problem in a way that had been tried in the past without success. His supervisor wondered, "Should I let him try it or just tell him we know that approach doesn't work?" He decided letting him try it would be useful experience. Perhaps you can guess what happened? With a new perspective and a little different twist, the newcomer solved the problem. Sometimes we learn wrong lessons from experience.

History has many examples of nations learning lessons from past conflicts that are ineffective in subsequent ones. For one, France in WWI emphasized offense and suffered devastating casualties. Prior to WWII, they emphasized defense instead, resulting in vast expenditures on the

Maginot Line for protection, a defense German panzer forces readily circumvented.

Expertise in a given area often creates a mental set preventing employing a novel approach. Computer specialists usually see a problem as requiring data analysis, even when a qualitative approach is more promising. Substantial advances in psychology have been made by neurologists and anthropologists; and several psychologists have been awarded a Nobel Prize for innovations in economics. A fresh perspective makes a difference.

Unnecessary constraints is another common obstacle we encounter in solving problems. On one occasion, I asked some of my students a simple question. "Yesterday I dropped a nickel on the floor. You know about 50 percent of the time it will have landed heads and 50 percent tails. Can you guess how it landed"? After a few moments of puzzled looks, someone invariably answered that it stood on end. How would anyone know? Instead of considering the probabilities of coin tossing, it helped to ask what are the probabilities of my bringing it up unless something improbable occurred?

By breaking out of such boundaries, we make progress with our problem-solving ability. Does an automobile need a driver? A spacecraft a crew? A library book? If such constraints are removed, ground-breaking opportunities often emerge. Judging whether to break traditional constraints, however, requires perspicacity (a well-polished crystal ball would also come in handy).

In facing personal problems, we also encounter restraints. A woman who feels victimized and close to a breakdown may assume she must stay with her husband

and work to resolve their difficulties. Once she accepts the idea that separating is another option, she becomes more confident in coming up with a resolution. Whether it be divorce, a temporary separation, marriage counseling, spending more time in activities away from home, or continuing to try to resolve their conflicts (but with a new attitude), a less constrained perspective helps.

Leaders are judged by their success in breaking away from past policies and practices that hamper progress, retaining those that have value and introducing innovative programs that produce progress.

Perception is relative.

Whether we see something as large or small, easy or difficult, fast or slow depends on some reference point. You see a bonus of $500 as small if others in your group receive $1,000; large if they receive $100. The reference point (or anchor) is influenced not only by group norms as in this example, but also by how often you have received bonuses of various sizes in previous years (frequency) and size of last year's bonus (recency). In negotiations, it helps to establish a favorable reference point from the start. An employee representative would want to start negotiations by pointing out other companies awarding large bonuses rather than complaining that last year's bonus was too small.

A variation of this is the "door in the face" tactic. Some national and organizational administrators initially make outrageous demands (the kind that would make you slam the door in the face of such a sales pitch) and then "compromise" to the kind of arrangement they were seeking.

The term contrasts with the "foot in the door" tactic of the salesperson who starts with getting a small concession as a step to a larger one. "If you decide to buy this exciting car you are considering, what color would you prefer"? As a college student, I once sold encyclopedias door-to-door. I was instructed to greet the potential customer with, "Good afternoon, I'm here to speak to you about your child's education." Invariably, I would be invited in to describe the wonders of my product.

Social Perception

Findings mentioned above apply to our perception of people as well. An awareness of mental set, unnecessary constraints, unwarranted assumptions and confirmation bias should help you be more accurate (and less prejudicial) in understanding others. In addition, research on social perception reveals how we make inferences about others from multiple sources, including their dress, physical appearance, vocabulary, facial expressions, speech patterns, eye movements, gestures, and posture. As in physical perception, judgments are sounder if based on accurate and relevant information. It is easy to miss key cues about someone and not know what they are really like. Conversely, too much information may be misleading. If you are hyper-vigilant and see significance in every raised eyebrow, finger movement and inflection in voice, you are likewise likely to misjudge people. When in doubt, find a tactful way to check it out!

Ben Franklin, realizing public perception of reality is as important as reality itself, cultivated a positive impression by his conduct, his dress and the associates he chose. In his early career as a printer, he made it obvious that he worked from early morning, until late in the day. In recruiting companions for the Junto, he focused on people of sound reputation. As he said, "Hide not your talents, they for use were made. What is a sundial in the shade?"

A well-known example of successful impression management was his decision to wear a coonskin hat when he arrived in France as American ambassador. The French were delighted at his pose as a plain, down-to-earth frontiersman, even though they knew it was showmanship.

Self-perception

Closely related to social perception is self-perception, or self-concept, a collection of beliefs about yourself. It originates in early years, based mainly on what your family tells you and how they treat you. It is modified over the years, by your accomplishments and by how others judge you. Were you older or younger than your classmates? If so, you will tend to compare yourself with them, rather than those your own age, in judging your abilities. This grouping has some surprising (or maybe not so surprising) outcomes. In one study, for example, most Canadian professional hockey players were found to have been born in January and February. Because they began school a few months before their cohorts, they were, on average, a little bigger, stronger and faster than other children, consequently, a little better at ice hockey. This slight difference at the start led to more ice time, more attention from coaches, more confidence, and more skill, so differences magnified as they matured.

Another bit of research comparing college students in highly selective universities with those of equal ability in less competitive ones has significant implications for high school and college choice. Called "Big fish, small pond effect," it found that your average students developed higher self-concepts in less selective schools.

Why? Because being above average in accomplishments gave their egos more of a boost than students of comparable ability who were below average in more selective colleges.

This research tells us social perception, just as physical perception. varies with our reference point, and our reference point is often peer group average.

I recall a student who believed his ability must be declining with more education instead of improving. His concern: "In high school, my scores on standardized tests were high, in college they were average, but my scores on the Graduate Record Exam are now below average."

Similarly, a student who is an excellent athlete in high school, and an above average one in college may not have the talent needed in the higher standard of professional sports.

Self-Concept

We frequently find students (and members of all occupations) whose self-concept hinders their progress including their ability to problem solve and communicate their ideas. This can be modified with experience. I recall recommending a student for a prestigious graduate award, based on his performance as an undergraduate. He declined, saying he was not "a brain" but "just a regular guy with a variety of interests beside academics." When he visited me after his first semester of graduate work at an Ivy League school, he mentioned he had done better than students from more elite schools, including those who had received prestigious awards. His self-concept had undergone a substantial change.

Another student, whose speech, dress, and demeanor made it difficult for him to obtain a position as an accountant did not believe he should change. "That's the way I am." "Why should I change? As Frank Sinatra crooned it, Love Me as I Am.

This attachment to a damaging self-concept is a frequent roadblock to achievement. We ask, "Why shouldn't I continue to be me"? Instead of "How can I improve"?

Collaboration.

Next, we will look more closely at problems requiring collaboration, from small groups of colleagues to vast international efforts.

You will recall how Franklin organized the Junto, a group of men who met regularly to discuss and attempt to solve a wide variety of issues. He assumed a group of intelligent and diligent people with different perspectives would do better at problem solving than anyone working alone. It was much like today's Rotary.

Some companies today encourage innovation by forming collaborative teams, task forces or brainstorming groups. They use a variety of approaches to share knowledge, promote new ideas and solve organizational problems. Here communication is crucial. We have seen that problem solving and decision-making require accessing and understanding information others have. Progress builds on previous progress. Moreover, we know communicating ideas to others helps clarify your own thinking; in addition, the feedback you get stimulates further reflection.

It is not enough to have promising ideas for solving group problems; in addition, as Franklin demonstrated, you need to communicate them in a clear-cut and convincing manner. Here is one of his many comments about this need:

When I advanced any thing that may possibly be disputed, I avoided the words certainly, undoubtedly, or any others that give the air of positiveness to an opinion; but rather say, I conceive or apprehend a thing to be so and so; it appears to me, or I should think it so or so, for such and such reasons; or I imagine it to be so; or it is so, if I am not mistaken. This habit, I believe, has been of great advantage to me when I have had occasion to inculcate my opinions, and persuade men into measures that I have been from time to time engag'd in promoting; and, as the chief ends of conversation are to inform or to be informed, to please or to persuade, I wish well-meaning, sensible men would not lessen their power of doing good by a positive, assuming manner, that seldom fails to disgust, tends to create opposition, and to defeat every one of those purposes for which speech was given to us, to wit, giving or receiving information or pleasure. For, if you would inform, a positive and dogmatical manner in advancing your sentiments may provoke contradiction and prevent a candid attention. If you wish information and improvement from the knowledge of others, and yet at the same me express yourself as firmly fix'd in your present opinions, modest, sensible men, who do not love disputation, will probably leave you undisturbed in the possession of your error."

Moreover, communicating ideas to others helps clarify your own thinking.

Some groups, however, miss out on valuable input because people hesitate to speak their mind. An authoritarian leader or an intimidating bloc discourages innovative ideas.

An additional issue affecting communication is that new ideas and products may affect income or reputation, so people are often reluctant to share them.

Benjamin Franklin never patented any of his inventions. He had a voluminous correspondence openly sharing his ideas and findings. He believed the resultant benefit to society outweighed any personal gain.

Today, dominant internet firms have developed databases on the characteristics of our entire population. This knowledge provides power to a select group of firms and raises the question, should they be required to share this information? A question with no easy answer.

Now that we have examined the intricacies of memory and problem solving, we will next consider how we can utilize these cognitive abilities in making positive decisions and avoiding deleterious ones.

Chapter 11.
Making Wise Decisions

Introduction
Problem solving and decision making are two closely related cognitive processes. In theory, problem analysis is taken on first, with its results providing information we need to make prudent decisions. In practice, the two processes interact. Improved problem solving facilitates decision making.

Life constantly throws decisions at us, some routine, everyday ones, others with a major impact on our lives. Outcomes for most of these are uncertain. If you wait until certainty, you will do very little. Perfectionists, including workaholics, perform well below their potential.

As Benjamin Franklin put it: "The man who achieves makes many mistakes, but he never makes the biggest mistake of all - doing nothing."

Individual and Group Decisions

Individual decisions
We start the day determining what to eat for breakfast and selecting what clothes to wear. These, like most of our everyday decisions, we handle quickly without much thought or concern. We open our email (some of which has already been filtered as Spam) and make our selections: delete, Spam, forward (with or without comment), respond (brief or lengthy), file, save (for action after reflection or obtaining more information.

Other choices, such as which college to attend, what major to select and what career to follow, lead to more significant consequences. You have no doubt heard more than one person say, "that was the worst decision I ever made in my life," or "that was the best decision I ever made." Decisions confront us every day. Just glancing at today's Philadelphia Inquirer reminds us of this.

One article describes how Aqua America, a water and sewer utility company in Southeastern Pennsylvania agreed to swap interest rates in buying Peoples Gas, a Pittsburgh Company resulted in a 3.6-million-dollar loss. Chris Franklin, CEO of Aqua, was quoted as saying, "If you had a crystal ball a lot of things would be different." How true!

In another article, Phillies GM Matt Klentak, in justifying deciding not to top the 300 million deal San Diego had offered shortstop Manny Machado, said, "sometimes you have to be willing to walk away." Also true!

Group Decisions

In additions to decisions you make on your own, you also participate in those made with your family, work groups, teams, community groups and other organizations, large and small. Most of what we know about individual decisions applies to groups as well, but you will see additional issues when you work with groups.

Probability

Understanding probability and utilizing it in your life will lead to success most of the time and eliminate procrastination based on waiting for certitude. Ben is right. "Nothing in this world is certain except death and taxes." Since you cannot be sure of the outcome of most decisions, you must base them on probability.

Subjective probability

Often, you must use your judgment and experience to predict the likely outcome of a decision. You may feel that a choice is right-an intuitive sense. Don't ignore that feeling, but also evaluate it rationally (and, when possibly, quantitatively).

If you were a physician determining what medical treatment to use for a patient, your diagnoses and treatments would be based partly on experience and judgment. In addition, a significant part of your decisions should be guided by a knowledge of probable outcomes of alternative treatments.

Life involves balancing multiple, often competing, goals. We need to sacrifice one to reach another. Let us imagine we are buying a house. We consider size of property, number of bedrooms and bathrooms, quality and appearance of the kitchen, reputation of the neighborhood, distance from job(s), quality of schools, and several other factors. We cannot expect to find a home meeting all our preferences, so we must compromise, sacrificing certain things we like and selecting one with most of the desirable features. In considering two or three homes, we may vacillate from one to another, attracted to a feature one has that others lack.

Benjamin Franklin came up with a process for weighing pros and cons of such dilemmas.

In a letter to Joseph Priestly, he provides a simple procedure for calculating tradeoffs. Franklin states: *"divide half a Sheet of Paper by a Line into two Columns, writing over the one Pro, and over the other Con. Then during three or four Days Consideration I put down under the different Heads short Hints of the different Motives that at different Times occur to me for or against the*

Measure. When I have thus got them all together in one View, I endeavour to estimate their respective Weights; and where I find two, one on each side, that seem equal, I strike them both out: If I find a Reason pro equal to some two Reasons con, I strike out the three. If I judge some two Reasons con equal to some three Reasons pro, I strike out the five; and thus proceeding I find at length where the Balance lies... tho' the Weight of Reasons cannot be taken with the Precision of Algebraic Quantities, yet when each is thus considered separately and comparatively, and the whole lies before me, I think I can judge better, and am less likely to make a rash Step; and in fact I have found great Advantage from this kind of Equation. "

To utilize this approach, first select your goal and collect relevant information (data) about it

Then list their pros and cons and evaluate the probability and desirability of each. Finally, you make your decision, implement it and learn from and reflect on the outcome.

A more quantitative version of the process would address the problem by ranking the importance (utility) of each pro and con on a scale of 1 to 10. Then rank the probability of each on a similar scale. When you multiply the rating for importance and the rating for probability for each and compare total scores, you will see whether pros outweigh cons and by how much.

. The process, however, is more valuable than the number. After relating and reflecting, you are better able to decide. Even the act of writing them down, helps you see issues more clearly and avoid procrastination.

At one time, I was offered a position as Director of a Counseling Center at a university in another city. Uncertain whether to accept the offer, I used Franklin's method. Starting with two columns, labeled Pro and Con, I wrote down the arguments for accepting or declining.

Pros:
Higher salary
   More responsibility
More prestigious
Better opportunity for professional advancement
   More modern facilities
   Immediate supervisors (dean and vice president) seemed good to work with

Cons:
Like current job, and feel successful in it
   Required to give up tenure and academic rank
Need to leave friends at work and in the area.
   Less able to help parents.
   Weather is harsh in new location.

On examining pros and cons I realized my reasons for staying put were basically emotional- I felt good about my present position and apprehensive about leaving it. The appeal of the prospective one was mainly rational-I judged it to be a good move for my future, financially and professionally.

As often happens in decision-making, an incident arose that tipped the scales.

I had been assured I would be welcome to teach a psychology course each term but had not yet met the Chair of the department. I finally succeeded in arranging an interview but was taken aback by his greeting. "You're a Catholic aren't you"? I responded with a puzzled 'Yeh-ess'? He then asked, "Do you think you'll fit in?" I said nothing, but thought, "I guess not." Normally. I would have addressed this indication of prejudice more directly and clarified the situation, but his attitude added enough weight to the con side for me to opt against making the move.

Objective probability

In other situations, you can compute the probability of an event, sometimes precisely, sometimes approximately. Your chance of being dealt an ace on the first card of a 52-card deck is exactly one in 13; A weather forecast of a 50% chance of rain is approximate, but more accurate than a subjective opinion.

Unfortunately, most people understand little about probability and ignore what they do know in their choices.

A few years ago, a popular TV game show, Let's Make A Deal, hosted by Monty Hall offered contestants a chance to win an expensive new car hidden behind one of three doors. A goat was behind each of the other two. Once a door was selected, the host would open one of the other doors showing a goat behind it. Contestants would then confront the option of staying with their original choice or changing it to the third door. Contestants agonized over their selection; members of the audience chimed in, some shouting "stay" and others "switch." Which choice is better? Well, changing your initial choice is twice as likely to get you a car as not changing. Still not convinced? Label the doors A, B and C. Assuming you select A and keep your choice you will win only one-third of the time. On the other hand, if you switch to the unopened door, you will win whenever either B or C is correct- two-thirds of the time. This logic applies no matter which door you first pick. Cynical readers may question the integrity of the show. Maybe all three doors would reveal a goat behind them, and the probability of driving away with a car would drop to zero. I am a more trusting soul.

How tuned in are you to basic probability? If you bet on roulette and lose three times in a row, do the odds favor a win on your next bet? No, the odds stay the same as for each of your first three bets, so you have no good reason to increase your bet (or to bet at all).

Which lottery ticket is more likely to be a winner, 111111111? or 275412896? Since most winners look more like the second number, the majority of people feel it has a better chance of winning. In fact, the probability of either number winning is the same (very low).

Here is a less obvious one. If you toss a coin three times, how often will you get one head? At first thought, 1/3 seems to be an obvious answer. Let's check. Suppose we imagine tossing three coins several times. The eight possible outcomes are HHH, HHT, HTH, THH, HTT, THT, TTH, and TTT. Of the eight, three come up with exactly one head: HTT, THT, and TTH. Therefore, the probability of three flips of a coin producing exactly one head is 3/8 or 0.375, a bit more than one-third.

Using Probability

Americans spend approximately $150 billion each year on sports betting, mostly with only a rudimentary sense of their chance of winning.

Worldwide, trillions of dollars are invested in stocks and related ways to increase income. Here, expertise in judging probability of gain or loss is invaluable.

. "Decisions must be data driven"! has become a mantra for a host of organizations and their top people. It makes sense to collect relevant data to be able to make an informed decision. But the key word here is relevant. Deciding what information will help should be your priority, rather than mining vast amounts of data hoping to reveal a handful of valuable nuggets. I prefer turning this mantra around and saying," Data must be decision driven"!

Usually we find ourselves juggling several variables that affect the outcome of a decision. Certain of these carry more weight (or have greater utility) than others, so we should measure those with greater precision. Also, we must weigh potential "gain against pain," being cautious if the outcome of a low probability event would be disastrous.

Psychologist Daniel Kahneman was awarded the Nobel Prize in Economics in 2002 for his research demonstrating that the utility expected from a decision is subjective. A potential financial gain from an investment may not be worth the pain of an equal financial loss. So, whether you would invest in a project promising substantial income but running the risk of bankruptcy depends on how serious a problem you consider bankruptcy.

In choosing to market a new drug that improves a disorder in 80 percent of patients, but produces an adverse reaction in five percent, a pharmaceutical company must compare potential gain and loss (or benefit and harm).

Accurately predicting the probability of an event can be crucial. When hurricane Katrina raced toward the U.S. Gulf Coast in August 2005, the Hurricane Warning Center predicted its probable path, its expected intensity and its effect on communities it would strike. It was closely monitored, and as more data emerged, predictions became more accurate. It soon became clear it would hit New Orleans and its impact would be serious, perhaps catastrophic. Federal, state and local officials faced a crucial decision- what steps should they take and how soon should they take them. Act early, even though the danger was uncertain? Recommend or require an evacuation? One crucial question was how far the Mississippi would rise. Evidence indicating it was most likely to crest two inches below the top of the levee might seem reassuring. More significant, however, was the 30% chance of it overflowing, which it did.

In retrospect, information was available to significantly reduce suffering from the hurricane but understanding and communicating its importance and coordinating emergency efforts presented major stumbling blocks.

Organizational decision making

Organizational budget planning provides a familiar instance of the need for relevant data. For years, I had a personal interest in my colleges budget where estimates of income and expenses determined whether faculty would receive a salary increase, and, if so, how much it would be.

More recently, I sat in on a presentation of budget planning for ACTS Retirement Life Communities as a resident of one of the corporation's numerous communities. It is an ongoing three-year project of constantly updating projections as more recent data becomes available.

It starts with calculating (or estimating) costs of food service, health care, security, maintenance and social and physical fitness activities.

Then it considers any necessary renovations and repairs, followed by desirable improvements and expansion.

Income projections are also developed, mainly entrance fees for new residents and monthly apartment fees. Variables that influence cost include: the housing market, minimum wage and wages paid by competitors, social security payments, taxes, health insurance fees and benefits, food prices, and cost of construction.

Input is obtained from residents and staff of each community about priority items.

Based on this material, administrators determine increases in fees and projects or programs to initiate.

This is an example of well-planned organizational decision making.

Basis of ineffectual decisions

"To err is human." Although we want to do things that are most likely to improve our lives and least likely to hurt us, we also possess tendencies that interfere with that objective.

Emotions

We aim to make rational choices, but our emotions also influence choice. Grappling with problems triggers emotions. Controlling them is part of the solution. Let your emotions help drive and sustain your efforts; don't allow them to disrupt your focus on the target!

When our drive to reach a goal is stymied by a roadblock, we often lose sight of our goal and act out of frustration. We burst into anger, sink into apathy or compulsively persist in the same behavior that has failed time and time again.

Wishful thinking, or optimistic bias, is a tendency to see things in a positive light and underestimate difficulties. We become so excited and upbeat about an undertaking that it distorts our perception and interferes with clear thinking.

Fear of failure

Negative emotions like fear and worry can get out of hand and disrupt our judgment.

Apathy and avoidance. It is easy to fall into a routine of avoiding tension and challenge. I have frequently heard employees say, "I don't get paid to think." This is the drone mentality. Utilizing and developing critical cognitive abilities enables you to develop appropriate initiative and assertiveness to lead a fuller, more productive life,

Prejudice, (and arrogance and self-centered thinking.) We all have our prejudices and at least a touch of self-centeredness. Sometimes arrogance is thrown in too. It helps to approach problems with an open mind and a willingness to consider evidence objectively. Success is often impeded by having a preconceived notion of what the solution entails. Prejudices often contribute to this. We hold tightly to views on important issue such as how to advance education, improve health, reduce crime, and motivate employees, which run counter to objective evidence-often overwhelming evidence.

Emotional immaturity

Researchers have discovered that differences between adolescents and adults in decision-making are not due to a lack of logic or reasoning, but to emotional immaturity.

This lack of maturity (which is not confined to adolescents) is characterized by low impulse control, poor emotional regulation, and difficulty delaying gratification and resisting peer pressure. I remember a college senior telling me that one of the main things he learned in college was to set his own priorities and to make his own decisions. Rather than going along with what other students were doing, he had learned to take charge of his life.

Miscommunication

Miscommunication provides material for both comedy and tragedy. A Three Stooges skit has Moe telling Curly: "I'm gonna hold this spike steady, and when I nod my head, you hit it with the hammer. Got it?" Curly responds "Sure, when you nod your head, I hit it with the hammer." Moe says "Right!" followed quickly by "Hey, wait a minute, wait a minute!"

Cases of tragedy and near-tragedy abound. In a U.S. military exercise in the Middle East, the Navy was defending an aircraft carrier against attacks by planes from our Air Force. One Navy pilot radioed his controller that he had an attacking plane in his sights and asked, ": What should I do?" "Shoot it down"! the controller replied, not realizing the aircraft had live ammunition. Shoot it down, he did. Fortunately, both crewmembers parachuted from the plane safely.

Time Pressure

What to do when you must come up with a decision before a deadline, or without occupying too much of your time? Instead of striving for an ideal solution, settle for a satisfactory one. Why spend needless time, energy and

resources for a minor difference in outcome? This
approach is called Satisficing.

Competitiveness

Sometimes competition facilitates decision making
sometimes it interferes with it. Have you ever been in a
negotiation or other competitive situation where you forget
about everything except winning?

Universities take on excessive debt to build a bigger
stadium or field house than competing universities, just as
all kinds of organizations get themselves in trouble by
determining to do something unessential to beat out a
competitor.

That's when competitiveness hurts. A series of
research studies with subjects competing for a financial
reward (they could gain or lose money) found participants
believing they were winning if they were losing less
money than their competitor. Don't let your competitive
drive divert you from your true goals!

Cognitive Limitations

You will recall several common characteristics that
hinder our ability to solve problems mentioned in the
previous chapter including complexity of the problem.
mental set, unnecessary constraints, unwarranted
assumptions and confirmation bias.

These are worth repeating along with additional ones
we confront in making decisions.

Information overload

Information overload is a disconnect between amount
we accumulate and our ability to assimilate it and use it
effectively. A university administrator I worked with was

described by one of his colleagues as "a brilliant light that shines in all directions except straight ahead!" Eliminating extraneous and irrelevant information helps us focus on our goals, but just the sheer volume and complexity of available data makes that a common challenge today

Findings from market research showing that customers are more likely to buy a product when offered a few choices rather than many also show the influence of information overload. An excess of options slows the process. Narrow your choices to a few desirable ones, then decide!

Analysis Paralysis

Involves over-analyzing a situation so that you fail to act in a timely matter (If you tend to postpone things, maybe you're not a procrastinator after all, but simply a victim of analysis paralysis!).

Cognitive biases

We screen out or minimize evidence that is inconsistent with our set of beliefs (our mental set) rather than approaching choices with an open mind. We also tend to accept or reject information based on our attitude toward its source. Certain people, organizations, or groups we see as more trustworthy than others. Do we believe scientific research or traditional religious teaching; Fox News, CNN or Facebook; the judgement of experienced members of our profession or innovative ideas of bright newcomers?

We also tend to believe what we hear most often and from the greatest number of sources. We think, "if everybody is saying it, it must be true. Aim for the best decision, not the most popular one!

Timeliness of information acquisition. Primacy and recency

In accumulating material to guide us in our deliberations, we obtain some early in the process, some later. Which influences us more? The answer is "it depends."

Often our thinking is unduly influenced by initial information that shapes our view of subsequent information (called the primacy effect). It readily serves as a reference point, or anchor, against which newer material is judged. Conversely, more recent material often tips the scales because we either ignore or forget more distant material (the recency effect). Learn to evaluate whatever contributes to your decision without regard for when it came to your attention.

Cognitive inertia is reluctance to change our usual thought patterns to adapt to new circumstances. We are constrained by unwarranted assumptions. Viewing a problem from a new perspective or "thinking outside the box" often helps

Incremental decision-making

Small steps in a given direction leading to a series of similar steps. This is also known as the slippery slope. Ask yourself, "would I be doing this today if I were starting from scratch (using zero-based decision making) rather than following habitual practice"?

Illusion of control: We tend to believe we have more control over events than we really do. Hedge your bets and be ready for the unexpected!

Framing Effect

How information is presented influences decision making and judgment. Being told a surgical procedure has a 90% chance of succeeding makes it sound more acceptable than hearing it has a 10% fatality rate.

Group decision making

We know problem solving and decision-making require accessing and understanding information others possess. Progress builds on previous progress. So, collaboration provides access to a variety of relevant knowledge present among group members.

You will recall how Franklin organized the Junto, a group of men who met regularly to discuss and attempt to solve a wide variety of issues. He assumed a group of intelligent and diligent people with different perspectives would do better at getting things done than anyone working alone.

Quite a few companies today encourage Innovation by forming collaborative teams, task forces or brainstorming groups. Using a variety of approaches, they share knowledge, promote new ideas and solve organizational problems. When done well, it has a positive effect on an organization.

Why? Because when we are involved in decisions that affect us, we are more likely to accept and implement them and are better able to coordinate our activities with others. This holds true especially when we feel respected and appreciated during the process. In conducting group discussion, keep this in mind. What else should we be alert to about group decision making? Well, first and foremost, that the purpose is to decide and to implement, not just discuss. Whether decisions will be made by a leader after getting a sense of the group's opinion, by a majority or plurality vote, or by some other method, should be clear to everyone.

We must also be alert to group dynamics. Competition can get groups off track with everyone trying to outdo one another; or, instead, simply going along with the group (group think) and be more concerned with pleasing others than candidly addressing issues.

Thinking Creatively

Convergent and Divergent Thinking. We draw on two kinds of cognitive processes, convergent and divergent thinking, in problem solving and decision-making. The first involves pulling information together from a variety sources and using this knowledge rationally to solve problems, make decisions and achieve our objective.

One illustration of using convergent thinking comes from research in the sports world where fans regularly question officials calls.

Would major league baseball be improved if umpires' calls of balls and strikes reviewed by instant replay? To answer this, researchers reviewed tapes of thousands of pitches, comparing calls made by umpires with what the tapes revealed, Their findings? Umpires missed the correct call about one-third of the time on close pitches. More importantly, mistakes tended to favor the home team! Does this mean baseball should introduce instant replay to review umpires' calls? Well, other kinds of data bearing on this decision might be collected, e.g. effect on length of games, before determining to implement it.

Divergent Thinking. involves exploring possible ways (including new and creative ways) to address an issue or solve a problem. It is "thinking outside the box."

Most objective tests, including teacher-made and standardized multiple-choice questions (as well as so-called tests of IQ) measure the kind of factual knowledge and logical thought involved in convergent thinking. Essay and oral tests more likely require divergent thinking.

Albert Einstein is considered a gifted divergent thinker. He asked questions and then did thought experiments, rather than conduct experiments in a laboratory, to find answers. For example, he wondered what it would be like to ride on a beam of light. This kind of speculation inspired his theory of relativity.

As Einstein said, "Logic will get you from A to B. Imagination will take you everywhere."

Much of Ben Franklin's achievements stem from his talent for constantly making observation and measurements and then testing them. Even while he was traveling by ship, we may recall, he was constantly checking currents, marine life, and meteorological phenomena, demonstrating the intellectual curiosity and methodology of a scientist which mostly requires convergent thinking of high quality. But he was also a divergent thinker.

He wondered if continents had moved or if seas had covered substantially more land in the past. He speculated about population change in species and its implication for the future. On observing the first ascent in a balloon, he predicted a future for air travel. On the same occasion he conjectured "it is winter over every part of the earth" at high altitudes.

An award in his name The Benjamin Franklin Creativity Laureate Award, which is presented annually by The Smithsonian Associates and the Creativity Foundation "recognizes and celebrates influential thinkers, innovators and catalysts in the arts, sciences and humanities, in both traditional and emerging disciplines."

Positive psychology recommends we follow Franklin's lead and develop both our divergent and convergent thinking skills while solving problems, making decisions, completing projects and attaining goals.

My own education through high school emphasized convergent thinking. We were told what to learn and tested on it.

I had expected college to be a continuation of this kind of factual learning, but at a more demanding level. Instead, I found I was expected to think. Faculty constantly bombarded us with questions, several factual, others requiring reflection, speculation and imagination. This experience encouraged reading and discussion outside of class. It gave me an enthusiasm for education. It exemplified the adage "Give students information and they will learn facts; ask them questions and they will learn to think." To my disappointment, graduate study returned to a demand for convergent thinking.

Creativity can also play a role in everyday life. In preparing a meal, instead of following a recipe as directed, try variations to provide a new culinary experience. In decorating your home or workplace, introduce innovations to give them a personal touch and you a feeling of satisfaction.

Playfulness also involves creativity. Cultivating it enriches your social life.

Summary

To sum it all up, developing and utilizing your cognitive capabilities promotes your ability to accomplish your goals (and maybe realize your dreams).

Yet, as we have seen, our brain has built in limitations just as the rest of our body. Fortunately, we have developed tools to compensate for these limitations, some readily available and easy to use; others requiring special skills and extensive training. We will next consider how to select and utilize tools to enhance your development.

Chapter 12.
The Power of Tools.

Introduction

When you think about self-improvement, your cognitive abilities, emotional control, interpersonal skills, and persistence natural come to mind. Equally important in today's world is facility with technology. It can enrich your personal life, enhance your career and help you become a better-informed citizen.

History

Early History

What would we see if we could travel back in time and look at the lives of our early ancestors? For one, we would find them utilizing primitive tools. Developing this ability provided early hominids an advantage over other species in competing for resources; it enabled them to survive and even thrive in a wide variety of environments throughout our earth.

They constructed spears and arrowheads for hunting game and implements for igniting fires, and these played a major role in early human progress. We use terms such as "The Stone Age" and "The Iron Age" for different segments of our pre-history based on the predominant material used for tools during a given epoch.

It is no surprising that tools also served as weapons in competition between individuals, tribes and nations. What does history tell us about their role? Well, it provides a continuous record of the impact of new weapons: huge catapults, enabling Mongol invaders to smash walled cities of Europe, British longbows enabling them to strike down enemy forces, machine guns, tanks, dive- bombers, intercontinental missiles and nuclear weapons producing increasingly powerful destruction.

In contrast to tools designed to kill, are those developed to save life and reduce suffering: think of new drugs, surgical tools, vaccines, and dental equipment. Diseases that once caused worldwide death and disability have been wiped out or greatly curtailed.

Our ancestors' knack for communication and coordination also enhanced human progress. We realize how important language was, and, for communication at a distance we know they employed blasts on horns, beats of drums and smoke from fires. It may be hard to imagine a time when communication was almost exclusively oral and face-to-face limited to those you were close enough to see and hear. Everyone exchanged information by speaking and listening. They convinced others or were persuaded by them; they hammered out compromises face to face.

You probably recall that in ancient Greece public speaking (rhetoric or elocution) was a mark of an educated person. In Greek theater, comedy and drama were major ways of touching emotions and stirring audiences to action.

Before sound amplification, a stentorian voice was a major asset. Benjamin Franklin was so impressed by the volume of one preacher's voice that he paced out the distance from the church to find out how far from it his voice could still be heard.

How did this emphasis on public speaking influence the initial reaction to the printing press? It meant that books were initially seen as an aid to speaking. Memorization would no longer be necessary; speakers could read material to their audience. Only gradually did books become tools for silent reading in search of information or pleasure as we use them today. New discoveries bring unrecognized possibilities.

Ben Franklin constantly pursued new ideas and shared them openly. He published and wrote frequent articles for newspapers, engaged in extensive correspondence, and started a lending library.

Still, for years, slow and inaccurate communication hampered efforts to understand events in our world. You might have to wait for passengers arriving by ship or stagecoach to catch up with news. In war, battles raged, and men died well after a was over.

With the advent of the telegraph, news spread more rapidly to and from any place where telegraph wires could be strung (including by cable across the Atlantic Ocean). Increased speed in communication did not necessarily mean a comparable increase in accuracy. Humorist Finley Peter Dunne has his barroom philosopher Mr. Dooley answer the question: "which general was responsible for victory?" in the then-current Spanish-American War. His response was "whoever got to the telegraph office first."

Later history
When we think about Ben Franklin, one of the first things to come to mind is how he embraced technology and saw it as contributing to our pursuit of happiness.

We have mentioned 24-hour clocks, bifocal eyeglasses, lightning rods, the Franklin stove, refrigeration, flexible catheters, swim fins and odometers.

He was also always on the lookout for devices others had created that would help him and his community. Think of his well-known quote, "A discovery that is not good for something is good for nothing." Ben encouraged others to cooperate on improvement projects using new technology such as installing lightning rods, improving street lighting and paving streets.

The world recognizes him as an innovative trailblazer in early science.

. . Much of it amazed us; much of it changed our lives, our work, and our perception of our world.

Think of how the steam engine revolutionized transportation and manufacturing, and how the telephone, radio, motion pictures, TV, and Internet improved communication and entertainment. Compare our first computer, occupying a giant-sized room, with those today, most of which are smaller than the nail of your little finger. Technology stimulated comparable changes in other areas including education and the arts, and our exploration of outer space. It also made a major impact in the home where refrigerators, freezers, washers, dryers, dishwashers, microwaves, gas heaters and such acquired the well-deserve label "labor-saving devices." If you have seen devices used before these appliances appeared, you know that "housewife" was a full-time job-and a demanding one.

Resistance to new technology

Considering how many ways tools, technology and science have enhanced our lives, we might expect everyone to enthusiastically embrace them. In reality, our world has given most innovations a markedly mixed reception. If you wonder about whether science and technology have made life better or worse, you have plenty of company. Let's look at why.

Logical Reasons

A striking example of this concern occurred in 18th century *France*. An advertisement in a 1749 newspaper, offered a substantial prize for an essay responding to the question: "Has the restoration of the sciences and arts contributed to the purification of morals?" Rousseau, a German philosopher, captured the prize. He argued that science has had a destructive influence on our society. A simple, primitive life, in tune with nature, was a more satisfying life.

Do you agree that a primitive life with minimal technology would be a better life? Hardly. Yet, you may be reluctant to try new products. History provides abundant examples of skepticism and even hostility to anything new.

From our perspective today, we would think electricity would have been greeted as a godsend. Yet, when Edison first demonstrated electricity, one critic commented that while it was an interesting phenomenon, he could hardly imagine any use for it.

Alexander Graham Bell had a similar experience when he tried to convince Mark Twain to invest in his new invention-the telephone. Twain could see no use for it and declined.

Some products, like electrically- powered cars, fail to live up to expectations (at least so far). Devices for shuttling pedestrians faster and farther such as the Segway have been highly touted, but, as yet, have been rejected.

We have also seen new products and systems create unanticipated problems. Technology enabling us to do more and more, faster and faster also enables us to make more and bigger mistakes. I saw a minor incident of this at our university. A letter of acceptance intended for one student in one program was inadvertently mailed to every applicant to every program. Confusion reigned!

Many innovations have unforeseen consequences; help in some ways but hurt in others; or are of short-term benefit but cause long-term problems (like gasoline-powered vehicles that pollute our atmosphere). New and promising drugs may turn out to have side effects worse than disorders they are designed to treat.

Is a new product worth the time, trouble and cost? Is it superior to competing products? You, and other consumers, producers and investors must decide.

Moreover. government agencies must consider possible injurious effects that require curtailment or regulation. When we think of this issue, the Supersonic Transport (SST) comes to mind. With its supersonic speed and greater passenger capacity, it promised an upgrade in air travel. Yet, it soon fell into disuse largely because of its window-shattering sonic boom and resultant outcries from communities adjacent to airports.

In view of these and other cases of promising technology that failed, it is reasonable to be skeptical. Skepticism, however, shouldn't lead to rejecting products outright, but to investigating and evaluating them.

Psychological Reasons

We are creatures of habit. We do most things the way we have done them in the past and use previous habits as a basis for judging anything new.

In the early days of automobiles, a driver whose car had broken down, was typically taunted with, "Get a horse!" the traditional means of transport. When the 1939 World's Fair in New York first introduced television, a critic wrote that Americans would never accept a product that required them to sit still and watch. People habitually listened to radio then, and they could perform work or engage in other activities while tuned in.

We become accustomed to doing things in a certain way using tools we are familiar with.

At one time when I worked as a chemist, one of my duties was measuring liquid products using a pipette. By sucking on this tube and drawing the substance up to its desired height, I could measure its contents accurately. I had worked with it regularly and was confident of my skill. Thus, when a new product containing cyanide was to be tested, I continued with this same procedure ignoring possible danger. Not until a colleague reminded me that one drop could be fatal, did I demand a hand-controlled pipette.

We become attached to our possessions, including, cars and trucks, computers and cell phones. If robots become more human-like and more readily available to perform every-day tasks, emotional attachments we form with them will likely rival that with pets.

This emotional attachment you form with your possessions means you demand more from a product than what function it performs.

A new car promises to transport you quickly, safely, comfortably to your destination. That's a logical reason for buying one. So why would anyone spend twice the price of an inexpensive one? That's where psychological reasons enter the picture. Will it impress my friends and colleagues? Will I look foolish? Will it help me feel good about myself, or will I regret buying it?

Have you ever wished you could buy a powerful car, truck, boat or even a jet plane to give you a feeling of power and status? I have from time to time, although I am reluctant to admit it. Recently, driving through my neighborhood, I saw a cab from a huge tractor-trailer with a *For Sale* sign prominently displayed on its windshield. I fantasized about buying such an imposing-looking vehicle, imagining the reaction of colleagues when they saw me roar into the faculty parking lot. "Wow! That man is one powerful dude." Then, back to reality, I picture the Dean requiring a note from a psychiatrist to be permitted back on campus.

You might have noticed that an inexpensive feature with psychological appeal will often tip the scales in favor of selecting a car costing many thousands.

Your ego influences a wide variety of your activities including purchasing furniture and clothes, selecting music and participating in or watching sports. I have been around long enough to experience the high we get when "our team" wins a Superbowl, World Series, Stanley Cup, NBA and NCAA championships. The entire city of Philadelphia burst with pride each time. We celebrated wildly, and we spent freely during our celebrations.

Your ego can even endanger your life. Many safety devices are resisted or rejected because users feel freer or more rugged without them. Seat belts, helmets, safety goggles, dust masks are examples that come readily to mind. Despite clear evidence that helmets reduce injuries for cyclists and athletes, we have seen continued resistance to getting them adopted. In factories, machine operators, more than you might think, disengage safety devices if they find them annoying. And I know a firefighter who mentioned that some men he works with rib him because he wears a protective mask during a fire.

Our egos even influenced space exploration. Initially, engineers designing space capsules saw men riding in them simply as passengers without any control of their vehicle. Test pilots ridiculed potential astronauts, saying that they were not actually flying their spacecraft, but simply "Spam in a can." Astronauts, in turn, insisted that spacecraft must have flight controls and windows. Subsequent early flights showed the value of skilled pilots who had some control over their spacecraft. Since then, however, improvements in technology have made control from the ground highly reliable. Will we see astronauts in future space exploration? Maybe, maybe not!

Gender Issues

Besides difficulties we all face in learning and utilizing technological tools, girls and women face other barriers including discrimination, self-concept and fear of failure.

Although we all learn from an early age to use tools to shape our environment, more powerful and more technical tools have traditionally been intended for men. As children, boys were encouraged to use toy trucks, construction machinery and other such "masculine" gear. Girls were directed toward toy versions of devices used for cooking, sewing, cleaning and other kinds of housework as well as those employed in traditional women's occupations-secretary, teacher, nurse.

Changes have occurred over the years. Prior to World War II, relatively few women drove cars and fewer yet owned one. While change is especially evident with the automobile, more and more women now work with a greater variety of tools and more embark on scientific and technological careers. Educational institutions are removing gender barriers and encouraging women to consider opportunities in science. Even so, girls still receiving mixed messages about science and technology, and women are still underrepresented in STEM careers.

Consider this, the Society of Women Engineers now has only about 30,000 members worldwide a miniscule percentage of the total of over 10 million engineers.

Other minorities are also underrepresented in STEM occupations. Together they provide an important pool for future expansion.

In summary, various reasons discourage us from learning science and technology including cognitive and psychological ones. On top of this, poorly designed equipment and systems, which we will treat in the next chapter, play an important role.

Organizations, as well as individuals struggle with adopting new technology. Owners of major league teams, for instance, were initially resistant to radio broadcasting and later to telecasting for fear this would hurt attendance. I had a personal experience with this in my youth. Our house was adjacent to Philadelphia's Connie Mack Stadium with a clear view of games. The A's management refused to admit newsreel cameramen for the 1929-31 World Series, fearing the option of seeing its highlights in movie theaters would hurt attendance. As a result, three newsreel companies paid us to film games from our rooftop. Newsreel showings, of course, had zero effect on attendance. Today, profits from television rival income from ticket sales and the worth of a major league franchises have skyrocketed.

While sports franchise owners learned to adjust and prospered; other organizations failed to adapt and collapsed as a result. Sears at one time dominated the market for distant customers but were slow to accept new technology. Competitors moved in quickly to provide that service, and Sears suffered.

Evaluating New Technology

Sources of information

New technology is anything but easy to learn. It requires time and effort and a willingness to admit you don't know something worthwhile.

Fortunately, you have multiple sources of information at hand.

One is advertising. Eye-catching advertisements alert us to new and purportedly useful products. We soon learn, however, not to take such claims at face value. Companies marketing new products emphasize their worth, downplay their limitations. So, Caveat Emptor!

Children learn at an early age to be skeptical toward advertisers' pitch for products. In the movie *A Christmas Story,* Ralphie is initially all agog over getting a "Little Orphan Annie decoder ring" enabling him to decode secret messages sent during his favorite radio program. Disillusionment arrives with his very first secret message- an ad for Ovaltine, its sponsor's product.

I also recall my young daughter's response to a TV sponsor's description of a "marvelous new toy" with "I bet it's a piece of junk."

Other, more reliable sources of information include news reports, magazines and journals, the web (including consumer ratings), classes and workshops, tutoring, networking, and manuals. Select sources that work best for you. When mulling over purchasing a product, take time to determine resources available to help you master it.

Making Smart, Logical Decisions

In choosing a product, keep in mind what you have learned about decision-making.

It is stressful to many of us, and stress affects our judgment. Keep stress under control; learn to be confident and relaxed. You rarely have time or resources to evaluate every decision thoroughly. Push on! Don't procrastinate! Spend your time and effort on important decisions; make others quickly, or delegate. Consult at least two reliable sources before deciding. Don't come up with a hasty decision based on one expert's opinion. Faulty group decisions often stem from a recommendation by one person-one who knows more than the group, but not enough to provide a high-quality decision.

We might think having numerous options would produce better decisions. An unfortunate truth is more options make decisions more difficult. Narrow your initial choices, preferably to two, then weigh pros and cons of each. Modern technology offers far more choices than previously. It also provides procedures to facilitate our decision making.

Emotional (psychological) Influences

What do we look for in new technology? Certainly, to accomplish tasks, but also to help us feel more competent, independent, up-to-date, powerful or respected. Be alert to these psychological appeals influencing choice. You can boost your ego without being misled by it.

Psychological motives drive decisions, not only in individuals, but in organizations. Administrators may take pride in owning the newest, most powerful and most expensive product or system. Others value a reputation for frugality, tradition, conservatism and skepticism.

Other considerations in deciding on new technology include how readily you can learn it, and how smoothly you can utilize it. Human factors and engineering psychologists strive to provide technology that is easier to use, more comfortable, less frustrating and safer, a laudable goal, and one toward which we are moving. We will devote our next chapter to this.

Organizational decisions

Most of us not only face individual decisions, we also contribute to those of organizations where we work. Throughout this chapter, I have emphasized psychological findings that should be helpful for both your personal use of technology and that of organizations. In our next section, I provide a case that highlights many issues an organization confronts in updating products, including whether they will live up to claims of the producer. Many highly touted products fail to do so.

In this case, the U.S. Army was determined to build a vehicle for transporting infantry superior to a new Russian one. Complications involved in the development and procurement process are played out in the film, *The Pentagon Wars (1988)*, a dramatization based on true events. The vehicle produced for the Army was designated the Bradley Fighting Vehicle. Here is Wikipedia's description of it:

"The M2 and M3 Bradley Fighting Vehicle is a lightly armored, fully tracked transport vehicle that provides cross-country mobility, mounted firepower and protection from artillery and small-arms fire. It is used in mechanized infantry and armored cavalry combat." W

Air Force Lt. Col. John Burton, in running the vehicle through a series of tests, fears it may turn out to be a deathtrap. In his attempt to evaluate it properly, he is constantly frustrated by higherups pushing for its completion and acceptance with little concern for its suitability.

This film depicts one problem in procurement, i.e. how to determine if a product will live up to its claims. Failure of many highly touted products to do so often leads to litigation, and manufacturers of military equipment are a frequent target of such suits.

Another industry often sued by states and feds is pharmaceuticals. Accused of marketing drugs for conditions for which they haven't been approved, companies have settled out of court for millions of dollars (without admitting any wrongdoing).

Unfortunately, the primary concern of most organizations considering new technology is, 'will it increase profits"? Effect on jobs, environment and community are secondary considerations. A perennial hot-button political issue is government regulations that restrict companies in order to protect the public.

As a result, we find some defects corrected, some not. At one time, I read that the model Ford I was driving, would sometimes slip from Park into Reverse and possibly cause an accident. I was watching my mail for notice of a recall to correct this defect. Instead, the letter I received contained a sticker to attach to my dashboard-a warning not to leave the car in *Park* when its motor was running. Rather than incur the cost of fixing a defect, they chose to endure the wrath of costumers.

Using Technology to Improve Our Lives

Ben Franklin lived a life full of curiosity and a penchant for trying and enjoying new products and new experiences. Positive psychologists find this approach a source of fulfillment. They recommend you try it. Ben Franklin is someone to emulate. You certainly have an ever-increasing variety of products available that promise to improve communication, coordination, recreation, health, education, transportation, food preparation, decision making and other facets of your life.

It is up to you to keep current through reading, networking, consulting with those with expertise and basically being proactive. Go where the action is. Seek out products that best suit your needs and employ them to best advantage. Retain valuable ones and put aside those that add little or nothing to your life.

Meanwhile, here is a brief list of recommendations.
Start with your values and set priorities consistent with them. Consider new technology's value for family, job, health, community service, finances and just plain fun.

Be positive. Tools provide opportunities to enrich your life. Welcome them with enthusiasm and take advantage of them.

Set realistic limitations. You can't do everything. Enjoy what you can do.

Decide wisely. Technology brings problems as well as progress. Know when to say "No."

Don't obsess over mistakes. You will hit plenty of potholes on the road to success. Persist! It will pay off.

Learn how to best use new technology. Become competent with it. We have mentioned many sources enabling you to do just that.

Our next two chapters will continue and broaden your perspective on technology. The first addresses how to make technology user friendly, particularly the findings of human factors psychologists who specialize in this discipline. The second will discuss our latest in computer technology and point out what looks to be particularly useful.

Chapter 13.
Making Tools User Friendly

Introduction

Human factors psychology, human engineering, human factors science, ergonomics (or just plain human factors) involves using psychology to improve the engineering and design of products, processes, and systems. Its goal is to reduce human error, increase productivity, and enhance safety and user satisfaction.

Those who design technical products always knew they had to be used by people yet, they had a limited understanding of the skills needed to use them efficiently and safely. So, we inevitably find a disconnect between a product's capability and its performance, particularly in new, complex technology. It was often challenging to find someone able to use it proficiently. Typically, a tool was designed to perform a job, and workers selected and trained to fit the job. Human Factors Psychology reverses this process building technology geared to human capabilities.

User-unfriendly Technology.

Adding to difficulties in adopting new technology is that so much of it is designed to perform a given function with little consideration for those who use it. You will encounter examples in your home, your work, on the road and in your community.

Do you ever feel incompetent when you have difficulty figuring out which microwave button to push, whether to push or pull a door or what directions in a manual mean? If so, you have plenty of company. The problem often lies, not with you, but with product design that is far from user-friendly.

Keyboards

Examples of poorly designed products abound. A classic case is the organization of keys on typewriters (known as QWERTY design based on the location of the first six letters on the top row of keyboards). It requires you to use fingers and combinations of fingers that are less efficient than others (I commonly hit Caps Lock key instead of A). At one time our federal government conducted an extensive research study looking for a more efficient arrangement of keys. They found one that improved training time, accuracy and speed. Typing would be faster and easier, and they would save a considerable sum of money. Since it would also involve retraining for experienced typists, it was, unfortunately, never adopted.

In the home

Our homes provide abundant examples of poorly designed products. For years, typical kitchen stoves have had four gas burners, two in front and two in back. But which knob turns on which burner? An easy error is to place a pan on your back burner while turning on your front burner. Unless you are wearing a fireproof sleeve, you are a victim of poor design.

Other examples of products in homes that cause problems include tea kettles that scald your hand when you pour boiling water; frozen food packages with nutrition, refrigeration, and cooking directions in tiny print (or on its opening flap you tear off and discard); shower handles that easily confuse hot and cold or tub and shower; tiny print on medicine bottles, and furniture that might topple on you or one of the children.

Doors and windows

Have you encountered doors that puzzle you? A common source of confusion is whether a door opens in or out. Thus, the wag's question, "Do you need push or pull to get somewhere in this company"? It may also be unclear which side of a door you should use (left or right). In addition, some doors slide, and others require you to push a button.

People sometimes become trapped between two sets of doors, confused over how to open either of them.

Windows, particularly those so clear that they are practically invisible, are a common hazard.

We have all seen birds fly into them, and people do too. At one time, my office was on the first floor adjacent to the main entrance. Doors were clear glass, and students would bump into them from time to time. Then one day, a student rushing out of class, smashed into the glass door. I spent several minutes removing shards of glass from his hair and clothing. Fortunately, he escaped with only minor injuries.

My son-in-law tells of a similar, more frightening experience when his family was on vacation. His young sister, running from their motel room to the pool, smashed into a sliding glass door. She was cut badly, and may not have survived, but by good fortune, a surgeon, also on vacation, was nearby and saved her life.

Automobiles

The cars we drive involve so many controls and so many displays that we inevitably encounter some that are anything but user-friendly. One problem involves the wide variation from car to car. A quick look at your speedometer should tell if you are within the speed limit. In my previous car, when the needle on its display pointed straight up, I knew I was moving 60 mph; on my present car, it points up at 80 mph. Other differences that require you to break old habits include controls for windshield wipers and headlights that must be moved in the opposite direction from in previous cars, and those for opening trunk, hood and gas cap in different locations from car to car.

For instance, when stopping for gas, I must ask myself: "Where is the gas cap." On my wife's car, it is on the opposite side from mine. If I wait until I pull into a service station before asking this, I may have to move to the other side of the pump.

At one time, I picked up a rental at the Los Angeles Airport and was speeding along a freeway in heavy traffic. As it began to grow dark, I went to turn on my lights. But where was the light switch? Since I couldn't take my eyes off the road for more than a few seconds, I spent several anxious minutes searching, groping for the switch (turning on my windshield wipers in the process) until I managed to locate it and turn on my lights.

Another time, I was driving along a dark road in heavy rain when I noticed that the rain had subsided. As I reached down to turn off my windshield wipers, I suddenly caught myself. To turn them off, I simply had to push a button on the dashboard. However, a similar button located right next to it would turn off my headlights. A common fault in design is controls that are easily confused or unintentionally activated.

Signage

In traveling from place to place, you have no doubt been confused by signs intended to provide direction and information. Most are not as ambiguous as "Fine for Dumping", or as ludicrous as one in a restaurant in Spain, "This restaurant only serves water that has been passed by the manager."

Well-designed, well-lighted and well-placed signs is an obvious need on our streets and highways.

We have made considerable progress in enabling motorists to see needed information, understand it and absorb it in time to respond.

Still, some drivers struggle to understand road signs, and some provide examples of the adage "It is impossible to make anything foolproof, because fools are so ingenious." One driver, when pulled over for going 80 mph in a 65-mph zone, argued that he was just obeying signs that plainly read Rt. 80. The officer countered that it was a good thing he stopped him before he turned onto Rt. 120.

In yesterday's newspaper, a columnist criticized a bit of signage at Philadelphia's Airport. As motorists approach it, they encounter signs to turn one way for arriving flights and another for departing ones. It also lists "Parking" next to "Arriving Flights." Travelers who want to park and depart, do not usually realize they must follow directions for arriving flights. and thus, often turn the wrong way. They must wind their way through the airport, exit and drive back to start over again.

Warning signals

Like signs intended to inform us, warning signals should alert us to action. A sonar operator on a submarine scanning a screen spots some activity. Is it an enemy, or merely movement in the water.? Does a warning light indicate a problem with a car's engine or a defective light? Should you stop at once or ignore it?

We may ignore or be slow to respond to a warning if we are uncertain whether it is a true emergency or a false alarm. Have you ever been in a hotel when a fire alarm sounded? What did you do? Many guests call someone at the front desk (who usually knows no more than they do), wait to see what others are doing, or search for signs of smoke or fire. Better instead to get out at once. Otherwise, it may be too late.

Medicine

Inadequate medical technology and its misuse still poses a serious problem. Even simple modifications in tools and procedures can be the difference between life or death.

First, a minor incident. My primary care physician removes wax from my ears from time to time. Typically, he held a pan under my ear and flushed the ear canal until the wax was cleared. Preparing the paraphernalia and performing this procedure was time consuming, and treatment a bit uncomfortable, but it worked. Last year, I had it done at a nearby walk-in clinic. There, a physician used a different tool, a pointed metal probe, to dig it out. It was so painful that I was ready to run out of the office screaming. Then he said, "Oh! you're bleeding," which I was. I had to consult a specialist to treat the damage.

This year, I asked my primary care physician to do it. "Sure", he said, "I have a new tool for this job." He took out a narrow flexible tube with a tiny light on one end, inserted it gently into my ear and in a few seconds removed the wax. Not a bit of discomfort. He mentioned that the new tool cost under $20. The right tool used by a skilled person makes a major difference.

Mistakes in medical treatment stemming from poor design are often tragic. In one case, a child died in a hospital because a nurse administered the wrong medication. She picked up a bottle of the size, shape and color as the correct one. Only tiny print on the labels distinguished them. A more obvious difference in the two bottles would have saved a child's life.

The military

Military technology is complex and demands swift decisions. Mistakes are inevitable. One instance took place at West Point during artillery practice. A cadet accidentally selected a long round rather than a short round during artillery exercise. Consequently, the shell, instead of heading for its intended target, flew well past it, across the Hudson River and over an adjacent town. It exploded in an open field. By good fortune, no one was hurt.

Aircraft

I have previously mentioned numerous problems with aircraft. Equipped with far more displays and controls than automobiles, they demand quicker interpretations of the meaning of multiple gauges and alarms. Planes also require quicker and smoother responses.

Over a period of several years, a number of crashes, civilian and military, occurred when a plane inexplicably dove straight down into the ground. Investigations concluded that faulty design of a display was the culprit. Intended to tell whether a plane was climbing or diving, it consisted of two horizontal lines, representing horizon and airplane. If the plane on the display is above the horizon line, it is climbing; if below, descending. Regrettably, it was easy to confuse these two lines. A pilot, believing his plane is nearing a stall, looks quickly at the display to confirm his feeling and thinks it is. He pushes the controls forward, producing a rapid dive leading to disaster.

From time to time we also read of a passenger plane shot down because it was mistaken for an attacking military plane.

Communications

Cell phone, iPad, Twitter, Facebook, Skype and ever more new products of information technology enable us to communicate rapidly and directly worldwide. Entire libraries of information, reflection and opinion are literally at our fingertips. It holds out a promise of an educated citizenship and increased understanding throughout the world. It is so complex and changing so rapidly that it seems impossible to stay current in it and easy to err in using it.

Sad to say, our new technology also disseminates rumors, misinformation, conspiracy theories and hate messages faster and further and provides a platform for harassment. It also enables spin-doctors to gather extensive data about us and use it to influence our opinions, our purchases and our votes.

Manuals

If you happen to ask an engineer "how do I use this new device"? You may get the response R.T.F.M., meaning READ THE F-ING MANUAL! (or "read the full manual", if you prefer). It seems obvious. That's what manuals are for. Yet, most of us have been victimized by manuals that are misleading or incomprehensible. I recently purchased a new heater for my home and had difficulty adjusting its thermostat, a seemingly simple task.

Checking the accompanying manual, though, left me scratching my head. I found sections on installing a thermostat and removing one, but zilch on how to adjust one. Other manuals suffer from information overload. When I first bought my cell phone, I thought I was astute in requesting a manual. I was handed one of over 100 pages, mostly gobbledygook. I was constantly muttering, "Where is the stuff I want?"

Another type of overload in manuals stems from manufacturers' concern about litigation from harm caused by their product. Manuals are now crammed with pages of warnings. "Do not eat this product." "Not to be heated in microwaves." "Keep away from young children." And on and on.

Workshops

Workshops offer a natural way to learn new technology.

Have you attended any? Specialists who teach them know technology. Regrettably, they often have trouble explaining it. I have been in workshops offered for faculty in which the instructor concludes that all faculty are stupid; faculty, in turn, become convinced technicians speak another language. Both are frustrated.

History

Some folks have always experimented with designing and modifying products in order that they might be used more effectively. Ben Franklin is one of the most celebrated. Another, from the early 20th century, is Lillian Gilbreth, one of our first woman psychologists. She, and her husband Frank, an engineer and a pioneer in time and motion study, formed a consulting team specializing in improving efficiency and safety in a wide variety of occupations. They introduced improvements in tasks required in manufacturing, surgery, and even in managing the household. One task that initially seemed an amusing curiosity, an efficient way of taking a shower, was adopted by the military to save time and conserve water. After her husband's death, Dr. Gilbreth continued to manage her practice for many years. Her exploits are chronicled in the best-selling book, Cheaper by the Dozen, written by two of her children and made into a popular movie back in 1950. They provide a humorous retrospective on growing up in a large family with an efficiency expert and a psychologist for parents.

World War II
Except for a few such pioneers, human factors emerged as a recognized area of research and application during World War II. Suddenly, a vast number of soldiers, sailors and marines encountered new, complicated weapons and weapons systems, mostly poorly designed and exceeding the capacities of the recruits. Much of the human factors research was devoted to airplane safety and proficiency. Since I went through flight training with the Navy, and subsequently served as a flight instructor, I saw numerous examples of deficiencies in equipment (sometimes with catastrophic consequences). I was intrigued with the work psychologists were doing to improve safety and efficiency. The need was striking, with

the number of pilots lost in accidents rivaling that in combat.

Expansion of applications

From research in WWII came studies of human performance in a variety of situations. You may have seen the results in advances in motor vehicles and highway signs, but it has also improved proficiency in conducting surgery, monitoring surveillance screens, designing aircraft and spacecraft, performing factory jobs, presenting information, arranging workspace, and carrying out household tasks. Designers began to realize they needed to incorporate characteristics of users into their designs.

What do professionals in human factors psychology do? As we might expect, they conduct research on human abilities, and limitations that are particularly relevant to designing and evaluating products, machines, tools, equipment, and systems. They utilize this knowledge in enhancing safe, satisfying, and successful performance. They aim for more user-friendly technology.

Person-machine system

Human factors professionals work within the person-machine system. They focus on functions performed by people and demands placed on them whenever they work with machines or other technology. In this interaction a person must interpret input, decide what action to take, activate appropriate controls, then note the effect of this action and adjust. Human factors psychology improves this process by helping design displays that can be interpreted more accurately and controls that can be operated more effectively.

Airplanes are a familiar example of a person- machine system. In performing various maneuvers such as taking off, landing, turning, climbing, diving, navigating, bombing and dogfighting, and coordinating objectives with other pilots and those on the surface, pilots must handle considerable input. They draw on information from direct observation of the environment: apparent altitude, objects in their flight path, wind direction, visibility and weather. They also note input from the plane. Is the engine running smoothly? Does the plane feel as if it is vibrating or close to stalling? Is there a worrisome odor? Much needed information, however, must be obtained from technical devices, such as displays, gauges and alarms. A pilot is required to coordinate information from these varied sources, do it swiftly and accurately and decide what action to take. At times, they miss or misinterpret important input.

Once input has been interpreted and decisions made, pilots employ the proper controls. But sometimes controls are confusing, poorly placed, or difficult to operate. In one case I recall from flight training, we moved from a plane in which a lever on the left side lowered its landing gear to one in which a lever in that same location released a smoke bomb. Needless to say, smoky landings were common.

Modern fighter planes have far more controls. So many, in fact, that a pilot activates a different one with each finger and with motions of the head.

Traditional views and empirical evidence

Sometimes research in human factors comes up with results that surprise us. If we were to decide driverless cars should have a distinctive color, what would be your color of choice? Red seems an obvious answer. Yet human factors research with emergency vehicles tells us accidents are far greater for red fire trucks than for those using a lime green color.

To a casual observer, two brake lights on the back of an automobile might seem enough, but evidence shows that adding a third light significantly reduces rear- end collisions.

Do machines need humans?

An alternative to user-friendly person-machine systems is to take the person out of the system, by introducing devices that perform processes automatically. The thermostat is a simple example of this. Before its introduction, temperature in a house was controlled by its residents' actions. If they felt cold, one of them would add another log to the fire or toss a shovelful of coal into the furnace. Thermostats automatically add heat when the temperature falls below a given level and turn on air conditioning when it gets too high. Yet, as we know, mechanisms malfunction. For one, I recently found the air conditioner in my apartment continually running, blowing cold air in. At the same time, my heater was blasting away generating more heat.

Pilotless planes and driverless cars have been tested successfully and may soon be commonplace. However, they still have glitches to iron out and consumers concerns to overcome. Demonstrators against driverless cars recently attacked some of them with clubs and knives after a pedestrian was struck and killed by one. In this instance, a monitor riding along failed to sustain needed attention- an instance of failure on both parts of a person/machine system.

When machines can perform complex processes automatically, do we still have a place for workers?

Usually we need someone to supplement machines and systems and to monitor them in case they malfunction.

Wherever we employ monitoring, a human factors perspective can make it more effective. We now use visual surveillance in more and more situations: cameras at traffic lights, body cameras for police, backup cameras for motorists and for military surveillance. Russia even uses forward-facing cameras on vehicles as evidence against floppers who throw themselves in front of a slow-moving vehicle then sue.

Rather than stop a motorist for speeding, some police departments are simply taking a photo of an offender's license plate.

Information obtained from our new technology still requires humans to interpret it. Surveillance cameras contribute to security, but someone must review visual information and decide whether it is useful.

Hazardous machinery

Much of our technology is not only inefficient, but also outright dangerous. When the Occupational Safety and Health Administration of our Department of Labor (OSHA) was formed by the Occupational Safety and Health Act of 1970, around 14,000 workers had been killed on their jobs in the previous year. Although U.S. employment has almost doubled since then, fatalities from industrial accidents is now roughly one third of that figure. Over the same period, serious workplace injuries and illnesses has declined from 11 per 100 workers to 3.6 per 100 workers. Attention to making machinery safe paid off.

We have likewise seen a marked decrease in fatalities from automobile accidents. Human factors psychology's contribution to automotive design and highway safety has played a significant role in this. One of the ways traffic has been improved is with the introduction of the E-Z Pass to eliminate toll booth bottlenecks.

Challenges and opportunities

Other areas, including medicine, surgery, pharmaceuticals, and computer information systems have been slower to incorporate human factors research into their work. Consequently, both provide challenges and opportunities. So does an increasing market for devices geared to needs of special populations including those requiring assistance in vision, hearing, language, cognition, mobility, balance, and physical strength.

Chapter 14. Technology to Enrich Your Life
By Margaret (Peg) McManus, Ph.D.

Technology as a Tool to Support and Enhance Positive Psychology

Introduction

Technology, we have already stated, "can enrich your personal life, enhance your career and help you become a better-informed citizen." Indeed technology, when used wisely, knowledgeably, and securely, helps us to improve our lives, our research and communication—and it can also promote and support positive psychology in our lives. Martin Seligman, in his Handbook of Positive Psychology, explains that positive psychology reinforces our personal strength and resilience, characteristics supported by technology. Technology can help us to improve our interpersonal skills, perseverance, and purposefulness. To understand how technology can help us to achieve these goals, we first need to understand technology's basic structure and how it is used in so many practical ways in everyday life.

Overview ofComputer and Telephone Technologies

Knowing the basics of computer and telephone technology enables us to delve into how these technologies can support and promote positive psychology. From the Abacus to the ZBook, computing technologies have evolved over the centuries. Sliding beads on an abacus to vacuum tubes, transistors and integrated circuits for components; punched cards representing one's and zero's to eye movements for input;

punched paper tape to video images for output; simple step-by-step instructions to complex machine-learned algorithms for programs; roomfuls of big machines to a tiny integrated circuit in a cell phone for hardware—these are some of the radical ways that computing technology has evolved from bulky "dumb" machines to intelligent devices over the years. For many decades we used Moore's Law to measure how quickly technology evolves, as the number of components in an integrated circuit doubled every two years, increasing its processing speed. Now we simply know that new devices and apps appear almost daily! With the creation of interconnected computers, now globally connected in the Internet, we communicate to others around the room and around the world. The input and output (data signals) can be sent through hard-wires or wirelessly, even using satellites 22,000 miles above the earth in a stable orbit. "Apps" are the modern day programs which run on a gamut of technologies, from smart phones to tablets to laptops to desktop computers. Apps provide us with the means to obtain movies and music, do calculations, play games, read the news, and importantly to meditate and exercise.

The telephone was seen as an innovative but disruptive technology in the 1870s from its first transmission of "Mr. Watson, come here—I want to see you" by Alexander Graham Bell. The telephone ousted the telegraph as the principle means of long distance communication. (https://www.thoughtco.com/history-of-the-telephone-alexander-graham-bell-1991380). In the late 1800's if you wanted to use a telephone, you had to set up your own line to connect with whomever you wanted to speak! By the end of the century, you could use a switch to connect to the line that you wanted and dial a number of pulses to indicate whom you were calling. Also at that time, you could use a pay phone to call someone else, depositing your coins at the end of the call. By the middle of the 1900s, phones used touch tones instead of pulses and a rotary dial. In the 1970s, phones became cordless and by the 1990s, they also became digital with the incorporation of integrated circuits. The first mobile phones were actually similar to two-way radios, such as those used in taxis in the 1940s. The iPod, made by Apple Corporation, was the foundation for our current mobile/cell phone with computing technology, connection to the Internet via wireless technology ("wifi"), touch screen, audio and video recording and playback. Using our mobile phones, we can contact friends, family, businesses and many others at virtually any time and any location. We use our "smart phones"--actually hand-held computers---to look up information on the Internet, take photos, run apps, and –oh yes—make a phone call. This pervasive communication supports our busy lifestyle very well.

Positive Technology

Let's consider how technology can aid and support us in using positive psychology. We'll look at the present types of positive technology through the eyes of Tchiki Davis, founder of the Berkeley Well-Being Institute and at future technologies through the eyes of David B. Yaden, Johannes C. Eichstaedt, and John D. Medaglia, researchers in psychology departments at the University of Pennsylvania and Drexel University.

Types of Positive Technology

Tchiki Davis in her article "What is Positive Psychology?" in <u>Psychology Today</u> notes that there are many technology tools available now to aid us in achieving positive psychology, such as happiness apps, stress sensors, gratitude achievers. She generalizes these into five types of positive technology: Informational, academic, applied, passive, and mixed types.

The Informational Type of Positive Technology

Informational technology provides information (obviously) on ways to achieve positive psychology. For example, articles in online and paper-based psychology magazines, medical resources, self-help books and social media provide information about how to achieve a positive attitude. Information may be given about methods to reduce stress, eat healthily, or build your immune system, especially in trying times.

However, one of the challenges of the informational type is the need for us to verify the integrity of the source. You can verify if an informational website is an authentic source by carefully examining the name of the web site, especially its domain type (.com, .edu, .org, .net). Additionally, you would need to use your own initiative to actually put the suggestions into action appropriately for your own benefit.

The Academic Type of Positive Technology

The academic type of positive technology provides us with structured assignments, lessons, or activities. These activities would need to be repeated consistently and frequently to becoming a lasting and effective habit. For example, the website Berkeley Well-Being Institute provides online exercises to aid us in achieving well-being. The exercises include directions and dialog boxes in which we enter our response; our information can be saved or printed for our files. In the <u>Prioritizing Positivity</u> activity, as shown in Figure 1, we are asked

Figure 1. Screen Shot of Prioritizing Positivity Activity from Berkeley Well-Being Institute
(<u>https://www.berkeleywellbeing.com/emotion-activities.html</u>)

to make a list of things that we enjoy and then post the list on a Pinterest board. For example, I would include DIY (do-it yourself) crafts, home décor and gifts on my Pinterest board.

In <u>Happiness Values,</u> we are asked to list three emotions that we value. Next we are asked in what behaviors do we achieve them and how often we exhibit them on a frequency basis. I value calmness, confidence, determination, hopefulness, and serenity; I can achieve calmness through deep breathing.

Figure 2. Screenshot of Happiness Values Activity from Berkeley Well-Being Institute (https://www.berkeleywellbeing.com/)

In <u>Mental Time Travel</u>, we use our imagination to imagine ourselves happy in the future. An exercise would be to imagine that we have become happy by realizing that we each matter in this world and then by imagining this environment. For example, I might imagine that I have more confidence and see myself in the future with more confidence.

Figure 3. Screenshot of Mental Time Travel Activity from Berkeley Well-Being Institute (https://www.berkeleywellbeing.com/)

However, challenges can arise from the academic type of positive technology. We might find it cumbersome to use technology to record our feelings or we might become bored with this activity because it doesn't involve other people directly.

The Applied Approach to Positive Psychology

The applied approach is achieved by practicing a technique while we are doing another task. For example, we might use Mindfulness while we are taking a walk. Mindfulness causes us to remain in the moment, not allowing our minds to wander. We focus on our breath in various parts of our body.

Figure 4. Screenshot of Mindfulness Activity from Berkeley Well-Being Institute (https://www.berkeleywellbeing.com/mindful-activity.html)

We could also use the Calm app to help us to achieve mindfulness. It provides various exercises to help you to meditate, get more restful sleep, listen to music to help you relax, watch videos to help with relaxation and body stretching.

**Figure 5. Screenshot of Calm.com App on a Cell Phone
(https://www.calm.com/blog/about)**

The challenge with the applied approach is similar to that of the academic type—we could possibly run out of motivation or interest to continue using the technique at all or in a beneficial way.

The Passive Approach to Positive Technology

This technology helps us build skills unconsciously as a result of external cues, not directly to create well-being. This could be achieved by using positive social media or a gift-giving app. For example, many shopping websites first ask you if you wish to donate to a cause. For example, when I visit the Amazon.com website, I am asked if I wish to donate to a charity, thus increasing my social connection.

Figure 6. Screenshot of Amazon Donation Box (https://www.amazon.com/)

The challenge with the passive approach is that it might not be significant enough for us to feel a difference in our own positive thinking.

The Mixed Combination of Approaches

A mixed combination of two or more positive technologies could also be beneficial. For example, there could be "Happiness Games" which combine academic and applied use of technology to build happiness or self-esteem, such as the apps SuperBetter, Happify, and MindBloom.

Potential Problems with Positive Technology

Positive Technology is a fairly new field and is still incurring "growing pains." For example, many of the technologies are based on instinct or are not developed by experts. Additionally, there might not be thorough research and data about their effectiveness and efficacy yet. However, we can view these issues as a challenge to ourselves to become experts or to emphasize the need for clinical research.

Future Technologies in Positive Psychology
David Yaden, Johannes Eichstaedt, and John D. Medaglia at the University of Pennsylvania and Drexel University (https://doi.org/10.3389/fpsyg.2018.00962) study about future technologies in positive psychology, focusing specifically on machine-learning algorithms on big sets of data, non-invasive brain stimulation, and virtual reality.

Machine Learning Algorithms on Big Sets of Data
An algorithm is a set of explicit instructions to solve a problem. On the other hand, machine-learning is a computer algorithm without explicit instructions. It makes inferences, predictions, and models by using training data from a large data set. In our current world of social media, Yaden and his colleagues describe their study of machine learning using two types of social media, Facebook and Twitter. They used machine learning algorithms on nearly 2,000 Facebook users to learn about their life satisfaction levels, an aspect of Positive Thinking. They then applied the results to the Tweets of tens of millions of Twitter users to estimate their life satisfaction level. They then superimposed the results to a map of the United States, showing the life-satisfaction levels of people across the country, as shown in the following map, using county-level scores.

Figure 7. Big Data Analysis of Geo-Located Tweets (Yaden et al.)

Non-Invasive Brain Stimulation

Non-invasive brain stimulation is accomplished through different technologies, such as magnetic signals and light signals sent from an external source through the brain. Transcranial magnetic stimulation (TMS) may be used to supposedly enhance brain function or well-being, specifically increasing cognitive performance, mathematical ability, attention span, problem solving, memory, and coordination, as well as treating depression and chronic pain. While scientists do not completely understand the mechanism by which TMS influences the brain function, they do know that it activates brain axons, causing them to fire action potentials.

Light stimulation, known as Photo biomodulation (PBM), uses high or low powered laser or LED sources on the brain. It has been used to help patients with depression, stroke, PTSD, addiction and insomnia. It has also been shown to have increased the blood flow in the brain to enhance cognition.

However, the ethics of the use of TMS and PBM is under discussion. It may be very helpful for persons suffering from depression, but it is questionable if it should be used to enhance a normal person's abilities.

Virtual Reality

Virtual reality (VR) provides us with the experience of being <u>inside</u> a three dimensional environment, even being able to manipulate objects inside the environment. It can help us to understand the environment and communicate with a partner in the actual environment. Often positive emotions and feelings of awe are generated while in the VR. Some VR can also be used to track facial expressions and eye movements. VR can be a tool to offer us experiences which we would not normally have, such as travel to an international city. I had an opportunity to explore underwater worlds using VR at the Franklin Institute Museum in Philadelphia. My grandson and I each donned VR headsets and explored these worlds, while simultaneously talking with each other about what we saw.

Scientists might be able to use VR to study the well-being aspect of positive psychology—how to achieve well-being using VR and how long it lasts.

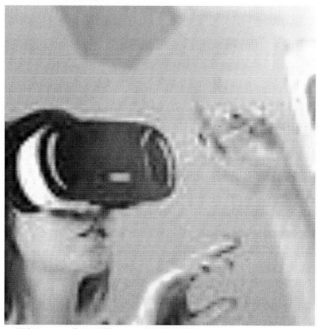

Figure 8. Virtual Reality Technology
(<u>https://www.vrs.org.uk/virtual-reality/what-is-virtual-reality.html</u>)

Applied Technology in Everyday Life

We have just discussed how Positive Technology itself can help us to achieve the benefits of Positive Thinking and even how we can measure our level of achievement. Now we turn our attention to other applied technology in everyday life that can also promote Positive Thinking, but in an indirect way. We address a variety of technologies here: <u>communication</u>, <u>social media</u>, <u>the Internet of Things</u>, <u>big data and analytics</u>, <u>entertainment</u>, <u>assistive technologies</u>, <u>artificial intelligence and robotics</u>, <u>gaming</u>, and <u>cloud computing</u>. Usage examples of these technologies come from various industries, such as government, medicine, health care, education, finance, and manufacturing. Because technology evolves rapidly and advances come quickly, by the time you read this book, new technologies may have been invented!

Communication Technologies

Early in history, humans communicated by signs, symbols, and then language. Letters, telegraph and telephone evolved as communication means and devices. Now with telephones, we can talk with one, two, or even hundreds of people who are located elsewhere. With video conferencing, which runs on the Internet, we can also see the video image of other people on the call. We use video conferencing to connect with our family and friends, our business partners, and our teachers; we can chat, have virtual meetings, use telemedicine, see webinars, and attend class, using products such as WebEx, GoToMeeting, and Zoom. When we attend the session, we see the video of all of the other participants in gallery format, as shown in Figure 9. Not only can we talk with others, we can collaborate with them by sharing and jointly editing documents and drawing on a whiteboard.

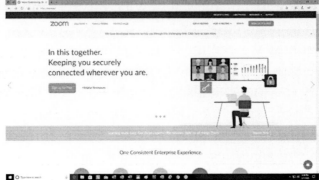

Figure 9. Screen Shot of Zoom Platform for Virtual Meetings (https://zoom.us/)

Educators use video conferencing to teach online courses, connecting with the students synchronously, that is, at the same time. When I teach online courses using Zoom or GoToMeeting, I can immediately reply to my students' live questions, and I can show them solutions to homework exercises. Educators also can use a Learning Management System (LMS) to connect with the students asynchronously, that is at different times and locations. Through the Canvas LMS, my students obtain their assignments and take their tests online at any time they choose and is convenient to them within the parameters of the due dates that I specify in the syllabus. I post their grades in the LMS' grade book and the students view them there. The LMS is also useful for face-to-face (F2F) and hybrid courses, a combination of F2F and online, as it provides an infrastructure for course materials.

So using communication technologies running on the Internet, we can learn new information and build social skills, thus helping us to enhance our Positive Thinking.

Social Media

We can use our computers, laptops, tablets, or smart phones for social media-- "forms of communication through which users create online communities to share information, ideas, personal messages and other content, such as videos," according to Merriam Webster. We can choose from many different social media platforms technologies, such as FaceBook, Twitter, Instagram, YouTube, and TikTok, to name a few.

As a FaceBook user, I can learn about the benefits of Positive Psychology, as from the Positive Psychology topic and its link to "Leadership and Positive Organizational Psychology."

Figure 10. Screen Shot of FaceBook Page for "Positive Psychology" (https://www.facebook.com/)

I can join a group, such as "Positive Psychology" which currently has 125,000 (125K) members! You can join in online discussions in the group, read event announcements, watch videos, see photos, and access files such as theses, forms, and papers.

Figure 11. Screen Shot of Positive Psychology Group Facebook Page (https://www.facebook.com/)

We can use social media to a degree to help us form new friendships, connect more with existing friends, have a sense of community or togetherness, learning about topics. However, we need to be aware of some disadvantages for us as "casual" users—spending too much time on social media, possibility of someone "hacking" our account to obtain our private, personal information. To prevent some of these issues, it is important that your information is secure. In my FaceBook page, when I click on the question mark for Quick Help, I am given a list of common questions about security settings. For example, the responses to "What can I do to keep my account secure?" I am given many recommendations, such as protecting my password and not sharing my information.

Figure 12. Screen Shot of FaceBook Security
(https://www.facebook.com/)

Twitter enables you to connect with other people through "microblogging," that is writing very short messages, thoughts, questions to other. You can use it to "follow" another person to read their "tweets" or postings, or to view photos or videos. At the twitter.com service, I entered the term "positive psychology" in the search bar, as shown in Figure 13. From the results shown, WISE National seems like it could be helpful for Positive Psychology in encouraging us to give gratitude for good moments.

Figure 13. Screen Shot of Twitter Tweets for "Positive Psychology" (https://twitter.com/explore)

Internet of Things

More than 20 years ago, Kevin Ashton coined the term "Internet of Things" (IoT) for the network of objects connected via the Internet, with the things creating data. The concept of IoT actually existed since the 1970s, then known as pervasive computing and embedded computing. For example, a Coke machine at Carnegie Mellon University could tell the computer programmers (who had created an embedded program in the machine) if a cold drink was waiting for them.

Today we use smart phones which have GPS systems to find directions via its GPS, wearable technology, such as a Fitbit to track our number of steps per day, and apps in our cars for navigation and diagnostics. Businesses use the IoT for inventory management, doctors read data from their patients' heart monitoring devices, and our homes turn on the lights themselves!

Kuva 1. Internet of Things. Lähde: Huffington Post

Figure 14. Internet of Things
(https://www.huffpost.com)

But how does the Internet of Things relate to Positive Psychology? (https://www.psychologytoday.com/us/blog/the-digital-self/201902/its-not-iot-its-iol-the-internet-life) John Nosta extends the concept of the Internet of Things to the Internet of Life! It's not just that things are connected, but that connectivity can benefit us and facilitate our lives. "The blending and mixing of technology and humanity is both complex and ambiguous," says Nosta. A person can wear a stress monitoring device, such as the Garmin wearable which not only detects stress but gives you relaxation breathing timers.

Figure 15. Garmin Wearable Stress Tracker (https://www.garmin.com/en-US/blog/general/which-garmin-wearables-have-stress-tracking/)

Big Data and Analytics

For some of us, looking for a friend's telephone number had meant using the white paper pages of the telephone book. Peoples' names were arranged in alphabetical order making them easy to find. If I were looking for a plumber, or other such home service, I would use the yellow pages in which all the plumbers were grouped together. New telephone books of white and yellow pages were updated and published annually.

But what a difference there has been in data technologies in 30 years! Storage of data has evolved from paper-based to electronic databases. An entry from our personal phone book is stored as a single record in an electronic database. We use our smart phones as our "white and yellow pages" by saving our friends' cell phone numbers and email addresses in our phone's electronic address book. We can look up a Philadelphian's phone number in the online white pages.

Figure 16. Screen Shot of Philadelphia, PA White Pages (https://www.whitepages.com/white-pages/philadelphia-pa)

When we want to look for a plumber, we open our web browser to the Internet and do a search for "plumber in Philadelphia, PA." The result is not

Figure 17. Web Search for "Plumber in Philadelphia, PA"

only a list of plumbing services, but also a list of related search terms, such as "best plumbers in Philadelphia." We then simply click the mouse on the link, shown in blue, and that web page is displayed on our screen.

Not only can we use databases which others have created, we can create our own databases using software such as MS-Access or Structured Query Language—that's a topic for another book!

The size of databases has grown significantly over the years, storing huge quantities of data—thus being called "Big Data." Big Data sets are too large to be handled by traditional data processing systems; however the large size of data provides sufficient data to be analyzed for trends. For example, my health information including my doctor visits, procedures, and medications is stored in my Electronic Medical Record (EMR) in my doctor's office associated with Jefferson University. My information as well as the information for other patients are stored in its large database. A great advantage for me is that I can look up my medical history using a portal connection to the database—through secure, password-protected access to the data. The login screen for the Jefferson Health System, shown in Figure 18, illustrates that I can communicate with my doctor, refill prescriptions, access my test results, and manage my appointments. An advantage for doctors and researchers is that they can analyze the big data of thousands of EMRs to determine medical trends, such as the occurrence of certain medical conditions in a specific population.

Figure 18. Example of the Jefferson Health System "MyChart" Portal

Other examples of Big Data are Google's search index, Facebook's user profiles, Amazon's product list. The U.S. Government's data.gov website provides links to many, many data sets available to all of us, such as climate change. As shown in Figure 19, I used the Education selection, and then selected the Integrated Postsecondary Education Data System to find the trend of the number of students enrolled in postsecondary institutions from 2000 to 2020. The trend shows 23 million students enrolled in 2000, moving to a high of 29 million in 2010, and decreasing to 26 million in 2016-2017. We might wonder why there was a decrease, and then find out through more research, it could be because of a decrease in the college-age students at that time.

Figure 19. Screen Shot of "The Home of the U.S. Government's Open Data (Data.gov)

Figure 20. Screen Shot of National Trend of Students Enrolled in Postsecondary Institutions (https://nces.ed.gov/ipeds/TrendGenerator/app/answer/2/2)

The U.S. Census Data provides many interesting examples of Big Data, especially because this year (2020) we are doing the decennial census. At its web page, I can select a topic to explore. For example, by selecting

Housing, I can find data about affordability of housing, such as "who can afford to buy a home in 2009?" I traced through the Topics (Figure 21) and then the section on Housing (Figure 22).

Figure 21. U.S. Census Data
(https://www.census.gov/topics/)

Figure 22. U.S. Census Data on Housing
(https://www.census.gov/topics/housing.html)

The chart shown in Figure 23 shows us in the first row of data that a home with 30-year financing costing less than $20,000 can be afforded by 30,816,000 families or by

16,055,000 married couples. Although these data are provided for 2009, with the new 2020 census upcoming, we expect that similar, current data will be available.

Figure 23. Housing Affordability
(https://www.census.gov/data/tables/2009/demo/housing-affordability/h121-13-02.html)

Big data are also used in Recommender Systems, which can recommend a product or service to you based on your previous choices and on other consumers' trends. You might have received a recommendation for a best-selling book after you have ordered one book online.

Big Data and Analytics can impact our Positive Thinking. By being able to find data about a topic of interest and to learn about the latest trends gives us great knowledge and can help us to make sound decisions.

Sometimes this process can make us feel frustrated, until our persistence prevails leading to a successful search.

Technologies for Entertainment

In the early days of the television in the 1950's, it was simple to turn a TV on or off by simply pressing a button on the TV. TVs have evolved so much that they now connect to the Internet to enable us to view from thousands of productions; tablets and readers are our digital books, and smart watches can be our fitness monitor. When we connect our TV, computer, tablet or watch to the internet, we can stream audio data to hear a podcast or stream video data to watch a movie. Streaming sends the audio and video to the device in a continuous stream; we hear and watch the signals as they are sent in groups. You might have noticed that sometimes you need to wait for the signals to buffer, that is, be received, causing the screen to temporarily freeze. Table 1 provides a list of some providers and the main kind of content that you can obtain.

Streaming Service	Content
Amazon Fire	Digital media player that streams audio and video to a high definition TV from a home internet network
Amazon Prime Video	Amazon original shows and HBO shows
Disney+	High quality shows
Hulu	New and classic shows
iTunes	Music

Netflix	TV shows and movies, including originals
Roku	Device that allows access to streaming services
Spotify	Music
YouTube	Videos which any subscriber can post and anyone can view
YouTube TV	Sports, news, and entertainment

Table 1. Current Audio and Video Streaming Services and Devices

Thanks to the wide array of offerings from streaming services, we can gain cultural understanding of others, develop critical thinking, increase our knowledge, learn a new skill, and even listen to "Positive Music" for mindfulness meditations at TIDAL, as shown in Figure24.

**Figure 24. TIDAL Streaming Music
(https://tidal.com/browse/track/50516188)**

Assistive Technologies
For people with disabilities, assistive technologies can enhance their learning, working, and daily living. These

technologies can be special-purpose computers, hardware and software for computers, tablets and smart phones, as well as unique devices.

Figure 25. Screen Shot of AbleData Web Site (https://abledata.acl.gov/)

The AbleData web site provides not only products by category but also an evaluation of the products.

Figure 26. AbleData Search Results (https://abledata.acl.gov/)

The category Blind and Low Vision provides us with many products—from the "Blind Abilities" Apple mobile application which provides podcasts and blogs "dealing with accessibility, technologies, devices and enhancing the opportunities in the job market for the blind, visually impaired and deaf-blind. The members share their experiences and offer advice including about life skills and everyday living. Their purpose is to "enhance the self-confidence to reach one's higher expectations in all aspects of living with Blindness."

Georgia Tech's "Tools for Life" web site is another resource for finding assistive technology. For example, when I searched its site for assistive technology for blindness, a list of free "My Favorite Apps" was displayed. For example, the "Text to Voice" app on your smart phone converts the text to speech which you can listen to.

Having technology which can assist the disabled provides them with Positive Thinking because they become empowered to improve their lives.

Figure 27. Screen Shot of Georgia Tech's Tools for Life (https://gatfl.gatech.edu/tfl.php)

Artificial Intelligence and Robotics

Artificial Intelligence (AI) was originally defined as computer systems that were designed to do what humans could do. Now, however, we view this area as what AI and humans can do together! We find AI in driverless cars such as Teslas and cars which even park themselves, facial recognition which gives us access to locked rooms, voice recognition to ask our device for assistance, translation to and from foreign languages, medical diagnoses, digital assistants which almost magically appear when we visit a retail web site or smart speakers that we ask questions, such as an Echo device. For example, I verbally asked Siri, the digital assistant on my Apple smart phone, "What is Positive Thinking." She responded with a definition of Optimism and a link to see more on Wikipedia.

Figure 28. Screen Shot of Digital Assistant Siri's

Responsive System on iPhone

We can even consider GPS (Global Positioning systems) on our smart phones as AI. Based on traffic and map data, a GPS can give us driving directions, using the best route without traffic delays, to our destination.

Robotics, machines which use AI to replicate human actions, help us in so many ways. Doctors use medical instruments operated by robotics to perform delicate surgeries, NASA uses robotic arms in space exploration, climatologist use drones to obtain weather information, children build robots in school, supermarkets use 6 foot tall robots equipped with vision to roam the aisles looking for spills and doing price checks, hotels use robots as desk clerks, airports use information kiosk, web sites use chat "bots" for you to ask questions via chatting online, factories use robots to build cars, and retailers use robots to manage inventory. We have seen that entertainment systems can provide us with a wide variety of content, and that content can be recommended to us by intelligent systems, as is done with Netflix and Pandora.

Figure 29. Giant Supermarket's Robot Marty (https://www.iqvis.com/blog/9-powerful-examples-of-artificial-intelligence-in-use-today/-)

Figure 30. Robots Taking Inventory (https://www.forbes.com/sites/gregpetro/2020/01/10/robots-take-retail/#578f53721720)

Robots can also be used for education, such as Robvi Robot, which supports children in their language learning, enhancing their self-efficacy.

Amazingly, some people are forming relationships with their own robots! The Roomba robotic vacuum seems to some people to have a personality based on its movements—eager, slow, and even grumpy! Scientists are studying why people form a trusting relationship with their robots. Lonely people seem to relate to their robot like a friend. Hospitals and health facilities often use pet therapy to soothe their patients. Robotic pets are now providing this consoling and therapeutic relationship, to combat loneliness and depression.

Figure 31. Robotic Pet
(https://www.cnn.com/2020/04/27/us/therapy-robot-pets-wellness-trnd/index.html)

Some people are worried about perceived negatives of AI, perhaps because they do not understand how it works or they think they might lose control or lose their jobs, or their data might be misused. However, Pew Research suggests a "values-based approach" to build intelligent devices "imbued with empathy that can help humans aggressively ensure that technology meets social and ethical responsibilities." To accomplish, perhaps there might need to be a regulatory or certification process.

Gaming

Gaming can help us to improve our minds, especially regarding memory and cognitive thinking. Games available in print and online newspapers include crossword puzzles, Sudoku, anagrams, KenKen and many more. Brightfocus Foundation, which focuses on Alzheimer's, macular degeneration, and glaucoma research and prevention, provides games to help us improve our memory (Figures 32 and 33). Of particular interest in its web site, shown in Figure 32, that it also clearly provides ADA compliant web viewing: notice that the text size can be enlarged (A A) and the contrast can be changed from a white background to a black background. You can also subscribe to a provider such as Lumosity (Figure 34) or Staying Sharp from AARP to train your working memory and improve your cognition.

Figure 32. Screen Shot of Memory Games by

BrightFocus Foundation
(https://www.brightfocus.org/alzheimers/memory-games)

Figure 33. Screen Shot of Daily Sudoku by BrightFocus Foundation
(https://www.brightfocus.org/alzheimers/memory-games/sudoku-daily)

Figure 34. Screen Shot of Lumosity Memory Games
(https://www.lumosity.com/en/brain-games/memory-games/)

Other types of games available online are word games, crosswords, math games, action games, time management, solitaire, card games, and sports. Playing mentally active and challenging games and learning new games can help us to stimulate our brain and cognition. In addition to games, we can challenge our brains by simply working on our memory—memorizing shopping lists or items in a room.

By learning new games, we can improve our brain health. We should avoid frustration at trying "too much" and try a gentle and graduate approach to learning new games.

Cloud Computing

The "cloud" is more than moisture in the air! Cloud computing supports data storage, management and processing, through a network of computer servers on the Internet, rather than on our own local computer.

Figure 35. Screen Shot of Cloud Computing (https://www.pcmag.com/news/what-is-cloud-computing)

Cloud computing is useful for many users from the everyday consumer to large scale businesses. As everyday consumers, we can use a cloud service to store our documents and photos, to obtain office-productivity software such as word processing, choosing from a variety of providers.

Provider	Cloud Services
Microsoft Azure	OneDrive - for storage; Office Online – for Word Processing, PowerPoint, spreadsheets and OneNote; Gaming; Knowledge Mining, Analytics, IoT
Google Cloud Platform	Gmail, Calendar, Docs, Sheets, Slides, Hangouts, Maps (with accessibility settings), Earth, Photos, Meet (for video meetings); collaboration
Apple iCloud	Word processing, spreadsheets, presentation; collaboration with Pages, Numbers, Keynotes; storage; photos, videos, files
Amazon Web Services	iCloud - storage of anything you buy from Amazon Prime and Kindle, such as music, videos and books; Website hosting; robotics, VR, AI, machine learning; analytics, gaming

Table 2. Current Cloud Computing Providers and Their Services

You can access the cloud by using your own device—computer, tablet, or smart phone—and connect to the provider's cloud services through its web site. Or, you could use a device that is dedicated cloud hardware, such as the Google Chromebook. The Chromebook, which looks like a laptop, runs Google's web browser Chrome and directly connects you to Google's cloud services. Many elementary school students use ChromeBook for schoolwork with Google Classroom, especially for virtual learning.

Businesses often use larger scale cloud services, such as a customer relationship management system (CRM), a data analytics program, AI, or IoT in the cloud. For example, universities use an enhanced version of SalesForce, a CRM, to track prospective students, and health service providers to track interactions with potential patients or clients. IBM's Watson includes both AI and machine learning facilities and its Community World Grid invites everyday and business users to allow their computers to share their resources through the cloud in the solution of large problems, such as potential treatments for COVID-19. On a simpler scale, Google provides tips to the user, including a "Stay in the Moment" tip, a reminder about mindfulness (Figure 36).

**Figure 36. Google.com Tips
(https://about.google/intl/en/products/?tab=wh&tip=do
-not-disturb)**

Cloud computing can be beneficial to us as we pursue Positive Thinking. Cloud computing provides us with computing resources that might not be easily available, such as services through the web or Internet. We can work on documents in a shared environment collaboratively enhancing our productivity. We can meet with our friends virtually to reduce feelings of isolation and improve communications. We can share our photos electronically to enhance our sense of family. The challenge of the learning curve to use the cloud can be daunting but could be mitigated by online help and digital assistants.

Evaluation of Technology for Positive Thinking – Advantages and Challenges

We have seen a wide gamut of positive psychology technologies per se and other technologies which can be used to promote positive psychology. The advantages of using these technologies are many: these devices, apps and systems help us to focus on aspects of positive psychology, they provide us with sound and meaningful information to enhance our knowledge, they provide us with structured and applied activities, and they can even indirectly affect our sense of well-being. Through the everyday use of technology, our communication skills are enhanced, we become more sociable, we connect our devices to our life style, we use big data to analyze large scale data, we use streaming entertainment to gain a cultural understanding of others, we use assistive technologies to compensate for a disability, we use robots to help us with our chores, we play electronic games to improve our memory, and we access many services and shared knowledge through cloud computing.

Challenges may deter some from the effectiveness of these technologies. Some may get frustrated during their learning curve or the need to continually update the systems. Using the systems can be costly and time consuming.

Conclusion

It is our hope that you will find that the advantages of technologies for positive psychology strongly outweigh their challenges. Smart devices and applied technologies support our interpersonal communication skills, information awareness, self-esteem, and mental cognition which should help to build our own sense of positiveness.

References

8 Examples of Robots being used in the hospitality industry. Revine. https://www.revfine.com/robots-hospitality-industry/. AARP Games. https://games.aarp.org/ Retrieved May 20, 2020.

Accessible Tech.org. Assistive Technology. *Accessible Technology in the Workplace.* https://accessibletech.org/assistive-technology/.

Able Data. Tools and Technologies to Enhance Life. https://abledata.acl.gov/. Retrieved May 6, 2020.

Amazon Web Services. *Amazon.* https://aws.amazon.com/. Retrieved May 20, 2020.

Apple iCloud. *Apple.* https://www.apple.com/icloud/. Retrieved May 20, 2020.

Anderson, J. and Rainie, L. Artificial intelligence and the future of humans. Pew Research Center. December 10, 2018. https://www.pewresearch.org/internet/2018/12/10/artificial-intelligence-and-the-future-of-humans/

Apple iCloud. *Microsoft.* https://azure.microsoft.com/en-us/solutions/. Retrieved May 20, 2020.

Artificial Intelligence and the Future of Humans (2018). https://www.pewresearch.org/internet/2018/12/10/artificial-intelligence-and-the-future-of-humans/.

Berkeley Well-Being Institute.
https://www.berkeleywellbeing.com/emotion-activities.html.

Big Data. https://techterms.com/definition/big_data.
Accessed May 6, 2020.

Calm. https://www.calm.com/blog/about.

Davis, T. (2017). What is positive psychology?
Psychology Today. Posted 12/7/2017.
https://www.psychologytoday.com/us/blog/click-here-happiness/201712/what-is-positive-technology.

Dickson, B. What is artificial intelligence? PC Magazine.
May 3, 2019.
https://www.pcmag.com/news/what-is-artificial-intelligence-ai

Eight brain-training games for memory. (2014).
Alzheimers.net Blog. November 5, 2014.
https://www.alzheimers.net/11-5-14-brain-training-games/
Retrieved May 20, 2020.

Escalante, A. (2020). Scientists confirm that your Roomba
does have a personality. *Forbes Magazine*. May 15, 2020.
https://www.forbes.com/sites/alisonescalante/2020/05/15/scientists-confirm-roomba-personality/#7594ac26623b.
Retrieved May 20, 2020.

Gabbai, A. (2015). Kevin Ashton describes the Internet of
things. *Smithsonian Magazine,* January 2015.

https://www.smithsonianmag.com/innovation/kevin-ashton-describes-the-internet-of-things-180953749/

George Petro. (2020). Robots take retail. *Forbes Magazine*. Jan. 1, 2020. https://www.forbes.com/sites/gregpetro/2020/01/10/robots-take-retail/#578f53721720. Retrieved May 20, 2020.

Georgia Tech Tools for Life. https://gatfl.gatech.edu//assistive.php

Google Products. https://about.google/intl/en/products/?tab=wh&tip=here-to-help. Retrieved May 20, 2020.

Griffith, E. (2016). What is cloud computing? *PC Magazine*. May 3, 2016. https://www.pcmag.com/news/what-is-cloud-computing. Retrieved May 20, 2020.

Hamblin, M.R. (2016). Shining light on the head: Photobiomodulation for brain disorders. *BBA Clin*. 2016 Dec; 6: 113–124. Published online 2016 Oct 1. doi:10.1016/j.bbacli.2016.09.002 and https://www.ncbi.nlm.nih.gov/pmc/articles/PMC5066074/

Happiness Games. https://www.psychologytoday.com/us/blog/click-here-happiness/201711/ten-plus-happiness-games-and-activities

Hindo, J. (2020). World Community Grid joins in the fight against COVID-19. May 14, 2020. https://www.ibm.com/blogs/corporate-social-responsibility/2020/05/world-community-grid-joins-in-the-fight-against-covid-19/?lnk=ushpv1811. Retrieved May 20, 2020.

Housing Affordability. https://www.census.gov/data/tables/2009/demo/housing-affordability/h121-13-02.html

How the Telephone Was Invented. https://www.thoughtco.com/history-of-the-telephone-alexander-graham-bell-1991380.

Hoyt, J. (2018). Brain Games for Seniors. *Senior Living.* May 18, 2018. https://www.seniorliving.org/life/brain-games/ Retrieved May 20, 2020.

Garmins. https://www.garmin.com/en-US/blog/general/which-garmin-wearables-have-stress-tracking/ Retrieved May 3, 2020.

Internet of Things. *Tech Target.* https://internetofthingsagenda.techtarget.com/definition/Internet-of-Things-IoT. Retrieved May 1, 2020.

Internet of Things. *Huffington Post.* https://www.huffpost.com.
Kim, A. (2020). Some Florida seniors isolated with Alzheimer's and dementia due to the pandemic are getting robotic therapy pets. *CNN.* April 27, 2020. https://www.cnn.com/2020/04/27/us/therapy-robot-pets-wellness-trnd/index.html Retrieved May 20, 2020.

Knorr, E. (2018). What is Cloud Computing? Everything you need to know now. *InfoWorld*. October 2, 2018.https://www.infoworld.com/article/2683784/what-is-cloud-computing.html. Retrieved May 20, 2020.

Memory games. *Bright Focus Foundation*. https://www.brightfocus.org/alzheimers/memory-games. Retrieved May 20, 2020.

Merriam Webster Dictionary. **https://www.merriam-webster.com/dictionary/social%20media**.

Moore, B. The Best video streaming services for 2020. *PC Magazine*. https://www.pcmag.com/picks/the-best-live-tv-streaming-services, Retrieved 5/18/2020.

National Center for Education Statistics. Trend Generator. https://nces.ed.gov/ipeds/TrendGenerator/app/answer/2/2.

Non-invasive brain stimulation: Application and implications. (2015). *National Institutes of Health*. May 5, 2015. https://www.ninds.nih.gov/News-Events/Directors-Message/Directors-Messages/Noninvasive-Brain-Stimulation-Applications-and-Implications.

Nosta, J. (2019). It's not IoT. It's IoL: The Internet of Life! *Psychology Today*. February 25, 2019. https://www.psychologytoday.com/us/blog/the-digital-self/201902/its-not-iot-its-iol-the-internet-life. Retrieved May 2, 2020.

Pinterest.com. https://www.pinterest.com/.

Recommender systems. http://recommender-systems.org/
Roybi. https://roybirobot.com/

Seligman, M. (2010). Positive psychology, positive prevention and positive therapy. *Handbook of Positive Psychology*, http://www.positiveculture.org/uploads/7/4/0/7/7407777/s eligrman_intro.pdf

The Internet of things delivers the data. AI powers the insights. *IBM Blog.* https://www.ibm.com/internet-of-things?p1=Search&p4=&p5=b&cm_mmc=Search_Bing-_-1S_1S-_-WW_NA-_-artificial%20intelligence%20software%20companies_b&c m_mmca7=71700000061085371&cm_mmca8=kwd-81501451787042:loc-190&cm_mmca9=&cm_mmca10=&cm_mmca11=b&gcli d=CI-Xi5WVtukCFdXtswodHRgJDQ&gclsrc=ds. Retrieved May 20, 2020.

TIDAL streaming music. https://tidal.com/browse/track/50516188. Retrieved 5/18/2020.

U.S. Department of Health and Human Services. What are some types of assistive devices and how are they used? https://www.nichd.nih.gov/health/topics/rehabtech/conditi oninfo/device

Virtual Reality Society. What is Virtual Reality?
https://www.vrs.org.uk/virtual-reality/what-is-virtual-reality.html

What is AT? *Assistive Technology Industry Association.*
https://www.atia.org/home/at-resources/what-is-at/.
Retrieved May 6, 2020

Which Garmin wearables have stress trackers? Garmin.
April 28, 2020.

Wikipedia contributors. History of the Telephone.
https://en.wikipedia.org/wiki/History_of_the_telephone

Wikipedia contributors. (2020). History of the Telephone.
https://en.wikipedia.org/wiki/History_of_the_telephone

Yaden, D.B.; Eichstaedt, J.C ; and Medaglia, J.D. (2018).
The Future of technology in positive psychology:
Methodological advances in the science of well-being.
Frontiers in Psychology. 18 June 2018
https://doi.org/10.3389/fpsyg.2018.00962 and
https://www.frontiersin.org/articles/10.3389/fpsyg.2018.00962/full

Chapter 15.
Emotions, the Engine That Drives Us

Introduction

We have seen in earlier chapters the pervasive influence of our emotions on how we think and act. They are a natural part of our makeup. But where do they come from? Do they stem from varied childhood experiences, or are they, at least to a degree, a part of our nature? Charles Darwin in his book Emotions in Animals and Man emphasized the innate nature of emotions; additional evidence since then has shown that Darwin was right. From birth, emotions, being a natural part of our makeup, have a major impact on our lives. They are the engine that powers our actions. Understanding and mastering them is a key to a satisfying, successful life. Controlling and utilizing them makes our lives more satisfying and successful, and this chapter intends to help you do just that.

Psychology enjoys a long history of research in this area, especially in grappling with emotional problems. We have strengthened our understanding, treatment and prevention of the emotional struggles that plague so many people. More recently, as we have seen, the positive psychology movement has laid emphasis on understanding our healthful emotions. How can this emphasis help each of us lead a more joyful, satisfying life? In addition, we will call on Ben Franklin as a model of someone who employed a constructive approach in coping with his own emotions, both positive and negative, and in dealing with those of others.

Understanding Our Emotions

We might compare our efforts to control our emotions with a rider trying to rein in an elephant. If a rider shouts, "go right" into an elephant's left ear, in which direction will he go? The answer: "whatever direction he feels like." The elephant represents our emotions, the voice of the rider, the voice of reason. This analogy depicts our emotions as so powerful that our rational mind is incapable of handling them; from time to time it seems they are. Yet emotions, like elephants can be trained, but it requires persistence. Keep in mind, the earlier you start the better!

Controlling Emotions

We have all seen plenty of cases of emotions out of control, more openly in childhood and adolescence. A boy who bursts into tears at slight setbacks, a girl who throws a temper tantrum over the least frustration, a child who is terrified for no apparent reason. Similar debilitating reactions smolder in many adults, often, but far from always, buried in our subconscious or under only partial control. Consider the case of a man who walked into my office for a counseling session. Sandy-haired, square-jawed, casually dressed and friendly looking, he had been fired from several jobs where he had been a proficient worker. His problem? Whenever his boss criticized him, he became enraged and smashed his face. Once he decided to seek help for this problem, he quickly learned to rein in his temper. In fact, in our second counseling session he told me he had been ready to take a swing at his boss, but then thought, "What would Dr. Rooney think?" Just making a commitment to change and discussing it with me provided incentive enough to start improving.

Positive emotions

Fortunately, most people are not so dominated by anger or other harmful states. In many children, adolescents and adults, warm and fuzzy sentiments prevail. We see sunny dispositions, ready smiles, and calm confidence. Most of us experience a wide variety of emotional states, positive and negative, mild and intense. Among any random group, we usually see greater differences than among Snow White's Happy, Grumpy, Bashful along with the rest of the Seven Dwarfs. Whatever your normal disposition, happens to be, you will always run across certain circumstances that produce strong passionate reactions (negative or positive). Since your natural response (fight or flight for instance) is often unfortunate or even detrimental, you will benefit from pushing yourself to develop more efficacious ways of responding.

Keep in mind when we speak of emotional control, we do not mean inhibiting or denying emotions. A case in point is bravery, which is not an absence of fear, but an ability to carry out courageous deeds despite our fears. Another way of putting it is, we can do the right thing rather than what we feel like doing. Often a few particular emotions are problems for us. We can follow in Ben Franklin's footsteps if we want to develop a more satisfying emotional life. Throughout this book, as you no doubt have come to expect, we will continue to draw on his experience, as well as what contemporary psychological studies teach us.

Biological Basis of Emotions

Meantime let us venture into biological processes underlying emotional behavior. Don't worry about technical detail. It is enough to know the basics of how our brains, hormones and in particular our autonomic nervous system are all involved. Let's start with our brain. We have long known of an increased ability to deal with our impulses as we move from adolescence to adulthood. Criminal justice professionals have time and time pointed out that if we can get young people through their teens and early twenties without getting into serious trouble, they should be all right. Recent research has discovered brain changes underlying this. As adolescents move through their high school and college years, their brain continues to mature, increasing their ability to learn impulse control. This tells us we should put more emphasis on developing self-discipline and emotional control in our schools and colleges.

In short, maturation of our brain affects our temperament. So do other biological processes, including hormonal differences. People often ask if men and women differ in emotional expression and control? And, if so, is it based, at least in part, on hormonal differences? The short answer is "yes" but the implications of biological gender differences is often exaggerated.

The most important biological system to become acquainted with in understanding emotions, however, is our autonomic nervous system. It controls the functioning of our internal organs, including heart rate, digestion, respiration and sexual arousal. Although its action is largely unconscious, we can learn to develop a useful degree of voluntary control over it.

Let's see how this system works.

The autonomic nervous system

This system has two complementary divisions, the sympathetic and parasympathetic. Often they act in opposition to one another, one activating a particular physiological response and one inhibiting it.

Our **sympathetic nervous system** goes into action when we are angry or afraid or when we experience other such strong emotions. It activates what we call a fight-or-flight response, diverting blood flow away from our gastro-intestinal tract to our muscles, increasing our heart rate, and pumping oxygen into our lungs. It increases our strength and energy and quickly mobilizes our bodies for action. Other species have similar systems. An ability to fight or flee more effectively when threatened has had survival value for both individual and species. Life today is certainly not free of threats and challenges that naturally arouse our emotions, but in today's world such biological responses can be more harmful than helpful. Increased heart rate and blood pressure, inhibited digestion, and rapid breathing contribute to a variety of physical disorders that are common today. Our stronger emotions are not the only culprit here. Weaker constant nagging worries, fears and irritations cause this system to be responding as if we are constantly in a state of emergency. Such emotions invariably affect our thought processes, narrowing our attention and distorting our judgment. If strong emotions are like the rush of a geyser, nagging emotions are like the constant drip, drip, drip of tiny drops of water. Each causes damage.

Improving our ability to respond to these challenges is the main intent of this chapter.

Our **parasympathetic** is a more slowly activated system. It predominates when we are relaxed and feeling good. It slows heart rate, lowers blood pressure, facilitates digestion, reduces pain and improves confidence. If the sympathetic nervous system prepares us for fight or flight, the parasympathetic prepares us for rest and relaxation. It preserves our resources; it has a calming effect. For example, we are less easily provoked to anger if we are in a good mood.

Knowing the long-term value of avoiding frequent activation of our sympathetic system, should we simply avoid conditions that arouse it and spend most of our time engaged in relaxing, enjoyable activities? Unfortunately, life is not so simple. We are bound to encounter stress every day. We need to develop habitual ways of handling it without excessive sympathetic arousal as well as ways of returning smoothly to a relaxed state when stress subsides. Some people do this readily: they can argue heatedly about an issue and move quickly to performing other tasks effectively. I remember a union representative who epitomized this. When arguing for employee benefits during contract negotiations, he might jump out of his chair with jaw jutting out and eyes throwing daggers. A short, wiry man with a Scottish accent, he would shout, bang the table and threaten to call a strike. Once negotiators hammered out an agreement, he quickly bounced back to a calm and congenial state, accepting contractual compromises and moving on smoothly to plans for implementing the agreement. Most people are not like that. They continue to stew over an issue: their bodily functions remain in "fight or flight" condition and they have difficulty concentrating on other tasks. We naturally believe situations we run into are the culprit producing our emotional reactions. But that's not really so- it's actually our interpretation of these situations.

Coping with Our Emotions

From either perspective, learning to employ confident, relaxing responses rather than tension-producing ones, helps us cope with stress and feel more in control of our lives.

How can we do this? We have a variety of approaches available to help us activate our parasympathetic system and counteract tension.

Relaxation techniques

Progressive muscle relaxation. An early approach contributing to this was progressive muscle relaxation, developed by American physician Edmund Jacobson in the early 1920s. He used it for treating hypertension, heart disease, headaches, and digestive disorders. As previously mentioned, I first encountered this technique during navy flight training at Chapel Hill, North Carolina during World War II. In place of calisthenics, we were directed to lie on our bunks and follow directions being broadcast over a loudspeaker: "Now your left foot is relaxing, now muscles in your lower left leg are relaxing." We joked that its main value consisted of getting us out of calisthenics. In truth, I found it effective in dealing with stress and improving performance. Over the years, I have continued to utilize it myself and to recommend it to others, at the same time incorporating newer, better-known approaches. It is a relatively simple process. You start by lying down or sitting in a comfortable place, selecting one part of your body, perhaps your left foot, and focus your mind on relaxing it (or, as Jacobson recommended, first tense your muscles a bit before relaxing them). You gradually move through the muscles of your body ending with multiple tiny muscles in your face, neck and head. If you lose concentration, just return to the process once you realize you have drifted. It is best to incorporate it into your schedule once or twice a day for five or ten minutes or so. It helps counteract tension throughout the day. Moreover, it is helpful as an aid to sleep, particularly if you wake up during the night and have difficulty getting back to sleep.

An additional benefit to practicing muscle relaxation is that you soon get to recognize tensions you had previously never noticed. In driving a car, for example, do you tense up even in routine driving? Or during an important meeting? Once you become sensitive to this (maybe tension in your neck or gripping your hands), you are able to counteract it early, rather than have it persist and spread. This awareness may be even more valuable than the practice sessions themselves.

2. Controlled breathing. Another procedure for countering stress is controlled breathing. You simply take slow deep breaths into your diaphragm (your belly as well as your chest), and then slowly exhale. It is best to breathe in through your nose and out through your mouth. Controlled breathing can be an alternative to muscle relaxation. Better yet-use them together.

3. Relaxing music. Soft melodious music is a boon to many people in search of relaxation. Franklin, convinced of its value, used it himself and recommended it to others. He developed the Glass Armonica, consisting of a series of glass cylinders attached to a wheel (actually, a mechanized version of glass tumblers containing varied amounts of water, which, when rubbed with the fingers, produced pleasant tones.) It enjoyed considerable popularity for its melodious music. On one occasion, Franklin used it to relieve the suffering of one of his

friends, Princess Izabella Czartoryska of Poland who was confined to her bed, suffering from depression accompanying a serious physical illness. Franklin visited her, sat by her bedside and played soothing music on his armonica for several hours. She was deeply moved by its music, and tears came to her eyes. Franklin, looking at her compassionately, said "Madame, you are cured." Immediately the melancholia lifted, and she became relaxed and contented.

4. Visualization. Another technique I recommend as an aid to relaxation is visualization. Here you allow your mind to visualize a scene, selecting a relaxing one such as lying on a beach watching a sunset, fishing in a pond or sitting on a grass-covered hillside or a mountain top.

More mundane scenes work as well. Counting sheep has been used as an aid to sleep and relaxation since the distant past. An imaginary walk through a familiar place is likewise relaxing

You might want to experiment with different scenes (buildings and fields in your college campus, rooms and grounds at a workplace or restaurants and views at a vacation resort).

Then again, visualization is helpful in preparing to perform complex or stressful activities. Visualizing yourself performing each step in giving a speech or playing a game of tennis before the event facilitates successful performance.

Athletes and fans. Most professional athletes are under considerable stress. In fact, one professional football player, a member of the Philadelphia Eagles Superbowl champions and a pro bowl selection, missed important games because of a panic disorder. He is not alone; many athletes suffer performance deficit of various types caused by stress. To assist in handling performance anxiety that goes with the pressure of the profession, most pro teams include mental health professionals on their staff. A number of players also employ their own psychological consultants.

In addition to players, fans likewise experience passionate highs and lows, at times, to extremes. Kicking the TV when frustrated by poor performance of a team is not as uncommon as we might think. Emotional arousal may have more serious consequences. Some years ago, when La Salle's basketball team was one of the top-ranked teams in the nation, I saw the effect on its fans. Most were elated and enjoyed the celebrations; more than a few, however, suffered from the stress. One of our college's vice presidents, a man in his sixties had to stop attending games after passing out several times from excitement. Moreover, the team physician, a friend of mine in his fifties, suffered a fatal heart attack during a tightly contested tournament in New Orleans.

Meditation. Muscle relaxation, controlled breathing and visualization are all useful tools in dealing with stress; so is meditation. For centuries, meditation has been a common practice in both Eastern and Western religions. In employing it, devotees take time to put stresses and strains from everyday life aside, instead reflecting on the mystery, wonder and ultimate values in life's journey. Repetitive prayer and/or music often accompany such spiritual meditation. Today, meditation is usually taught without a spiritual component; I believe it to be a valuable part of it.

Modern psychological practice features several types of meditation for you to consider. All emphasize the role of attention. For example, in Zen meditation you focus your mind on your breathing, ignoring any thoughts that may intrude. In focused meditation, you concentrate intensively on one particular object, such as a vase or a rose. In another type, transcendental meditation, you make a sound (hum) or repeat a mantra selected to keep all other images and problems from intruding on your thoughts.

In yet another type, mindfulness meditation, you simply accept whatever comes to mind from moment to moment without evaluating it or holding on to it. Your mind is much like a boat drifting in the water without any particular destination, just going where the currents take you.

With practice, you can reach a meditative state, obtaining its benefits within a few minutes. Today, meditation has an estimated ten million practitioners.

Progressive muscle relaxation, controlled breathing, visualization, and meditation discussed above are all procedures designed to reduce stress while also inducing a desirable level of relaxation. They can be invaluable when we find ourselves in situations in our everyday life that produce tension- something most of us encounter regularly. Still, what is stressful for one person may be a constructive experience for another.

Overcoming performance anxiety.

One common source of stress, as we have mentioned, is performance anxiety, in which we worry about our ability to perform at a certain level. Here, keep in mind; "competence breeds confidence!" A well-prepared student is less likely to have excessive anxiety than an ill-prepared one when facing an examination. This holds for athletic performance, business meetings (or presentations), the military and really in all occupations. Remember the one about the tourist asking for directions in New York. "How do you get to Carnegie Hall?" he asks. The reply: "practice, practice, practice!" Unfortunately, people often prefer not to think about an upcoming event rather than practice for it. College students illustrate this when they party, to avoid thinking about (or preparing for) an exam.

How to practice

Moreover, when you practice, do it productively. Practice that is as similar as possible to the desired performance is especially valuable. In preparing to make a presentation to a group, silently reading it repeatedly, is of some help; delivering it aloud is better; videotaping and reviewing it, is better yet.

You may have heard people say, be careful not to over-prepare; that too much time spent in preparation produces poorer performance. That's not the case. The mistake is lengthy preparation of the wrong kind. In my early years of teaching, I must admit, I spent considerable prep time learning more and more details about the psychology I taught, but too little time thinking about the students. How to stimulate their interest? How to facilitate their learning?

An extreme case of the wrong kind of preparation is a case of a faculty member I recall who decided to buy a car, though he had never driven one. After he practiced for his driver's test by carefully studying a book on how to drive, he considered himself thoroughly prepared. Needless to say, he failed his test miserably.

Watching a pro hit a golf ball, is better than reading a manual, but taking a club in your hand, then hitting a number of balls under the watchful eye of an instructor is better yet.

We have discussed ways of developing our abilities elsewhere in this book, but a few reminders are in order when we are considering the role of competence in reducing anxiety, at the same time enhancing feelings of satisfaction and well-being.

Different tasks require different kinds of preparation. Some, such as learning a foreign language, require considerable memorization followed by frequent review to prevent forgetting; other tasks require developing insightful understanding; still others require practicing a skill followed by utilizing feedback from an expert.

To reiterate briefly, learning to relax so you can approach challenges with confidence is a giant step in self-development.

Emotional interference

It helps as well to be able to recognize feelings you are experiencing and know what is triggering them. At times this is obvious. When your spouse criticizes you unfairly, you explode with anger; when you hear a rumor that layoffs are pending in your department, you worry; when your team wins an important game, you are elated. Often, however, you are unsure of exactly how you feel or why you feel that way. You may even deny your experience: "Mad? I'm not mad. Something like that doesn't bother me at all." Such denial is common. Clients in personal counseling with tears in their eyes may deny feeling sad. Helping them recognize and accept such emotions is one of the first steps in assisting them. Such denial occurs regularly in everyday life, most obviously in childhood. One of my daughters, when she was about three years old, acquired a fear of dogs after being bitten by a neighbor's collie. Afterward, when the two of us were walking around our neighborhood, she might suddenly say, "Carry me Daddy, I'm tired," whenever a dog came in sight. She wanted me to hold her but preferred to say she was tired rather than admit her fear.

The positive use of negative emotions.

Just as pain is a sign something is wrong that requires attention, negative feelings tell us something is hurting us. Use this awareness to learn to respond more effectively. Emotions such as anger, worry, sadness, disgust, embarrassment, and disappointment can motivate you to take positive action. For example, when Ben Franklin appeared before a judge in England in an attempt to represent the grievances of the American Colonies, he found himself growing increasingly angry at the judge. He felt treated with a distain that reflected the distain the British felt for the colonies. As a result, he withdrew his support of the Crown, instead throwing his efforts into the fight for American independence.

In general, it is counterproductive to suppress or deny unwanted emotions. Instead, learn to use them to motivate you in productive ways. Let people know you are angry, especially when you are angry at them. If your anger is justified, people will respect you for it, if you express it effectively.

I recall watching the Republican Convention back in 1952. General Eisenhower and Senator Taft were rated evenly in the race for the presidential nomination. Eisenhower, popular, but inexperienced in government, came across as rather bland. This perception changed dramatically when his opposition tried to seat a group of southern delegates favorable to Taft. He leaped from his seat, grabbed the microphone, spoke out forcibly and angrily against this maneuver. Eisenhower's reaction struck an emotional chord with his audience. People realized he would fight for what he believed in. I know he convinced me.

Other negative emotions can motivate us in a positive way. We see plenty of instances of reasonable fear, productive worry and normal grief. Unfortunately, we also see far too many instances in which these emotions trigger negative, even disastrous, outcomes. The man who punched his boss, I mentioned earlier. One of my colleagues felt like punching the Dean when frustrated by his intransigence; instead, he drove his fist into a wall, breaking his hand in the process. We see too many instances of road rage when drivers become so furious at other motorists that they end up smashing their car into them. Certainly, those who carry guns must be able to contain their passions. Otherwise, as we see too often, the outcome is another tragedy.

Responding to worry and fear.

Worry about possible danger or failure may motivate us to work harder and plan better, but much worry is anything but productive. A fire in New York prompts a woman to call her son, for fear he may have been harmed; an accident on a highway, upsets a man who worries that his wife might have been involved. Television news focusing on disasters (shootings, fires, accidents) plus programs bringing violence and horror into our living rooms, fuel unproductive worry and anxiety.

A classic illustration of the impact of the media on our emotions is Orson Welles's radio broadcast, of an episode of Mercury Theater's War of the Worlds on Halloween 1938. This program, featuring aliens from Mars invading

Earth, produced nationwide alarm including outbursts of panic. When repeated a few years later in a Latin American country, listeners became so enraged at this deception they stormed the station, demolishing it.

Reinterpreting stressful situations.

We see certain circumstances as tending to trigger unpleasant feelings. More accurately, as we have mentioned, it is our interpretation of the situation that leads to our reaction. The reaction of listeners to the War of the Worlds broadcast varied dramatically depending on whether a listener believed it to be a news broadcast or an entertainment. I recall my father reassuring a terrified neighbor who came pounding on our door to warn us of the "invasion" that it was "only a show."

This point is particularly relevant in cases of apparent failure. If we try something that doesn't work out the way we hoped, have we failed? Maybe not.

Thomas Edison put a positive spin on his attempts. "I have not failed 100 times; I have discovered 100 ways that do not work." Benjamin Franklin made the same point long before Edison: "I didn't fail the test; I just found 100 ways to do it wrong." James Joyce made a similar observation in his own literary style: "A man of genius makes no mistakes; his errors are volitional and are the portals of discovery."

These are optimistic views many successful people have adopted. They do not let apparent failures or mistakes sidetrack them; instead, they push on, learning what works and what doesn't. Exploring new territory. In the process, they never hesitate to try something innovative or challenging for fear of making a mistake.

Albert Ellis, the psychologist who introduced Rational-Emotive Therapy, helped his clients reinterpret disturbing events with considerable success. He provides numerous occurrences from his own life. In one instance, he tells us of a time in his youth when he feared to ask a young woman for a date, lest she reject him. He decided to try a project in which he asked numerous women to go out with him, viewing it as a practice exercise for the future rather than a test of his personal acceptability. He soon became quite adept at meeting new women, gradually developing a reputation as a "ladies' man." More than a few of his critics believe he overdid it!

Changing our environment

Several additional circumstances in our lives affect our moods, our feelings, our general level of happiness: the section of the country we live in, our neighborhood, educational level, occupation, and kind of organization we work for. Sometimes we benefit from changing our situation, sometimes by adapting to it more effectively. As Ben put it, "The Declaration of Independence only gives people the right to pursue happiness. You have to catch it yourself." Positive psychology tells us the pursuit of a worthwhile goal fosters happiness. It is not to be found in a pot of gold at the end of the rainbow, but in the joy of chasing the rainbow.

Cultivating positive emotions.

Being able to understand and deal with emotions such as anger, worry and depression is only one aspect in the development of a healthy emotional life. Cultivating positive emotions is even more important. They not only enable us deal with stressful conditions more effectively, but they improve our decision-making, besides adding joy and zest to our lives.

Our positive emotions, though, may lead to negative consequences. Confidence, enthusiasm, optimism, love, passion, elation are all valuable, but unless combined with good judgment they can lead to disastrous decisions.

Sexuality

Sexual arousal is triggered by both external stimuli (what we see, hear, touch, smell) and by our thoughts and fantasies. Our autonomic nervous system is activated, sex hormones are secreted, and erogenous zones of the body prepared for sexual intercourse. At the same time inhibitory factors come into play. Negative emotions, such as fear of sexually transmitted diseases or pregnancy, moral censure and performance failure affect both arousal and the decision to become sexually involved with someone.

Emotional Intelligence (E.Q.)

Our ability to understand, control and utilize our own emotions (including enthusiasm, passion, anger, humor) plus recognize and relate to emotions in others is referred to as our Emotional Intelligence. To be effective in working in any organization it not only helps to be intelligent; in addition, it helps to be able to work well with other people, including supervisors, peers and those we supervise. People who have emotional intelligence are said to have a high E.Q. Benjamin Franklin, renowned for his people skills, obviously had it. Throughout his adult life, whether with tradesmen, artisans and merchants in the Junto, with his world-wide network of scientists and intellectual or in international diplomacy, typified the behavior of a person with high Social-Emotional intelligence.

This term was first popularized by psychologist Daniel Goleman in his New York Times best seller, *Emotional Intelligence: Why It Can Matter More Than IQ.* What sparked Goleman's interest in this topic was a number of little-recognized research studies indicating IQ had less influence on success than other traits.

My own doctoral research with college students, for instance, indicated that nonintellectual factors such as motivation, social skills and confidence had a marked influence on student achievement, persistence, satisfaction, and leadership.

Such findings are consistent with my belief (one I hope most people share) that college should involve more than intellectual development. A student does not just send a brain to college-the whole person shows up. Consequently, college should be a time of increased emotional maturity, social competence, and personal responsibility along with intellectual growth. After one's formal education has been completed, this growth should continue to flourish.

With increased recognition of the significance of E.Q., a number of schools have introduced programs designed to help children develop socially and emotionally. They have met with considerable success. Children learn to master their impulses, grow more self-confident, be more empathic. They improve academically as well.

Emotions and economics.

The idea that we are rational creatures whose behavior is best understood by studying our cognitive processes has been pervasiveness in our society. A striking example of this is traditional economic theory, built on the assumption that people make rational decisions trying to improve their economic well-being. While economists have long realized this is not strictly true, a rational view of economic decision-making has persisted in government, business and in most people's personal lives.

More recently, however, (October 2017), American behavioral scientist Richard Thaler, was awarded the Nobel Prize in Economics for his groundbreaking research He studied the questions: why do people make irrational economic decisions? how they can be encouraged to make better ones?

Utilizing such knowledge would help people avoid excessive, worrisome debts on credit cards, college loans, mortgages and so forth, It would in turn, encourage frugality in spending, perseverance in saving as well as astuteness in investing. A number of parents, nevertheless, feeling they owe their children whatever kind of education they want, accumulate debt, thus endangering their retirement income, instead of working with their child in planning an educational program within their means. The latter approach fosters student development in addition to protecting family finances.

Ben Franklin emphasized the importance of managing money wisely in order to have a productive, satisfying life. "A penny saved is a penny earned" is one of his best known yet least followed maxims.

Recognizing emotions in others

In clinical work, most practitioners have recognized the impact of the unconscious, even if they disagreed with Freud's theory. One sample of this is Theodor Reik, who wrote, Listening with the Third Ear. Reik stressed that to understand a patient (or anyone) you must attend to much more than overt content of what they say. You need empathy too, which means understanding and respecting their feelings. An extreme case of a therapist who is lacking this quality, would be one who hears a patient say, "things are going well with me now" while at the same time they are, trembling and clenching their teeth. If her therapist simply replies, "good, I'm glad to hear that," he has obviously missed a crucial message in their interaction. Most cues are subtler, involving "listening" to what a person is expressing through such indicators as tone of voice, facial expressions, body posture and gestures. Thus, a raised eyebrow, nodding head or shaking voice is communicating as much or more than the content of their conversation. The saying," what you do is speaking so loud, I can't hear what you say", could be applied to such cues as well as to other overt actions.

Children notice such emotional indicators even before they understand speech, they instinctively feel whether a parent is angry, sad or happy. This ability improves as we mature; additionally, effort and training enhance it.

For instance, law enforcement people with long experience learn to notice certain kinds of suspects. A narcotics agent waiting in a busy airport terminal, suddenly spots a woman who sets off an alarm in his mind. Why? He is not sure, but he focuses on her as a prime suspect. She, in turn, picks him out from the crowd. Something about him tells her he is a narcotics agent.

In addition to sensitivity to what a person is revealing from both conscious and unconscious sources, it is desirable to listen to what our own feelings tell us about an interaction   If we grow irritated, or bored, or depressed, it is likely the person is triggering something in our unconscious causing such a feeling.

Influencing others

While Freud based his theory primarily on clinical experience, he applied it to a wide range of human behavior. This he discussed in his Psychopathology of Everyday Life.

His nephew, Edward Bernays, came to America, applying ideas of Freud, and other students of human behavior, to influencing public opinion. He employed "third party authorities" for manipulating public opinion involved using further his clients' causes. "If you can influence leaders, either with or without their conscious cooperation, you automatically influence groups which they sway" he declared. In promoting sales of bacon, for example, he cited research, which found most Americans ate light breakfasts. Commonly, it consisted of a cup of coffee, a glass of juice and little more. He arranged to poll a large sample of physicians on whether a light breakfast or a substantial one fostered health. By a large majority, they recommended a hearty breakfast. He arranged for this finding to be published in newspapers with headlines shouting, "physicians urge bigger breakfast'. Other articles stated that eggs with bacon made a good breakfast. As a result, sales of bacon soared. Again, he followed his belief that a news story influences people more than an advertisement.

Today, advertisers, politicians, con artists, as well as a host of others are competing for your time, your money and your soul; they draw on a whole raft of psychological research on how to influence people, particularly through appealing to their emotions. Combining this with a technology that enables capturing voluminous information about your preferences, allegiances, and habits, their pitch can be quite effective. Understanding these emotional appeals provides protection from being unduly influenced by them.

Summary

All of this emphasizes that we are not only rational creatures but emotional ones. In our effort to become a better, happier and more successful person, nothing is more valuable than understanding ourselves (and others) as the emotional creatures we are. Emotions motivate us, foster our aspirations, and dominate our relationships.

As we have seen, they have a biological basis. Knowing how our sympathetic and parasympathetic systems interact helps us utilize a variety of approaches to control tension and relax; realizing that negative emotions are not so much triggered by situations we come across, as by our interpretation of these situations helps us think clearly in emotionally-laden encounters; and recognizing emotions in others enables us to interact with them more confidently.

People who demonstrate facility in recognizing and utilizing feelings and passions are said to possess high E.Q. or emotional intelligence, a talent as valuable as a high I.Q.

Finally, learning to cultivate and express positive emotions in our relationships with friends, family, neighbors, colleagues, in fact, everyone who comes into our lives, enriches and adds value to our own lives.

Benjamin Franklin provides an excellent illustration for us here. In his early years, he had difficulty with his moods, quick to anger, frequently worried as well as easily discouraged. Realizing these emotional states were interfering with his personal development, he devised a systematic program to rid himself of detrimental responses and foster those that were more beneficial. He gradually transformed himself into a man of calm confidence and unbounded optimism- a change that laid the groundwork for his future accomplishments. He concluded that feeling good and doing good go together, each supporting the other.

In our next chapter we will apply what we have learned to our personal development

.

Chapter 16.
Your Personal Development

Introduction

When you think back on all of Ben Franklin's remarkable accomplishments, it is amazing how he could achieve them. Was he just lucky? Hardly. They came about through a systematic program of self-improvement. Ben spelled out his approach for us, telling us what worked and what modifications he employed based on experience. His approach to self-improvement stressed systematic observation and experimentation just as he conducted his scientific research. To follow his example. Write down the ways you want to progress, work on one at a time and keep track of your progress. It takes some persistence, but it pays off.

Ben stressed that curiosity, initiative, observation, and reflection not only aid us in getting somewhere, but in adding zest to our lives. He pointed to fishing where we find more satisfaction in the activity than the outcome. "Some anglers." he reminded us, "cast the fish back in the water." A variation states, "I would rather hold a rod and reel in my hand than a fish."His message is straightforward: discover joy in the life you are now living as well as in future hopes.

Research in positive psychology supports Ben's approach and offers additional recommendations. It contends that you don't find happiness in reaching a goal, but in striving towards it and doing so with an optimistic attitude. Remember this! Self-improvement is not a onetime task; it's a natural and satisfying part of your everyday life.

Where should you start? Start with objectives consistent with your sense of values. Imagine the kind of person you want to be. Clarify your goals. Without purpose you will be like Yogi Berra when he said, "we drove to the wrong place, but we really made great time." It is easy to get caught up in a rat race and later find yourself asking, "Why am I doing this?" If, instead, your efforts are consistent with your values, you will know why.

Self-improvement

Once you have considered your values and decided what kind of person you want to be, what next? An invaluable early step is to understand yourself-your basic nature as a human being and what built-in resources you have. In an earlier chapter, we provided you with a kind of "owner's manual" for the brain including its power and complexity. For instance, realizing that your brain is made up of two systems, an intuitive, spontaneous, emotional one and a rational, problem-solving one provides background to help you direct and integrate your behavior. Your emotions are an engine that drives your behavior; your rational faculties a steering mechanism that controls and gives direction to your passions.

We are naturally active. As young infants, we cry, smile, babble, glance from one object to another and manipulate objects by pushing, pulling, lifting, turning and tossing them.

Maturation

As we mature, our brain, with its billions of neurons, acquires new connections enabling us to perform more complex activities. We continue to explore our environment, testing what we can do. We organize and classify our observations. We group objects and people in terms of similarities we notice. Fish swim, birds fly; girls differ from boys; some folks have light skin color, others dark. We wonder where we fit in this universe and how we relate to its various components. We experience and display a variety of emotions and desires. We laugh, cry, worry, love, and dislike. We learn from new experiences, but our learning builds on and interacts with our basic human nature.

How We Learn

We not only progress because of maturation of our brain (and other parts of our body), we also inherit a marvelous gift- our built-in ability to learn.

Just as arboreal studies enable us to shape bushes and trees, research in learning facilitates human growth. You have been learning all your life, and no doubt know a great deal about it, but believe me, understanding this process more thoroughly is well worth your effort.

We group learning into three main types: modeling, exploration (with reinforcement) and imagination. Psychologists have labored long and hard in their labs, performing meaningful research on each of them. Their findings provide a treasure trove for self-development.

Modeling or Observational Learning

Let's begin with how we learn by observing others. In Yogi Berra's logic, "You can observe a lot by watching."

However you state it, we interact with others, and model our actions after them. That's why it pays to associate with the right people. Observing them and interacting with them, enables us to acquire attitudes, perceptions and skills (including skills in interpersonal relationships) that foster healthy personal development.

From early childhood on, we do this modeling naturally. I recall an incident that was embarrassing to me (and even more so to my daughter). One of my little quirks was to take a drink of water without using a glass by putting my hand under the faucet and drinking the water flowing into it. Of course, I only did this when I was alone (except for the children, who were not supposed to notice). Later my older daughter came home from a dinner with parents of her new fiancé and told me they seemed upset when she took a drink of water in this way. I said, "You did what!" She replied, "Well, you do it."

Much of what children model from parents and other caretakers is unconscious and copied without thought or effort: gestures, facial expression, emotional responses, posture, and speech patterns. You may be surprised when you look into a mirror and see something typical of your father or mother looking back at you.

Parents serve as our earliest and most influential models but, we find others, real life and fictional, around us everywhere. For one, a child copies other children. In my own childhood, I recall a common reproach: "monkey see, monkey do" in instances of undesirable modeling.

A perennial concern about violence and crime depicted in movies, television shows and video games is their potential influence in fostering antisocial behavior.

Models from the media

I remember a striking instance of this from my early years. John Garfield, a popular movie star at that time, was usually cast as a "tough guy" who defied the law and led a daring and exciting life. A young tough in my neighborhood adopted "Garfield" as a nickname, emulating him by copying his hairstyle, swagger and muttered speech. He also flouted the law, finding excitement in actions like smashing windows and "borrowing" cars for fast, reckless joy rides. He was soon playing out his script in prison.

Past movies deliver numerous examples of widespread modeling from our media. A scene in the 1930's classic, It Happened One Night, shows Clark Gable undressing. When he strips off his shirt, moviegoers are in for a surprise- no undershirt. Sales of undershirts plummeted as American men modeled this movie star's example. When another film showcased Marylyn Monroe wearing glasses; sales of women's glasses soared, particularly in Japan.

In general, our media provide images for us to model for good or ill. One of the most appalling was the message that smoking was sociable, sophisticated, and fun. Unfortunately, several generations of Americans bought into it.

Modes in our life

Those we know and admire in our everyday life influence us even more. In my own experience during navy flight training, I found one of my instructors, a marine captain, to be a most impressive instructor. He was firm, clear, and confident, yet friendly and relaxed. Once I became a flight instructor, I adopted his approach and felt confident in doing so

In addition to discovering heroes in our everyday life, we encounter them in our reading. I was pleased to learn that President Kennedy and I had one thing in common-we shared a favorite book in our childhood (Billy Whiskers).

What appeals to us in a model.
History offers numerous examples of prominent figures who followed in the footsteps of someone they admired and used as a model.

You come across such a variety of people in your life, what determines which you emulate? Research on modeling identifies three main characteristics-power, likeability, and similarity.

Power. First, let's examine power. Although history warns us that power corrupts, we still admire, respect, and imitate those with power and influence. They get things done. They accomplish goals (hopefully ones we consider worthwhile). You can no doubt think of examples at all levels of responsibility, from world leaders to those in your everyday life, who impress you because of their power.

Which of your parents has most control at home? Which administrator you work with is most successful in getting a job done? Who among your friends and colleagues has most influence on your group?

That's what we mean by power.

One highly controversial source of power is the gun, and a major difficulty facing advocates of gun control is that gun owners view it as a threat to their feelings of power.

Likeability. Next, let's look at likeability. This is an obvious point, but one worth repeating: we tend to emulate folks we like. Still, I'm sure you can think of likeable, popular, enjoyable and interesting people, whom you would reject as models, such as the class clown, slick, joke-telling salesman, or exuberant, egotistical politician. Popular, but not admirable.

Similarity. Finally, let's consider similarity. Does a person have prominent characteristics in common with you? Thus, short men may be impressed by other short men who achieved power and popularity; and a woman archeology student may model after a successful woman in that field. This process starts early: a boy in a Boy Scout troop sees one of his leaders as similar to him; and a young man in prison learns by observing and copying other prisoners he identifies with.

Ben Franklin's Modeling Where do you find models to emulate? Our world is full of amazing people. The more you socialize the more role models you have available. You get to see how various individuals handle problems and confront challenges. That's why positive psychology urges: get to know successful people with an optimistic outlook. Ben Franklin certainly did.

He also devoured books, enabling him to draw on models from the past. One of his favorites was Plutarch's Lives or, Lives of the Noble Greeks and Romans. It presents biographies of influential men from Ancient Greece and Rome, arranged in pairs (one Greek, one Roman) and compares their common strengths and weaknesses.

Your models

Not only do we find certain people (real or fictional) as models, but we also select certain features of a person as right for us and reject others. (our judgment here is not static; as we mature, we often reevaluate our earlier views).

You no doubt encounter people in positions of authority and say to yourself "that's a good way to handle this kind of situation" in one instance, and "I sure don't want to act that way with someone I supervise" in another. I hold up Benjamin Franklin as a model whose life can teach us so much of value. Yet I would not want to relate to my wife and family as he did. Thus, we draw on our set of values and our judgment in our modeling.

As you attempt to change yourself, you will encounter disappointments. Modeling is not a "one and done" event. Some of your attempts at modeling will work out, others will not. You try out your new style just as you try on a new jacket to see how it fits, how it looks and how others react to it. Your friends and colleagues not only serve as potential models they also provide feedback about your actions: they praise, criticize, argue, shake their heads, roll their eyes, smile, and frown and in so many other ways serve as sounding boards. They encourage some things you do and discourage others. For modeling also depends on reinforcement, a kind of learning we will discuss next.

Exploration, Reinforcement and Punishment.

We not only learn from observing others, we learn from exploring our world.

We learn from our mistakes, and even faster from our successes. We also learn from mentally anticipating results of various actions without actually trying them out.

Some things we attempt prove ineffective; others work out well. Successful behavior is reinforced, and, over time, becomes habitual. Roughly akin to reward, reinforcement is highly effective in influencing what we learn, but the process is often misunderstood. Knowing how it works, advances our personal development and enables us to influence others.

Punishment, the opposite of reinforcement, is a painful, unpleasant, or disagreeable event that is effective in stopping or discouraging a given kind of behavior. Even more complex, it often has undesirable side effects. Nevertheless, it is important to understand it and know how and when to use it.

Reinforcement

Much reinforcement and punishment stems from exploring our environment. A child touches a hot plate, feels pain and quickly learns to avoid hot objects.

Those around us provide reinforcement. A parent holding a baby who begins babbling listens for utterances that sound like "Dada" or "Mama." The parent smiles repeats the "word" and in other ways encourages the desired response. This kind of learning through reinforcement continues throughout life. If you try a new restaurant and find delicious food, efficient service, pleasant ambience, and a reasonable price, you will want to return. Your experience was reinforcing.

Behavior that stops or reduces an unpleasant state is also reinforcing. If you have a headache, take an aspirin and the pain subsides, you are prone to take aspirin for headaches. Either way helps. You have learned something.

Punishment, on the other hand, makes it less likely that you will repeat an action. We may do so by introducing an unpleasant or painful stimulus, or by removing or decreasing a pleasant one. Thus, a slap on the wrist or a reprimand that hurts is punishment; so is withholding a child's dessert or permission to play videogames. Both forms make it less likely that a child will repeat this action under similar circumstances. The child has learned what not to do. Penalizing, however, does not teach a child to do the right thing. A child who is disciplined for being late for school can avoid being late by being on time or by not coming at all, and employees berated by a supervisor for doing a poor job, may resort to sabotage rather than improve.

Punishment, thus, is fraught with unintended consequences including sympathy for those receiving it and resentment toward (and perhaps retaliation against) those dishing it out.

What about physical punishment? For years, spanking, slapping, paddling, pinching and other such punitive measures were used on children at home and in school. Evidence gradually accumulated, however, that physical discipline detracted from healthy child development, particularly when accompanied by rejection and verbal abuse. Using physical force to control children's behavior produces a multitude of undesirable consequences including inducing anxiety, worry, guilt, timidity, anger, hostility, rage and a whole range of negative emotions. It also sets an unintended example: if others do something you don't like, hurt them. A classic example of this was a widely circulated cartoon showing a parent spanking a child and saying, "this will teach you to go around hitting people." Violence breeds violence. Better to emphasize a more positive approach in modifying a child's sanctions.

Keep in mind, though, that other, non- corporal types of punishment can be helpful and even necessary in teaching a child proper behavior and self-discipline.

Recently, a woman asked Pope Francis if it was all right to spank a child. His off-hand answer was "Yes, if it is done in a loving way." While I do not agree with the Pope about spanking, any kind of reprimand works better if the child (or adult as well) believes it does not indicate rejection or lack of respect, but is directed against certain, specific undesirable behavior. Better yet if a child sees admonishment as justified and intended to be beneficial. If criticism is applied thoughtfully, children realize that a parent is using it to help them learn; if harshly, they sense that their parent dislikes or rejects them. The relationship between parent and child and how both affection and criticism are expressed is the key to opening a child's mind to self- improvement.

Angela Duckworth, psychologist at the Character Lab of the University of Pennsylvania cites recent (2020) evidence that a combination of modeling and teaching appropriate behavior is more effective than either alone. Rather than make the traditional mistake "do as I say, not what I do" we should do as we say and say as we do. Consistency helps!

Modifying behavior. We are now acquainted with basic principles of reinforcement and punishment. How can we use this knowledge to modify our own behavior, and to influence others?

Isn't it easy to know when to use the carrot and when to use the stick? The reality is that a more thorough understanding of the power of these two forces provides a giant leap forward in improving yourself and influencing others. This knowledge will also make you a more informed citizen on such issues as the role of punitive methods and positives ones in our homes, schools, police, judicial system, and relationships with other nations. Let's take a closer look at reinforcement.

How can we know whether something will be reinforcing? A wide variety of experiences can be, such as those that generate feelings of success, accomplishment, recognition and approval. Keep in mind that whether or not something gives you pleasure will vary with your motivation and your interpretation of a situation. When you are not hungry, food is not normally appealing; when you are, food (including a tasty salad) is. If, however, you were expecting prime rib when invited to dinner, and are served a salad, it would hardly be reinforcing. If a colleague praises your work, it may or may not encourage you depending on your relationship and what you think is behind this praise. It is then far from obvious what someone might learn from a given experience. Although a child, praised for artistic work, tends to persist, and one who is criticized to give up, outcomes vary with circumstances. Thus, a teacher praising a child for earning a high grade would seem like an example of positive reinforcement. If, however, a child dislikes the teacher or places more value on student opinion, such praise would not have the desired effect.

Using an approach that you think will influence others also fails if "the others" interpret it as manipulative.

Resistance. We value our independence and resent attempts to control us. Reinforcement works best in achieving common goals. This subjective element means you must know others to effectively influence them. And to change your own behavior start with "Know Thyself". If you want to exercise more, ask yourself if going to a gym and noting your progress will be enough inducement for you to persist, or is some additional incentive necessary. If you decide more is needed, pick an option that would work best for you. Perhaps working out with a friend, reading a stimulating book or watching an enjoyable TV program while you exercise; or perhaps rewarding yourself with a healthy snack after you complete your workout.

You can also use punitive techniques to stop or reduce your undesirable behavior. If want to quit smoking, you might wear a rubber band around your wrist and snap it whenever you reach for a cigarette. You might also discourage unwanted behavior by denying yourself one or more of your usual pleasures if you slip.

Criticism is often a useful aid to behavioral change. In your own program of personal growth, learn to seek and value criticism. Friends with your interest at heart, and those with expertise in a skill you want to enhance are invaluable in your personal development. It is worth your time and effort to form friendships with open and honest people and to network with knowledgeable and talented colleagues who not only accept you but challenge you.

Winston Churchill is a good example of this. He was headstrong, quick to anger and resentful of criticism. Yet he listened to his wife, Clementine who emphasized her love and her pride in his inspiring leadership. Consequently, when she proposed modifications in his style, he listened.

Unfortunately, too many children fail to develop into responsible citizens despite, or because of, their home and school upbringing. Instead, they become involved in criminal behavior. Punitive action seems in order, and our judicial system must decide what kind works. We will address this in a chapter that considers how psychology can contribute to building a healthier society.

Competition is a common source of feelings of success or failure. It is a natural part of society and learning to compete effectively is a valuable talent. We use the performance of others as a yardstick against which to measure ours and to motivate us to improve. I think back to competition in the Navy where we frequently ran obstacle courses. Competition in scaling walls, climbing nets, navigating tunnels and, of course, running, was an incentive for me to persist and improve. I found exhilaration in competing, win or lose. Moreover, though I never won any races, beating more of my competitors and improving my time gave me a feeling of success. In this kind of race, every competitor can be a winner.

Some of us, however, view life as one big competition-if you don't win, you're a loser! Some competitions resemble lotteries. they have one or a few winners with huge rewards and one or more frustrated losers. In other competitions, both sides (and most participants) can be winners (win-win situations). Your own progress can be reinforcing. Many athletes keep a record of their personal best performance and compete with themselves. Anyone can do this.

Even in my current retirement community, I am drawn to our fitness center by the urge to top my previous performance and best competitors.

We can now summarize what we have discussed about how reinforcement and punishment influence learning.

We learn to do activities that reinforce us.

We learn to stop activities that punish us.

Some reinforcements and some punishments are more effective than others. What works best varies with each individual or group and each situation.

Timing of an intervention is important. Immediate reinforcements and punishments are more effective than later ones, particularly in initial learning. However, awareness that punishment or reinforcement is sure to come can serve as well. Thus, if a police officer stops you for a traffic violation, it is an immediate jolt, even though you do not get hit with a fine until later. If, instead, the officer simply takes a photo of your car's license plate and reports it, this delayed penalty will not be as effective. Nor does an end-of-term failing grade motivate a student as much as an early warning because the warning occurs at the same time as the unsatisfactory work.. In changing behavior, the key is to encourage improvement, even slight improvement, rather than wait for highly desirable behavior. The woman who responded to her psychologist's recommendation to praise her troubled teenage son whenever he did anything right by "but he never does anything right" illustrates this. When she finally forced herself to look for any little positive change, his behavior quickly became more positive. Better to be able to say, "There, that's a bit better" or "Keep working at it and you'll get it right" than say, "No, that's all wrong." Praising effort, despite poor initial performance, boosts persistence.

Likewise, appropriate reprimands, for minor deviant behavior, discourages more serious infractions. Student achievement is higher and major infractions lower when schools set high standards for behavior and enforce them; and police programs of "zero tolerance" reduce crime, despite difficulties in implementation and providing needed support.

At first, you should reinforce desired behavior or penalize undesirable behavior each time it occurs. Once it becomes habitual, you can gradually reduce your frequency of interventions. It is also better to reinforce intermittently rather than regularly. This occurs naturally with social media. Adolescents become addicted to social media because they find an item of interest every so often. They feel that they must keep checking for fear of missing something. Casinos program slot machines to provide similar intermittent rewards. Players never know when they might get lucky. They keep feeding the machine hoping for a win next time, held to it like medal to a magnet.

Internal or cognitive reinforcement (and punishment) is as important and as effective as external. We monitor our own behavior. Just thinking of doing what is right becomes rewarding and thinking of doing wrong produces guilt. Through this process, we develop self-discipline. Of course, the values one has determines what one believes is right; an egocentric politician and an altruistic medical practitioner differ dramatically on what they mean by "doing good."

Cognitive Learning

The last kind of learning we want to mention is cognitive learning. Here you use your imagination to consider ways of achieving your goals.

This capacity is unique to humans. It is not necessary to perform an action to learn its outcome; you can think it over, visualize possible scenarios, and anticipate where each will lead.

You can also learn from others' experience. We often miss out on this source of learning and must learn from our own mistakes. Parents frequently lament that their children too often ignore their advice, and they find themselves repeating, "I told you so."

Common folk wisdom affords countless examples of using our cognitive abilities to guide our actions: "use your head," "look before you leap" and "think before you act." Our cognitive faculties prepare us for undertakings both simple and complex. In driving to a distant restaurant, you think of different routes, estimate traffic and decide which way to go. In the same way, teachers prepare lesson plans, entrepreneurs develop business plans and scientists envision plans for space exploration.

We may think of learning as acquiring more information, but for personal development, imagination is just as important as knowledge. That's why your reading should include works of fiction that stretch your mind, stir your imagination and broaden your perspective. As Ralph Waldo Emerson put it, "Fiction reveals truth that reality obscures."

Our above description of what psychology tells us about how we learn, and change (modeling, reinforcement and cognitive learning) is a useful resource to draw on.

Steps in Self-Improvement
Realize the need.

Most people don't bother to change. They remain dissatisfied but simply drift along instead of working to improve. They fail to realize that the road to a happier life begins with changing themselves.

Ben's Franklin's realization that he did not write as well as he would like is one example of his habit of self-examination and search for a better life. In your own self-examination, start with your values. Ask, "What kind of person do I want to be"? "What do I want to accomplish? You might start with improving self-knowledge, social skills, self-esteem, financial position, spiritual life, health, or any other aspect of your life.

Or you might start with your job. Steve Jobs captures its significance when he advises, "Your work is going to fill a large part of your life, and the only way to be truly satisfied is to do what you believe is great work. And the only way to do great work is to love what you do. If you haven't found it yet, keep looking. Don't settle. As with all matters of the heart, you'll know when you find it."

Recognize and draw on your natural aptitudes and strengths, not your weaknesses. Successful people possess a multitude of weaknesses but compensate for them by using their strengths. Your successes invigorate you. You feel upbeat and ready to take on new initiatives, including tackling your weaknesses.

Developing and maintaining competence is worthwhile in every occupation, in every area of life and at every age. Keeping abreast of new technological developments, expanding vocabulary, polishing social skills, and improving and maintaining athletic and other physical abilities all enhance your feeling of competence and your quality of life.

Realize that you possess the power to change. I think of a custodian who mentioned to me that he was unable to quit smoking as an example of this. I simply replied, "Oh,

I bet you could do it if you decided to." He later thanked me for reminding him that he had the power to change.

Decide to act. To bolster your decision, make a commitment, put it on your to-do list; tell friends you're going to do it. Despite successes of self-help groups and individual and group therapy, the most common source of positive change is when you take charge and just go ahead and do it.

Develop a plan of action. You will recall that when Franklin determined to improve himself, he developed a thorough plan, listing characteristics that he wanted to change, setting priorities, and keeping a record of his progress. He decided that being orderly was his number one priority. Once he succeeded with this step, he moved on to his next. He set realistic goals, broke them down into small steps and kept a record of his progress. Today's research in positive psychology confirms that Ben's approach works.

A widespread belief that is only partly true is that we simply need to put more push into what we do in order to accomplish something. The anecdote of a passerby who comes upon a father and son having difficulty cutting a log with a two-handed saw is worth repeating. When the man remarks that the difficulty seems to be that the saw needs sharpening, the father tells him he is in a hurry and has no time to sharpen his saw. Quite often, we benefit from taking time to sharpen our skills, modify our habits or change our perspective.

Although sometimes it pays to work harder; more often it pays to work smarter.

Taking that first step. It helps to think and plan and decide, but it is essential to act. Too often, we fantasize about our hopes for our future yet fail to do anything concrete to make them come true. We need motivation and initiative. As Ben Franklin said, "Motivation is when your dreams put on work clothes

Keep a record of your progress. Use a system like the checklist Franklin employed or devise one that suits you better. It keeps you on track and reinforces your efforts.

Find ways of supporting your accomplishments. Know what kind of treats, rewards, or other reinforcements work best for you and use them.

You've reached your first goal. Congratulations! You feel a sense of accomplishment. Use this experience in planning your next project. You should embark on it with more confidence based on your initial success.

Common deterrents to self-improvement

Old Habits

You no doubt carry baggage from your past you should get rid of. Like an old pair of sweat socks that you hesitate to discard even though they hurt your feet. Obvious habits involving alcohol, drugs, tobacco, weight, exercise, temper, procrastination cause you to think, feel, and behave as you did when you were less mature.

One example is habits of speech. You acquire them when young without realizing how they will label you as an adult

Also, ask yourself, "Do I dress for success"? A good number of people give little thought to what they wear and its effect on their progress.

If you think, "I wear what I feel like," or "my friends all dress like this," you are allowing old habits to hamper your success. Or you may fail to distinguish between casual dress, business or professional dress and social or party dress thus showing up wearing the wrong clothes for an occasion.

A couple of examples come to mind. Some time ago, a recent college graduate came to me because he was having difficulty getting a job. An accounting major with good grades, he had interviewed for several openings with organizations, but was never offered a job. Wearing a garish jacket and tie, his hair long and wild and his speech crude, he appeared ready for an evening at a club, not a job interview with a business firm. He was adamant against modifying his appearance, insisting" I have the right to dress whatever way I like." In another case, a graduate student applying for an internship with a mental health agency showed up wearing spiked heels, a miniskirt and a low-cut blouse. She was dressed for a party rather than for counseling clients, yet she believed she was dressed to make a favorable impression.

You probably have acquired ways of thinking and acting that seem so much a natural part of you that you take them for granted. You might think that you should not say "No" to others, especially those in authority, or believe watching your money carefully is "not the way I am" or asking influential associates for assistance is being "too pushy." In a similar vein, ask yourself if you have views about building a positive reputation, and acquiring power and money that negatively affect your progress.

Need to please. It is natural for you to want folks to like you, particularly your family, friends and colleagues. One thing that hinders efforts to improve is that change often disturbs other people. Accustomed to how you have been they get upset when your actions differ from their expectations. When you say, "I don't like that kind of talk" when they insult you, instead of laughing it off, or if you say, "I'm sorry, I wish I could help, but I have another commitment" they may become irritated or angry. The "new you" that is surfacing will require adjustment on their part. Help them adjust, but do not let them block your progress.

Stress. Change produces stress. You will experience stressful moments during the change process. Be confident you have the know-how to handle it.

Fear of failure discourages new ventures. Expect roadblocks during your progress. Don't let that stop you. Act and persist. The only ones who do not have setbacks are those who do not try anything new.

Distractions and vacillation. Today's life is replete with time-consuming distractions. Set your priorities and stick to them. Follow Ben Franklin's advice, "Dost thou love life? Then do not squander time, for that's the stuff life is made of." Avoid dilly dallying. You have new worthwhile goals; experience the joy of working towards them.

Low self-esteem

If you lack confidence needed to move in a new direction, remember, your confidence will grow as you progress. At the same time, take advantage of activities mentioned throughout this book to bolster your self-confidence.

Negative emotions

Emotions play a major role in driving your actions. Worry, fear, anger, sorrow, frustration and other negative emotions act as potent deterrents to your improvement. Positive emotions, by contrast, build resiliency. They mitigate problems and frustrations of life and empower you to be more innovative and ready to take reasonable risks.

Resources for self-improvement

Here is a useful list of resources to speed your journey on your road to success:

Education. Today, opportunities for formal and informal education are everywhere. Select a place and program that is right for you and make the best use of its resources.

Self-help aids. You have countless self-help books, manuals, and videos available for your edification, including the book you are now reading. They can be a valued and practical part of your advancement. They are not, however, a substitute for professional help. Books offer suggestions for a wide audience; mental health specialists offer assistance based on individual needs.

On-the-job learning. Just about every job provides experience that adds to your growth, particularly if you spot opportunities and take advantage of them. For high school and college students, part-time work offers a valuable complement to formal learning I remember when my oldest daughter started a job in a five-and-dime store while in high school. I thought it would be useful experience in meeting a regular schedule, relating to people. and managing money. I soon found she was learning much more.

In my work in career counseling, I have often heard someone say, "Oh, I just had ordinary jobs; I didn't learn anything useful." After discussing functions of the job and requirements necessary to perform it, it quickly became clear how many skills, work habits and general know-how had been acquired.

One of the best ways to develop talent is through volunteer work and hobbies. If you have a passion that you cannot realize on your job, you can usually find it here.

Social interaction. A major part of personal growth involves relating to others in an upbeat, confident and effective way. Educational institutions, work settings, organizations of volunteers and special interest groups all provide settings in which you can benefit from healthy social interaction. So do churches, youth groups and business and professional organizations. Remember though, it is not the number of friends, but the kind of friends.

Nowhere is this more clearly depicted than in Claude Brown's epic autobiographical novel, "Man-child in the Promised Land" which chronicles his growing up on the streets of Harlem in the 1940s and 50s. After years of surviving poverty, crime and violence with his wits and his fists and support from his tight-knit gang, he realizes that all of them will soon be in prison or in the morgue. He resolves to change but knows the attraction of his pals and social pressure from his group will drag him along with them. Hence, he moves to a new neighborhood, cuts his ties with his gang and goes on to complete college and law school.

Learn to get along with a variety people, but close friends are a treasure. They add so much to your life that you should cultivate those who share your values.

Self-help groups. A wide variety of groups provide mutual support and encouragement to members with a common issue such as addiction, weight control, anger management, grief, disease or a common mental, emotional, or physical problem. Other groups focus on encouraging positive change. They work on areas of mutual interest such as education, child rearing or public speaking.

Professional resources. Several kinds of mental health professionals provide individual, or group help appropriate to a person's need. You have psychiatrists, psychologists, professional counselors, clinical social workers, and marriage and family therapists to choose from. They include specialists in addictions, career counseling, mental health, rehabilitation, marriage and family counseling, life skills enhancement, executive coaching and athletic performance. In selecting someone to work with, check their credentials including licensure and specialization. University psychology departments, primary care physicians, and nursing practitioners can lend a hand in finding a specialist who is right for your needs.

The above resources are readily available. All you need is initiative to profit from them.

We move next to a closely related topic, Interpersonal Relationships.

Chapter 17.
Positive Relationships
and Personal Growth

Introduction

Personal development does not take place in a vacuum, but in interactions with those you encounter as you move through life's journey.

Humans are, by our nature, social animals. Babies are completely dependent on others at birth and require holding and cuddling as well as feeding for healthy development. They have built-in mechanisms to get this. They smile, cry, grasp and make eye contact. They are attractive (or at least "cute").

Shortly, other innate tendencies emerge that facilitate social interaction, such as attempting to speak, crawl and walk. I often think we underestimate the role of these genetic-driven tendencies, so evident in early childhood, on our later lifestyle including the way we naturally relate to people.

Learning starts early too. Children imitate what others do, and encounter reinforcements and punishments in their early explorations.

Developmental perspective

This modeling and conditioning shaping our lives has its roots in our family.

Do you remember how your parents viewed other people and how they related to them? Were they trusting, suspicious, fun loving, cynical, indifferent, curious, concerned, ill-at-ease? Were their views widely different and, if so, which of them did you accept, and which reject?

And think of individuals you encountered (including those you ran into in biographies and fiction) and how their way of relating to people reflected parental views.

If you have read Bridge of Sighs by Pulitzer Prize winner Richard Russo you will see it played out in the life of its main character, Louis Lynch ("Lucy"). His father was an eternal optimist, who liked everyone and trusted them. His mother countered this with her shrewdness and skepticism. Lucy saw merit in both views but ended up being like his father, running a string of convenience stores they owned in the same easy-going way. His wife's views mirror his mother's fearing that this lovable guy who appealed to her so much must change, or their business will fail.

Like Lucy, your views of people and habitual ways of relating to them formed early in life before you were mature enough to evaluate them.

Now, you have the opportunity to examine them more objectively, take charge of your life and take steps to modify them as you will.

Understanding and improving yourself

Self-Concept Our effectiveness in interpersonal relationships begins with our view of ourselves-our self-concept.

Self-Awareness It also helps to recognize emotions we experience in our interactions and what situations trigger them. Early sensitivity to an emotion starting to erupt helps us act while we are still thinking rationally.

For example, a man who feels annoyed because his wife keeps talking while he is trying to concentrate on a project should address it early in a calm manner, letting her know he is working on something that requires his concentration for about an hour. If, instead, he waits until his anger builds up, he is more likely to come out with "damn it, don't you ever shut up," or something equally hurtful to their relationship.

Friendships. Another step to thriving is to widen your network of friends especially those with a positive outlook. This may be a good time to remember the role of the Junto. In it, Franklin and his fellow merchants and tradesmen exchanged ideas for building and maintaining a reputation for integrity, for networking outside the group and for improving their business and financial interests. Franklin credited this group with being a remarkable source for learning to work effectively with everyone else.

He also formed a wider network of associates from various backgrounds and made it a point to draw on their example. That is one reason he attended various church services. He heard homilies from a wide variety of preachers, drew on their ideas and incorporated effective methods of speaking into his own style. In a similar way, he cast a wider net reaching out to scientists, political leaders and other influential individuals and profited from their assistance.

Other prominent persons have done the same. Since early in his army years, General Dwight Eisenhower made it a point to stay in touch with his former commanders, learn from them and not hesitate to seek their help in furthering his career. When WWII suddenly struck, and an immediate need to identify highly qualified military leaders was evident. Eisenhower's name kept coming up.

Does such networking only work for people of prominence? Not at all! Any of us can benefit from it. A colleague of mine made it a practice to write to anyone whose accomplishments interested him. Over the years he developed a voluminous correspondence with a host of knowledgeable, helpful people.

I also read of a person who exemplified the out-going assertive networker He called a friend "I'm coming to Chicago for a couple of days. Anyone doing anything interesting that I should meet?" That's impressive networking!

Understanding and Influencing Others Power

Positions of power carry with them authority to require others to do what you ask. When we talk about power, we think of political leaders, CEOs of companies, union officials, presidents of universities, and Dons of the underworld.

The reality is any position with power provides opportunities to accomplish more. Don't hesitate to take on such responsibilities. They contribute to your understanding of people and ability to be effective in working with them.

Wealth also brings power and influence. For membership on a Board of Directors of a university, for example, I have heard it said that a person needs wit, wisdom and wealth- but the first two requirements can be waived!

We have previously mentioned the value of acquiring wealth as aid to increasing your influence and achieving positive objectives. Money can be used in so many ways. Using it wisely is a challenge.

Reputation

As a child, I remember my mother saying. "what will people think of you"? when I did something out of bounds. "Why should I care what people think"? was my unexpressed rejoinder. I have since come to realize that your reputation is important. Even before you meet someone, they start with expectations that influence your relationship, and, depending on what they have heard about you, may seek you out or avoid meeting you.

As Ben Franklin put it, "Hide not your talents. They for use were made. What's a sundial in the shade"? He made it a point to cultivate a reputation for industry, integrity and cordiality-a desirable person to know and work with.

Relationships and Influence

In addition to power we possess because of a position we hold and reputation we have acquired, we have influence based on relationships. Positive relationships produce positive results. Friends help friends. And a host of the right kind of friends enhances your influence.

Empathy

We have mentioned the value of understanding our own emotions and being comfortable with them. This is one-half of the secret to developing satisfying relationships. The other half is ability to recognize emotions in others; to understand, accept and appreciate how someone thinks and feels. This is empathy. Nothing is more important to most of us than to feel understood and respected.

Sometimes it is obvious how people feel from what they say, they express their feelings openly (what you hear is what you get). Often, however, a disconnect exists between the two and, unless you are a particularly skilled listener, you miss much. In fact, you may fail to understand their basic message let alone their feelings and motives.

A common problem in interacting with someone is that you are concentrating on what you want to say and only partly attending to them.

To be a skilled listener, you must be active, not passive. Ask for clarification, perhaps by saying, "let me see if I have this right," Also know when to be silent, and give the person (and yourself) time to think.

Often, instead, we simply jump to conclusions. Perhaps my favorite example is one from my own past. In my youth, I met a young woman who immediately said, "Oh, you look just like that pirate in the movie I just saw." Feeling insulted, I left her shortly with no interest in ever seeing her again. Later, when I saw that the pirate played the romantic lead, I realized she was complimenting, not insulting, me. Such misinterpretations are common in relationships.

Despite attending carefully to a person, your initial impression of his or her motives and sentiments may be erroneous. It helps to withhold judgment until you have tactfully checked your assessment. You might ask, "Tom, when you say you oppose this project, what is there about it that worries you?" or, "Helen, You say maybe we should break off our relationship, but I don't understand why?

Prejudice is a common contributor in misjudging a person. Not only do your prejudices influence your judgment, but so will your suspicion that a person you are interacting with is prejudiced. It is possible to be hyper-vigilant in looking for signs of prejudice and be misled.

Reinforcement and Punishment

Understanding how to reinforce positive behavior and "punish" undesirable behavior is essential in influencing others. Cognitive-behavioral approaches, that we have discussed, are particularly useful here. You will recall they stress that reinforcing positive thinking affects our actions and reinforcing positive acts affects our thinking.

Criticism is a common way of trying to change objectionable behavior. What we have recommended in helping children change also holds for adults. Criticize in a way that shows respect and appreciation, but that a specific change is in order. How to do this effectively depends on your relationship with the person, and your interpersonal skills. Some of us tend to resent criticism, some welcome it and even seek it out. I remember a colleague who was inclined to be outspoken and emotional at meetings. He was aware of this and asked me to please let him know if he was showing signs of getting carried away. We can all benefit from feedback of this kind.

Individual Differences

I often hear someone say, "I believe you should treat everyone the same way." Everyone, of course, is not the same. We need "different strokes for different folks".

Which ways of commending and reprimanding work with someone? Public recognition or private praise; an invitation to lunch or a thoughtful gift; a raise in pay or a promotion; free time or overtime; working in a group or alone?

On one occasion, well-wishers were congratulating conductor Arturo Toscanini on his performance. In response to their praise for how brilliantly he conducted the orchestra and how magnificently they played, he merely nodded and extended his thanks. Then, a woman who knew him well approached and said, "Oh, Arturo, you looked so handsome up there tonight" and he beamed with pleasure. Some compliments mean more than others.

This same point applies in penalizing an employee for being late or neglecting responsibilities or doing something aggravating. Is a private reprimand better than a public one? A letter more effective than an e-mail? A cut in pay superior to a loss of perks?

Consider this as a case in point. In one bit of research, a bonus paid in advance that had to be returned if a performance goal was not met, was more effective than waiting and paying a bonus if it was met. This demonstrates that punishment works. And it works best when you are typically reinforcing someone, and they know you can (and will) hold back reinforcement unless they perform satisfactorily. That's also why those working with children find removing privileges (including "time out") one of the best ways to foster healthy child development.

Emotional Quotient (E.Q.)

This may be a good time to revisit E.Q. For years, psychologists had considered intelligence (I.Q.) the most important determinate of success. As we mentioned in an earlier chapter on emotions, we now realize emotional intelligence (ability to understand and control your own emotions and to recognize and relate to the emotions of others) is equally influential. Benjamin Franklin exemplifies this concept. He understood people and he understood the value of forming emotional bonds with them. Of all the reasons for studying Franklin's life (and they are numerous) his ability to enable people to feel relaxed and upbeat in his presence and, in turn, ready to cooperate with him may be the preeminent one. Several events in his life illustrate this social proficiency. For instance, on one occasion when he was concerned about criticism from a competitor, he asked if he might borrow a valuable book from him. His rival felt flattered by the request, and their shared interest and enjoyment of a book soon turned this rival into a friend and supporter.

As Franklin recommended: "Do good to a friend to keep him, to an enemy to win him." Not only is he "turning the other cheek" to an enemy, but he is also turning him into a friend.

Unfortunately, a person with a high E.Q. may utilize this talent to manipulate people. When we talk about high-functioning sociopaths, for example, we mean bright and socially facile individuals who know how to tap into our fears, prejudices, hopes, hatreds, sympathies, loyalties and generosity in order to get what they want- usually power and esteem. Lacking a moral compass, sociopaths have little or no concern for the rights of others. We encounter them in all types of positions including unscrupulous lawyers, drug-dealing doctors, slash- and- burn corporate raiders, political demagogues and maybe even one of your coworkers or neighbors. Recognizing that our world has more than its share of sociopaths (and those with sociopathic tendencies) and understanding their techniques for appealing to our emotions, can help us protect ourselves against them.

In the world of business, companies have developed workshops for executives to increase emotional intelligence. Participants grow more confident and more effective in their leadership role. This should not surprise us, since most problems executives face involve emotional, rather than rational conflicts.

Social Support Systems

Another aid to a balanced and healthy emotional life is a social support system. Maintaining enjoyable relationships with family, friends and colleagues makes a major contribution to this. Sharing a meal, attending a musical performance and collaborating on a project not only offer sources of mutual enjoyment, but build resistance to stress. As research studies show, such support systems contribute to a longer and more satisfying life. In short, learn to relax, develop confidence and nurture friendships!

Friends and Social Activities

Close friends add so much to our lives. Sharing a tender moment of affection or a playful interaction with a very special person makes the day wonderful. Engaging in the everyday activities of life in our job, with our families and in our communities in ways that give us a sense of purpose; of doing something worthwhile; and of being part of something more important than ourselves generates an upbeat mood or sense of flow. In addition, hobbies and avocations, including music, art, theater, reading, movies, athletics, and such, contribute to a balanced emotional life.

Such activities help us express feelings of affection and provide a source of positive relationships.

Humor

You often see a different, more likable side of someone when dancing, or at a ball game or after swapping jokes you both enjoy. So, learn to share enjoyable emotional experience. You will like one another better and work better together. And although we like those who add humor to our lives, we like even better those who enjoy our humor. So, when a funny remark comes to mind, ask yourself whether the recipient will enjoy it or be annoyed. And when someone adds humor to your day, express your appreciation.

Ronald Reagan was a master of this. During his presidency, he even introduced the practice of having Vice President George Bush prepare a joke for cabinet meetings to get them off on a constructive note.

Ben Franklin, of course, had a well-deserved reputation for his wit. In his biography, we see how he practiced it and improved it, moving from a time where he was uncomfortable and only marginally successful to a style that had become a natural part of his persona.

Although sharing a laugh together helps build relationships, humor can backfire. A jokester explained the difference between comedy and tragedy thus: "If someone is hit in the face with a custard pie, that's comedy; if I get hit in the face with a custard pie, that's tragedy." So, humor can be a two-edged sword. It often has a bite to it, and some of us may feel the pain. Additionally, even though someone who initially hears or reads your joke may enjoy it, some down the line may be offended. This is especially true of jokes circulated on the internet.

Not long ago, several high-ranking judges and attorneys in Pennsylvania had their fun circulating "humorous" racist and sexist emails among themselves. Members of the public, however, were far from amused when they were exposed, and the resultant scandal did serious damage to their careers.

Cooperation

Throughout this chapter we have been emphasizing what we know about relating to others. One point to keep in mind is that working with a partner, or a group often accomplishes more and provides more satisfaction than working alone. You have heard of "lucky partners" where one person's strengths compliment the other and compensate for weaknesses, or where their interaction generates enthusiasm and confidence. One partner may be strong in technology, the other in marketing.

This is also the value of forming proactive groups and building teamwork.

In doing so, seek out individuals high in self-efficacy-they are typically also effective in collaborative activities.

Competition

It makes sense that understanding relationships not only enhances cooperation, it also boosts success in competing. Both the challenge of competing well and the joy of winning give us that upbeat feeling.

In some kinds of hostile or cutthroat competition, unfortunately, we can get sidetracked from our goal and direct our efforts toward hurting our opponent. Both sides lose, but those who suffer fewer losses consider themselves winners.

In one incident I witnessed, a man and a woman in a traffic dispute, jumped out of their cars and began shouting at one another. Suddenly, the woman leaped back into her car and rammed it into the man's. He, in turn, did the same to her car. The two continued this backing and smashing until police arrived to take charge.

It seems like an extreme case of trying to win a dispute by hurting your opponent more than they hurt you. Yet the Vietnamese war provides a classic case of this same thing on a far broader, more disastrous scale. On a regular basis, high level government officials ("the best and the brightest") assured Americans that we were winning despite the continued increase in our casualties because the Vietnamese were suffering even more. The American public didn't buy it!

Game Theory

In an earlier chapter on decision-making, we emphasized the value of knowing probability. If you can predict (or estimate) outcomes of various strategies, you can compete more effectively.

Game theory studies situations of this kind, applying probability to improving prediction and decision-making. Extensive research in this area is being conducted by psychologists and economists, and several recent Nobel Prizes have been awarded for this work. Much of it is done in Schools of Business, by large corporations and by the military.

It assumes that when individuals or organizations compete, they must consider what competitors are likely to do. It also assumes competitors will act rationally (this is the part that concerns me). In game theory, you analyze input of the probability of various actions by other participants to decide what is the optimum decision for you. Since numerous variables affect the outcome, analysis of this input can be highly complex.

. Often, however, we cannot calculate the probability of an outcome, but must estimate it (subjective probability). This is especially true in competitive situations where what opponents will do is uncertain (in fact, often intentionally misleading) and where emotions may override reason.

In this case, you must base probability on your knowledge of opponents' past performance and any cues you might pick up from their current actions.

A knack for recognizing emotions in others empowers you to be a winner in competition.

High stakes poker is a well-known example of skilled players gaining an edge on the competition by their ability to read body language and emotions at the table.

Many successful politicians, including more of our presidents than you might think, have been skilled poker players. These same skills leading to success in poker apply to everyday life. We compete constantly: vying with a rival firm for a lucrative contract and recognizing when a buyer is eager to make a purchase. .

Gamesmanship

This may be a good time to talk about gamesmanship. Moving from game theory to gamesmanship is quite a leap. It is easy to see why it has not been a popular subject of scientific research since it has acquired a dubious reputation. Yet it has a long history of affecting all kinds of competition. It has been called "Pushing the rules to the limit without getting caught" and "winning without actually cheating."

It also has a history of association with humor. Its unexpected ploys and one-upmanship strike a contrast with rational, traditional rules-of-the-game competition.

It's Lee Trevino tossing a rubber snake in front of Jack Nicholson during a golf match or Brooklyn infielder Eddy Stansky, distracting opposing batters by jumping up and down and waving his arms wildly as the pitch was coming,

The term gamesmanship was popularized by Stephen Potter 's humorous 1947 book, The Theory and Practice of Gamesmanship and the 1960 British comedy, School for Scoundrels, based on it. Featuring Ian Carmichael, as a well-intentioned nice-guy who is an easy victim of con men and colleagues alike. He enrolls in a "School of Lifemanship" headed by Alastair Sim and quickly learns tactics to be one-up on opponents. Utilizing them, he turns the table on a variety of manipulative persons including a used car salesman and his friend (Terry-Thomas) who has always had a knack for somehow making him feel inferior.

Politics offers a history of gamesmanship, with a wide variety of tactics used by politicians to inflate their own image and undercut opponents'.

President Trump, a prominent practitioner of gamesmanship, has moved it to a new level, and has reached far more of the public with it than any past president. He constantly tests the limits of his authority and, when necessary, backs off, at least for the moment. Is this immoral, unscrupulous behavior as his opponents charge? Or is it merely an escalation of traditional political hardball and gamesmanship? For, as humorist Finley Peter Dunne commented back when Teddy Roosevelt was president "Politics ain't beanbag."

In sum, making astute decisions involves non-rational, emotional variables as well as rational ones. Game theory would benefit from incorporating them into its research on competition.

What is acceptable legally or morally varies with the times and the situation. Prior to WW 11, and in its early stages, intentionally killing civilians was considered immoral. Thus, American bombers initially flew their raids during the day and directed them at military targets. In the later stages, whole cities became targets and civilians became the main casualties.

Common Situation for Interacting

Next, let's take a look at some kinds of interactions you might encounter, including recommendations that apply and how these vary with the purpose and setting.

In every case, prepare well in advance! Be confident, engaged and considerate during the interaction and be sure to follow-up afterward. Let's begin with the job interview.

Interviewing for a Position

Plan ahead. Make sure you have submitted a professional-looking resume that highlights your qualifications for the position.

Letters of recommendation count. Once, when my daughter was being interviewed for a position, the interviewer tossed one of her recommendations on his desk and scoffed "this can't be true, nobody could be that good"!

She retained her composer and simply said, "I wouldn't ask someone for a recommendation unless I were confident it would be a good one." Surprisingly, many job seekers miss that point. They ask readily available people without realizing they will usually write perfunctory recommendations of little worth..

Think about ways in which your education, work experience (including part-time jobs), military service, hobbies, travel, demonstrate competencies for that position.

Decide which experience to emphasize and which to simply mention. Some seemingly minor points may resonate with an interviewer. In the often-revived show How to Succeed in Business Without Really Trying, our protagonist happens to mention to the CEO that he was once a window washer. This sets off an exuberant response. A window washer! That's how I got my start with this company-as a window washer! And our job seeker has found a valuable connection.

During the Interview

Be appropriately dressed, using successful members of the organization as a guide. First impressions count not only with the interviewer but with others you meet during your visit. Be at your best throughout the day.

Take cues from the interviewer in using casual or more formal conversation. Know the interviewer's name and use proper forms of address. Be guided by what the interviewer says and does. but don't be distracted from what you want to accomplish!

Emphasize qualifications that demonstrate you are right for the job. At one time a colleague and I were each being considered for a plum assignment. Afterwards he told me I had been lucky to get it, but when he also mentioned that he had emphasized how badly he wanted the job (I had focused on how well I could do it), I knew it wasn't luck.

Also determine whether the job is right for you. Show initiative. Ask questions to clarify points e. g. "Mr.

Bernays, you mentioned the department provides some flexibility in overtime. How does that work out?" Do not start out with or overemphasize salary and benefits, but be sure to clarify them, and be ready to negotiate if need be.

Job interviews may involve lunch, a tour or a meeting with a group. In any case, be prepared.

Follow up. After the interview make a record of things you want to remember. Also write a note of thanks including an expression of your continued interest.

Meetings

Despite a common belief that meetings are a waste of time, many significant policies and practices of an organization originate in decisions and recommendations of committees.. Prepare

An administrator I worked with had his supporters and his critics, but I often heard, even from his critics, "You have to give him credit, he is always well prepared."

Look over the agenda well in advance and get clarification if needed. Review material relevant to topics under review and, where appropriate, discuss them with other members. This "meeting-before-the-meeting" often determines its outcome.

The meeting itself

Arrive early. Know the agenda and prioritize. Make important points with supporting evidence.

Listen and let others know you are listening- mention a speaker's name and repeat their point.!

Concentrate on both the purpose of the meeting and building effective teamwork. You want agreement, acceptance and commitment!

Follow up. See that decisions are carried out.

Teaching

One point we learn from teaching that is applicable to so many other situations is that it is not the amount of time you spend in preparation that is most important; rather it is how relevant preparation is to performance.

Supervising

A well-known mantra for administrators at any level is "be firm and be fair." It seems to make common sense but has just as often been misleading. Psychological research has clarified and modified it. Being firm does not work if you are harsh or hard-headed. The key here is setting clear performance goals. Those you supervise should know what is expected, how well they are doing and consequences of their performance (rewards and punishments).

Nor is being fair synonymous with treating everyone the same. Consider this. If working overtime is needed, rather than dividing it evenly, wouldn't it be better to divide it among those who want it? Employees have different abilities, interests and needs. Get to know them and utilize them!

Leadership research classifies some leaders as task-oriented, others relationship-oriented. In general, both are important, but which to emphasize varies with each person. Some employees are absorbed in their job, welcome any help with it but have little interest in how you interact with them. For others it makes a significant difference.

I remember a client who was thinking of changing careers. He had worked in sales for years with mixed results. In some jobs he was successful, in others (including his present position) frustrated. As we discussed his past work experience, it became clear that the crucial difference was in his sales manager. Working with one who had been supportive and encouraging, even on a bad day, he felt good about his job and had a fine sales record. On jobs where his supervisor was demanding and critical, he became discouraged, and his record reflected it.

After discussing his options, he decided to stay in sales, but, before taking on a new job, to discuss how he and his supervisor could work together to be most productive.

Buying, selling and negotiating

We are constantly involved in exchanging goods and services both in our job and our personal lives. What is something we want worth? What will someone give for something we have? Ben Franklin was an excellent judge of what was valuable and how to acquire it. In the process, he became a man of wealth and influence.

This may be a good time to remind you how Bernays, Freud's son-in-law, highlighted the impact of our emotions on how we spend our money. Since then, psychologists, economists and other behavioral scientists have accumulated a voluminous amount of evidence, much of it based on observing what makes someone successful in marketing products and services, something useful for all of us.

A look at a variety of situations familiar to most of us, will serve to illustrate practical applications of these principles.

Restaurant staff

If you dine out, even occasionally, you will surely notice that some of the staff do a superior job. You like them better and leave a larger tip. In fact, studies show that one server consistently earns substantially more than coworkers. Why? What we find is an emphasis on making the evening an enjoyable one for patrons. It helps to act as if you like them and are eager to please them; its better yet if you really do like your work and those you meet there.

Being sensitive to their moods and taking your cues from them helps. Are they in a hurry or relaxed? Happy or worried? Do they seem dissatisfied with something that you can help with such as location of their table or a place to put their coats? Connect with them. Introduce yourself (and repeat your name occasionally so they remember it); use respectful forms of address (avoid "you guys" which makes many of us cringe); make frequent eye contact and smile in a way that shows you like them.

Here are two of many research studies that bear on this. In one, a waitress was instructed to touch the male diner's shoulder lightly when she spoke to him. In another a waiter, at the end of the meal would distribute a chocolate mint to everyone and then, while looking directly in the eyes of the person who had asked for the check, say, "and this one is especially for you." In both studies, tips increased markedly. Specific behavior may vary. But the lesson is there. Let people know you appreciate them!

Buying a car.

One of my neighbors bought a new car every year from the same salesperson at the same dealer. He looked forward to this event as another annual happy occasion akin to Christmas and Fourth of July. He believed it was worth the price. His sales representative would call every year to let him know that new promotional material would be arriving, pointing out attractive new features that would help convince him (and family members) that another enjoyable experience was coming up.

I took a different approach, determined to find satisfactory transportation at a moderate price. On my most recent occasion, I checked information on the web and consumer ratings and narrowed my choice to two. I went to one dealer, but none of their selections appealed to me, so I tried a second. Here a salesman showed me a used car from the previous year with low mileage and a comprehensive warranty. I tried it, liked it, and after a bit of haggling over price and trade-in value of my current car, bought it.

A little effort saved me several thousand dollars.

I have not always been that successful. Members of the sales force sell cars every day; you buy one every few years. They know several ways to persuade you. A basic one is to help you narrow your choice to a couple of cars that appeal to you rather than offer too many options although throwing in a decoy choice (one that you obviously would not want) can help make the ones you like seem more appealing. Another device is to encourage you to get started on the decision-making process by making easier choices-giving you a nudge. "Are you looking for a new car?" "Do you have a color you prefer?" "Do you want one with automatic parking?"

During negotiations, a salesperson wants to be helpful. He is on your side. If you offer a lower price, he may suggest a way of adjusting your choice so it will cost less.

Or ask his sales manager if she could accept a lesser offer. Or indicate he could try to make it up on your trade-in.

He may ask you for a favor that you are unlikely to refuse. "Would you do me a favor and take a picture of me standing beside the car"? You agree; he offers you a copy of the photo, and you now feel more closely connected to him (and the car). As you will remember, this is often called The Ben Franklin Effect.

And when you have made a decision to buy you may find the final price higher than you realized. Do you go ahead with your purchase? If not, what will you say?

It doesn't matter much how you say it. Just say "No", even after an apparent agreement has been reached. "No, I changed my mind."

Selling a house

For most of us, our home is our most valuable asset and selling it is a stressful process. Assessing its value, making modifications before putting it on the market, negotiating with potential buyers, making settlement and arranging to move may seem overwhelming.

I dreaded the thought of it when I decided to move into a retirement community. An organization that works with such communities promised to save me the hassle, by buying my home and taking care of everything.

They would pay eighty five percent of market value as determined by two independent estimates. When I looked into it, I found that the estimates seemed low, and I would be required to spend $20,000 to make needed improvements.

I turned to a realtor who had been recommended by a friend. She suggested selling the house as is and letting the buyers modify as they wished. She also thought we should list it at s price substantially higher than previous estimates I had been given. On the first day it was listed, five buyers offered more than our list price.

Resisting the impulse to save myself what looked like an onerous job made a difference of $35,000! And it turned out to be relatively stress free.

An incident in the sale, illustrates another principle-value is relative. A person who drives ten miles to save ten dollars on grocery order of a hundred dollars, may be willing to spend a few hundred dollars extra for some minor feature when spending a few thousand dollars on a new car. It affected me during my housing transaction. One prospective buyer had met with me and told me how much it would mean to him and his wife to acquire this house. I took a liking to them and found we had much in common. When I later reviewed offers with the realtor, theirs was $ 1,000 below the highest bid. Nevertheless, I decided to accept it. Compared with the sale price of the house, the difference seemed small. Yet, if this nice couple would have visited me and asked if I would give them $1,000. I would have laughed in their faces. Objectively, 1,000 dollars is 1,000 dollars, but in subjective decisions, relative value often prevails.

Profiting from college

Higher education is a valuable investment. If you plan wisely and use your time productively, you will be prepared for a successful career, enjoyable relationships with friends and colleagues and a sense of well-being that comes with knowing you have used your time (and your money) well..

Focus on fit.

If you ask, "what is the best college in the country"? a handful of elite ones come immediately to mind. If you ask, "what is the best college for me"? the answer is more elusive. Yet, it is the one you need to consider. Which would be a good fit"? And our only reasonable conclusion is that many fine colleges are out there, most of which would work out well for you.

Begin with a broad search and narrow it down to a small number to look into more closely. Begin with your values and how you would like to develop as a person. Look for its mission statement and reputation, especially for undergraduate teaching. Check its cost and availability of financial aid.

Avoid being overly impressed by its athletic facilities, name recognition, or presence of prestigious faculty (whom you will never encounter). Check on class size and whether classes are taught by graduate assistants or faculty members. Don't let glitz distract you from essence!

I recall a group of graduates of a selective high school exchanging experiences during Thanksgiving week. Most complained about large classes, feeling isolated, having little contact with faculty and being in courses taught by graduate students who were struggling with learning English and absorbed in their own studies. Then one student who had selected a less prestigious college, spoke up, "I have the Chair of the department for my English Literature class which has 25 students, I'm enjoying the experience, have made some good friends and I'm glad I made the choice I did."

Plan ahead

Make your search an active process that in itself is a positive experience preparing you for future projects. Lots of valuable information is available out there but so is considerable misinformation and unsupported opinion. (friends who know far less than you may be vocal critics of colleges you are considering).

Consider the environmental press.

Unless you are a top student who thrives on competition and would still be able to lead a well-balanced life, think twice about highly competitive colleges. Research studies (called big fish small pond effect) find that students develop more self-confidence in a place where they perform well above average, while students of the same aptitude become less self-confident in a more competitive college where they perform below average.

And higher suicide rates at top-rated institutions is just the tip of the iceberg of mental health problems students experience. Some are obvious, many lie below the surface.

Keep in mind that you will be affected by what is expected (or maybe even demanded) of you- the institution's environmental press.

Which group will exert most influence on you, administration, faculty or fellow students? Studies indicate it is usually other students. So, make it a point to find a few friends that have values and interests similar to yours and who want to make college a positive, developmental experience. It's not so much the number of friends that matters. It's quality that counts!

I was taken aback by a recent newspaper headline that shouted, "College Presidents Say Binge Drinking is Their

Most Serious Problem." Our headline writer neglected to mention that it was *student* binging.

Quite a few colleges have well-deserved reputations as "party schools" where fellow students expect you to party throughout the night with liberal use of alcohol and recreational drugs; in many other colleges, where students are divided on this issue, "partying" is still widespread.

I have often heard graduates say how glad they were that they avoided drinking or drank very little, and instead developed a healthier program of social and recreational activities. As one student observed about the party group, "they missed so many wonderful opportunities." Or, as one of my faculty friends would remind his students, "You can't fly with the eagles if you hoot with the owls."

Treat college as an investment and keep your debt to a minimum. Don't allow size of necessary expenses to lull you into thinking that borrowing an extra thousand here and there to buy a car or go on an expensive vacation is "merely a small additional expense."

Plan your finances carefully, starting well in advance of decision time. Question, question, question so you can make well informed decisions. "How much reduction in tuition can I expect"? (Many students pay far less than the sticker price). "What percent of your students graduate in four year? (In some colleges, difficulty in getting into required courses forces many students to incur the cost of a fifth year). How many students drop out or transfer during or after their first year? (Maybe the image the place projects is a far cry from actual student experience).

It never hurts to ask. My son obtained a tuition waiver as part of an exchange agreement among colleges, including the one in which I was teaching. Because he changed colleges and majors, he needed to attend an extra semester (not covered by his grant) to graduate. I found out who oversaw the tuition-waiver program and gave him a call. When I explained his situation and asked if anything could be done to help, he simply said, "OK!" One phone call saved thousands of dollars.

Before applying for a student loan, investigate other sources of aid: grants, scholarships, assistantships, and work-study opportunities, from both the institution and outside sources. If you take out your loan first, it usually reduces your financial need and therefore your eligibility for aid.

My son-in-law managed to complete college in less than four years, by taking summer courses (at the part-time rate). It not only saved him a bundle on tuition, but it enabled him to hit the job market early and earn income while classmates were still paying tuition for their fourth or fifth year.

One decision on which educational counselors disagree is, "Should you work part-time during college"? That's because jobs can eat into time for study but can also add a valuable kind of experience (skills, knowledge and relationships) to complement what you learn in college. Earning money helps too! So, my answer is a qualified "Yes." Just as in any decision, weigh the advantages and disadvantages of available opportunities, then make your choice. And although you may have to forego some frills of college, don't cut back on essentials.

Romantic relationships

We have discussed friendships and partnerships and how to utilize and enhance them. Romance adds a new emotional dimension to relationships.

Falling in love can be a wonderful experience. It has been celebrated throughout the ages in story and song. At times, however, being in love is like riding a roller coaster.

Remember our earlier emphasis on resolving the all-too-human conflict between getting what you want and having concern for others? Nowhere is this resolution more important than in intimate interpersonal relationships. Romance, love and sexual intimacy is ideally a source of mutual affection, joy, exhilaration and fulfilment. Not only during sexual intercourse itself but in generating affection and contentment throughout the relationship. Many couples fall far short of this ideal. Moreover, it is not only self-centeredness that produces problems. A whole network of negative (and positive) emotions can be linked to sexual satisfaction: anger, fear, worry, resentment and hostility as well as laughter, and a variety of expressions of joy. Then too, relationships often founder from competition, dominance or submissiveness, and differing demands, expectations or sense of propriety. Building trust and sharing feelings with your partner goes a long way toward building a satisfying romantic intimate relationship.

Other countries and cultures
"If you want to understand people in your own country, spend some time in other countries." It's true. We are forced to reexamine many things we take for granted in our relationships. And differences we should be attuned to in our own country (socioeconomic, ethnic, regional, generational) stand out more clearly in international visits.

In preparing for my first visit to France, I heard two widely varied views from friends: "They hate Americans" and "you'll love it; wonderful people."

I soon came to see why. I came across some fellow countrymen who bridled at encountering someone who did not speak English and decided the appropriate response was to raise their voices a few decibels. The term "Ugly American" has its basis in folks like this as well as those who ignore customs of the country they visit and boast about how much they could learn from

With businesses becoming more globalized, employees are spending more and more time, in person and on the internet, interacting with cohorts throughout our world learning to adapt to other cultures. Doing this, increases your facility in all relationships.

Summary and Recommendations

We are naturally social beings. From infancy on, relationships are an inevitable part of our lives. Learn to enjoy them!

Positive relationships, including a social support system affect our happiness, success and longevity. For instance, in 2002, psychologists Ed Diener and Martin Seligman, conducted a study on the 10% of college students with highest scores on a survey of happiness. They found that the most prominent characteristics shared by students who were very happy were "strong ties to friends and family and commitment to spending time with them.

We learn ways of relating to those we interact with at an early age. These habits seem a natural part of our identity, but usually some are desirable, some are handicaps. A bit of modification is required (or sometimes a lot).

Positive psychology studies healthy relationships. Its findings offer a rich source of ideas for self-improvement.

View life as a journey. Plan for and look forward to your future but enjoy the ride and friends along with you. Gain sustenance from positive memories from your past. Positive memories foster a positive attitude.

Let people know you care for them

Don't take friends for granted. And don't assume they know you appreciate them- remind them and compliment them. A thoughtful gift, a caring note or a considerate act strengthens bonds of friendship.

Be involved in your community

The quality of the community where you live, and the organization where you work have significant effects on your life. Connect with like-minded neighbors and colleagues in order to maintain and improve your community and workplace.

Chapter 18.
Healthy Societies

'Today we are faced with the preeminent fact that, if civilization is to survive, we must cultivate the science of human relationships... the ability of all peoples, of all kinds, to live together, in the same world, at peace." FDR

Roosevelt's observation is even more apropos today. What is happening any place in the world affects every place in the world. Understanding our society, the groups that comprise it and other societies we interact with is essential for you to lead an informed and meaningful life.

Benjamin Franklin knew this. And from his work with tradesmen and merchants of the Junta and his involvement in developing the city of Philadelphia, to his work in forming the 13 colonies into a new country and gaining its place in the family of nations, he exemplified ways of accomplishing it. He firmly believed that contributing to society is an essential component of a successful life.

This is a complex process, so let's briefly review principles we have previously covered that will help guide you through our understanding of societies.

Emotions and Behavior

As we examine social groupings large and small, keep in mind what you have learned about the pervasive influence of emotions in driving our beliefs and our behavior. Our views of people of other nations are often a far cry from what they are really like.

In our lives today, globalization and advanced technologies permit all kinds of individuals and organizations to reach millions of people and sell a product, a person or a political movement. In the process, they cull and analyze vast information about each of us from Facebook and other social media and pinpoint "what makes us tick." What fascinates us? What makes our skin crawl? What makes us steaming mad? In short, what is our psychological makeup? The upshot of it is that manipulating people has grown to become a monstrous enterprise with huge financial rewards for successful practitioners. Russia, and no doubt other countries, have been bombarding the internet with misinformation (often couched in an appealing story) designed to divide and confuse us, and even sway presidential elections. Our media often pick them up and further circulate them (remember Bernays pointing out that a news story is more effective than an advertisement- and cheaper too). Counteracting such devious and dangerous activities has become a major challenge for all of us.

Prejudice

We have seen the importance of emotions, feelings and prejudices in our lives, yet most of us still expect to change people simply by getting them to "listen to reason." On occasion they do. Prejudice, unfortunately, is not rational.

Certainly, concerted actions such as legislation and protests have helped reduce discrimination with appeals to reason. To reduce prejudice, however, we need to tap into emotions. Sharing pleasant, productive or enjoyable emotional experience with other people does that. So does feeling empathy for their mistreatment.

Franklin tells us, "Be kind to your friends to keep them; to your enemies to win them." Quite a few people with deeply ingrained prejudices, have been moved to become advocates for equality because of new friends they have made.

Since prejudice distorts our judgments, it often leads to discrimination. One striking example I remember from WWII was the belief prevalent among military authorities that African Americans lacked the competency to become pilots. I heard the same prejudice from a number of my fellow navy flight instructors. They were actually frightened over being killed in an accident if they attempted to teach a person of color to fly. More recently, I spoke with one of the famed Tuskegee Airmen who broke the color barrier and distinguished themselves with their flying skills. He agreed that such distorted views constituted a major obstacle they had to overcome.

Think what it must be like being a member of a group that is a target of prejudice and discrimination. It makes it harder to enjoy a healthy emotional life. It is difficult not to let it affect how you feel about others and yourself. At the same time, prejudice hurts those who harbor strong prejudices, distorting their view of people and cutting them off from potentially positive relationships.

Avoiding Societal Conflict

Societal conflict has a long history. Looking back to the period following WWI, we find people and governments throughout the world searching for ways to preserve peace. The League of Nations made a major effort to do so, but handicapped by American isolationism and internal bickering, it proved ineffective.

Continuing in the search for peace, the Institute for Intellectual Cooperation in 1931 asked Albert Einstein to provide his ideas on how our world could avoid war. He did, so, and sent his response to Sigmund Freud as well.

The resultant correspondence between these two intellectual giants is worth revisiting.

Einstein believed incompetent world leaders was our main problem. We needed an intellectual elite in control. He realized, however, that the job demanded more than intellect, which is why he engaged Freud.

Freud postulated two causes of war, material and psychological. Material refers to conflict over limited resources; psychological to our two competing instincts which he called hadeotic and erotic. The former comes from the word "hades" or hell and the latter from "Eros" meaning love. More simply, a conflict between hate and love, self-centeredness and altruism.

Both men of genius were pessimistic about our chances of doing away with war, although Freud held that working on ways of fulfilling human desires would be a step in the right direction. Contented people don't want war

We can wade in on this debate and ask, "has psychological science learned much that can give us a hand with these problems today?" I am convinced it has, and progress in economics, governance, criminal justice, sociology, public health and related disciplines have too.

Psychology's influence is not so much from psychologists serving as experts in international affairs, but from experts in political relations at all levels understanding psychological principals and using them wisely and compassionately. A well-educated public will realize how much positive psychology can contribute.

I am likewise more and more convinced that having men and women in power who are brilliant is not the key (high-functioning sociopaths are too!). Nor need they be highly educated in results of research in international relations (they can call on advisers with expertise). More problematic is that those in power too often have excessive concern for themselves and too little for the common good. Being a good person is a necessary requirement for being a good leader. Not the only one, but certainly an essential one.

Classic Psychological Research

World War II, the rise of the Nazi party and the horrors of the Holocaust stimulated research in several related topics in psychology. Researchers sought to understand the effects of a charismatic demagogue's influence, and how conformity and obedience played a role in why their followers willingly participated in such despicable actions. Consequently, investigators wondered how authorities formed social contexts that brought about this blind obedience.

Obedience to Authority. Psychologist Stanley Milgram, for one, conducted research on why people obey authorities, even when ordered to do something dreadful. His findings were astonishing. Researchers ordered participants to deliver increasingly painful shocks to a subject (actually a confederate feigning pain) whenever they made an error in a "learning task." Participants continued to deliver what they believed to be painfully high, life-threating shocks on the experimenter's orders.

One of my nephews served as a subject in a replication of this study while a student at Georgetown University. I could see that his participation still bothered him when we talked a few years later. He justified his actions saying, "I figured it was OK since he was a professor and must have a good reason for what he was doing."

This, of course is the assumption too many people make about authorities, even misinformed, incompetent or sociopathic authorities.

Demands of the Situation. The Stanford Prison Experiment investigated how our behavior is influenced by the situation: our role, expectations, environmental press.

If you were a prison guard, for example, you know you must control prisoners. How do you act when in that position? Craig Hany, a doctoral student at Stanford University, decided to investigate this question under the supervision of prominent social psychologist Philip Zimbardo.

An experiment they devised startled everyone with its outcomes. They divided 24 student volunteers into two groups, one composed of prison guards, one of prisoners, and converted a basement at the University into a prison with conditions as realistic as possible.

Guards, in controlling the prisoners, quickly became hostile and cruel towards them. Prisoners, in turn, became more and more frustrated, unruly and ready to revolt. The experimenters had to cut their study short for fear of what might happen. In just six short days, this perfectly normal well-adjusted group of students had engaged in appalling behavior as a result of the demands of the situation. The lesson we learn is that almost any person can act badly depending on the circumstances. This has implications for other settings including police operations, psychiatric facilities and nursing homes.

You may recall the widely publicized case of prisoner abuse that took place in 2004 at the Abu Ghraib prison during the Iraq war. Photographs showing our military guards physically and sexually abusing prisoners and in other ways torturing. and degrading them made us want to cover our eyes.

It is hardly an isolated case. Even when guards know they will be penalized if detected abusing prisoners, records reveal it to be a common practice.

Yet, it varies from place to place and time to time. I remember a friend who was a POW in Germany during WWII. At the same time Nazis were exterminating Jews (and other innocent people) in concentration camps, German guards in the military prison where he was detained treated POWs decently.

Controlling Antisocial Behavior. Previously we have examined the socialization process from an individual perspective. At this point we readjust our lens to provide a societal view. What challenges does a society face in controlling antisocial behavior and reinforcing positive development? How can we improve rather than regress?

Let's begin with Thomas Sowell's observation,

"Each new generation born is in effect an invasion of civilization by little barbarians, who must be civilized before it is too late."

Child development. Any truth in this? Or, as some experts contend, will children naturally grow up lovable and loving, if not mistreated? I see merit in both views. Children need both loving care and direction. A newborn baby does not arrive as an amorphous mass nor as a barbarian.

At present, scientific evidence indicates that infants have built-in tendencies (modules in the brain) leading to exploration, assertiveness, anger, self-centeredness, and several additional characteristics requiring understanding, control and direction. When you hear someone say, "this child has a mind of its own!" They are absolutely right! Each brain is unique.

Children vary widely in characteristics affecting their socialization and adjustment. Some seem to naturally do the right thing; others are always in trouble. Differences in health, physical abilities, attractiveness, energy level, cognitive functioning and such, tells us that the nature of the needed support and direction, varies from child to child.

The family. A child's earliest support system is the family, and any structures that support a healthy family benefit the child. Sadly, too many of our children experience poverty, physical and verbal abuse, discrimination, rejection, violence or neglect. More parents than you might think still dish out corporal punishment despite clear evidence that it harms the child and promotes hostility and violence.

Education. The next major agency of socialization is our school system where many children thrive, and others learn more of the wrong kind of behavior.

Far too many students leave school unprepared for college, the work force or adult responsibility and devoid of a moral compass.

One of my daughters served as a volunteer in the Head Start program one summer. She was delighted with the way these pre-school children responded. They were excited about the experience, intellectually curious, friendly. and full of energy.

In the second half of the summer, she was assigned to work with children who had "failed" first grade (or had first grade failed them?). The contrast was unbelievable. They were discouraged, defeated, and depressed.

Corporal punishment.

Although we have seen the harm done by corporal punishment, the myth "spare the rod and spoil the child" still persists in some schools as well as some homes. Despite widespread efforts to eradicate it, the U.S. Supreme Court ruled (in 1977) that corporal punishment was permissible in public schools. Since then, 31 states have banned it (as of 2016). Worldwide, 48 countries, including Great Britain, now prohibit it. Yet, most of the world's children still live in countries in which such punishment is permissible.

Denmark not only prohibits corporal punishment in the school, but at home as well; the law requires that parents protect their children, not hurt them.

The media. We know that role models are a major source of learning. Today, children encounter a vast variety of models to emulate in the omnipresent media, including a raft of undesirable ones. Such models especially affect those boys who have no real-life male role model in their lives.

Violence in the Media. Does watching violence on television cause children to behave more aggressively? Back in 1968, when this question was being debated extensively, I was asked to write a paper on this topic. As I read study after study it became clear that watching violence does in fact encourage violent behavior in children. Even so, the effects are complex. The age of the child and several other variables have an impact. Then too, at times violence induces fear and anxiety. Subsequent research determined that violent video games produce similar results.

Here I take time for a brief digression. Just a few weeks after my paper, an article by psychologist Joyce Brothers summarized the same research and concluded it did not indicate any relationship between watching violence on TV and violent behavior. Perhaps not surprisingly since her review was written for TV Guide!

Dr. Brothers was a popular figure who first came to the public eye by winning the top prize on the game show the $64,000 Question in1955. The first woman who did so, she selected boxing as her topic and crammed to prepare for her opportunity. The resultant public recognition enabled her to establish a successful career hosting advice columns and television shows on popular ("pop") psychology.

Religion is one of the enduring sources of support for leading a positive life. People who follow religious principles, such as "Love one another" are happier and participate more in positive community activities

Youth Groups. For me, Boy Scouts and Sea Scouts played a significant role in my life from age 12 to 16, and friends I made there continue to do so. A wide number of other groups, including those supporting athletic activities, provide similar sources of positive socialization for our youth.

Gangs. Adolescents and young adults often form, or are inducted into, gangs involved in illegal activity and clashing with rival gangs. And we can draw a straight line from gang to prison. Convincing our youths to avoid gangs or to move from this gang culture to become responsible adults rather than prison inmates is a major challenge for our society.

Criminal Justice. Our complex criminal justice system, including our policing practices, our courts and our prisons have come under severe criticism today generating widespread public protests and demands for drastic reform.

To restrain those who have not been successfully socialized by family, school, or social agencies, we look to police to safeguard communities and "keep the peace." At times, they help get young people back on the right track. Far too often, they miss their mission. Accusations of police hostility and brutality towards African Americans has been a pressing issue fueling mass demonstrations demanding reform. Amnesty International has joined in, censuring the U.S. for the nearly 1,000 police killings per year with a disproportionate number of Black and Latino victims. What is the root of the problem?

Police culture.

As we have seen from research on control and violence, "police culture" is the main culprit. These research studies demonstrate that those whose job involves controlling the behavior of others come to emphasize their power, support one another in doing so and even dehumanize those they are intended to control. Add in anger, fear and racial hostility and you come up with an explosive mixture. As we might expect, the severity of the problem varies with the department and the individual police officer. Nevertheless, it is not just a case of some "rotten apples." It is a part of police culture.

The Courts. Judges have several options available including fines, probation, house arrest, community service and incarceration. In each case, they must decide which penalty will deter a lawbreaker from future violations, warn others of the consequences of criminal activity and protect the public. Our society considers juveniles separately since with greater maturity they often develop better self-control.

Ideally, courts should provide a way to reform offenders. On occasion that happens. More often they are sentenced to prison and hardened by their experience.

We currently have the largest prison population in the world, 2.2 million, more than half of them Black or Hispanic (let's not forget the million Whites as well), many of them wrongly convicted or sentenced to excessively long terms. I think of a former neighbor sentenced to five to ten years for buying marijuana for his friends at college!

Psychological research has revealed how behavior can be modified through the judicious use of reinforcement and reprimand. Why has it been so little utilized? Investment in incorporating this into our criminal justice system (in fact in all agencies involved in promoting prosocial behavior) would move our society forward dramatically.

Punishment in the past. Certain kinds of penalties in common use in times past, such as beatings, flogging and public hangings have been outlawed as abusive and cruel.

It was also ineffective. Much of our current practice is also.

In July 2020, the last public whipping post was removed from public display in Delaware. Between 1990 and 1945, 1,600 people had been subjected to this kind of abuse, most for petty offenses. Two-thirds of them were Black although Blacks constituted only one sixth of the population.

A friend and I, just out of military service in WWII went for a leisurely drive from our homes in Philadelphia in 1945. When we stopped for lunch, we were shocked to see signs COLORED and WHITE over the rest rooms. We had driven into Delaware. Little did we know that it was also the year of the last public flogging.

This past legacy of injustice reverberates today creating antagonism in our time for harsh punishment in times past.

The death penalty. The ultimate punishment, the death penalty, is still with us, although Amnesty International and other organizations have been working assiduously to eliminate it. Currently, two-thirds of the world's countries (but only19 U.S. states) have prohibited the death penalty. Pope Francis recently urged all countries to abolish it.

Prison. As for the American prison system, Craig Haney, since his research at Stanford, has been a tenacious advocate for prison reform through his research, writings, and court testimony.

Moreover, his work was influential in a United States Supreme Court 5-4 ruling that the California prison population must be reduced.

As an aside, I have a personal interest in his work since he was a student of mine in his first psychology course-and an outstanding one.

And when I think of problems with prisons, I can't help thinking of Lester Maddox, onetime Governor of Georgia. When asked what he was doing to improve the state prison system, he replied that he couldn't do much more unless they could start getting a better type of prisoner! Another case of shifting the blame away from those in positions of responsibility.

Stopping antisocial behavior. We can't just decry delinquency. Accepting responsibility and coordinating efforts to control disruptive activities would be a giant step in the right direction. Parents, schools, religious leaders, police, the courts and the public too often blame one another for delinquency and other aberrant behavior, rather than take positive action themselves.

Which move us to an oft-cited incident involving waiting for someone else to intervene-the Kitty Genovese case.

Bystander Apathy. In 1964, Kitty Genovese was murdered in front of her apartment. Thirty-eight of her neighbors heard her screams or saw her being stabbed, yet none of them made a move to assist her. Why the apathy? Psychologists began speculating and investigating that question.

Strangely enough, early studies, labeled the "bystander effect" discovered that the more people present, the less likely anyone is to act.

Darley and Batson then devised a series of enlightening experiments about helping behavior.

The Good Samaritan Studies. After recruiting seminary students for a study, they sent them to another building to prepare a talk. In one condition they told the subjects they were late, in the other that they had plenty of time. One task was to prepare a talk about the parable of the Good Samaritan. On their way to the building, they passed a man slumped in a doorway, moaning and coughing.

The researchers found that whether or not the seminarians were told to hurry had a major impact on helping behavior. In low hurry situations, 63% helped, in high hurry only 10%. Quite a few of them actually stepped over the victim! Ironically, this held true even for those going to speak on the parable of the Good Samaritan.

I once had a chance to be tested in a real-life situation. I was waiting to meet my wife where many Philadelphians met, at Wanamaker's department store, under the Eagle in the book section. Suddenly, I heard a woman's scream, coming from the mezzanine above. I looked around at the other people standing, seemingly frozen in place just as I was. I forced myself to the stairs. Just as I started up, a young man came flying down past me and out the door, shaking off a man who grabbed his arm. A few moments later a security guard, with another young man in tow, followed. He told us the two had attempted to rape a woman in the Women's Room. Why didn't we all rush to her aid at the sound of her first scream? I don't believe it was apathy. It struck me as more like a combination of fear of violence and confusion over what to do. That's why those in jobs requiring response to emergencies need extensive training.

Resolving conflict. In contrast to wondering why people follow authorities even those committing atrocities, psychologists also asked "how can we get groups to cooperate and avoid conflict"? A study attempting to throw light on this topic is the Robbers Cave experiment by Muzafir Sharif and Carolyn Wood, conducted over three weeks in a summer camp in Robbers Cave State Park, Oklahoma.

In this study, researchers split 22 eleven and twelve-year-old boys into two groups and placed them in competition with one another in various camp games. Valuable prizes awaited the winners. Both groups quickly developed hostility to one another. and in each group, aggressive boys took charge. In the final stage of the study, tensions were reduced through introducing a task that required cooperation between the groups (researchers disabled the camp water supply). More positive, problem-solving types stepped in as leaders and the groups began to work together.

We can hardly jump to firm conclusions based on this study. Still, it, and similar research, suggest the following:

Hostile and aggressive attitudes arise when groups compete for limited resources. As we have mentioned earlier, this hostility often hurts both groups.

Interacting with another group does not automatically better relationships between the two. Circumstances that foster positive attitudes such as working together for a common goal are particularly effective. Failure to give sufficient attention to this slowed progress in racial relations.

One way of generating positive intergroup relations is to find superordinate goals that promote cooperative efforts.

We have often heard it said that we need an invasion of aliens from outer space to assure that countries on earth would work together. Other global threats, however, such as our current corona virus pandemic, have provoked more conflict than cooperation, with too many instances of finger-pointing and too few looking in the mirror.

An award-winning 1966 film, The Russians are coming, the Russians are coming, offers a fictional look at how two groups in conflict might work together in an emergency. A patrol from a Russian submarine stranded on a sandbar at Cape Cod goes ashore and explores the area, uncertain what to do. Soon, in response to reports that Russians are invading, the chief of police and the head of the local veterans' group form a body of armed citizens to confront the perceived threat.

As the submarine captain and police chief flash their guns and exchange threats in a hostile shouting match, a small boy who had climbed up to the church steeple to see the drama, falls from his perch. Fortunately, his belt catches on a gutter, but this still leaves him hanging precariously in the air. Immediately, Islanders and Russians join forces to form a human pyramid and rescue the boy.

Organizational research. One of the most dynamic areas of research on groups has been Organizational Research. Most of us work in an organization. Psychologists have come up with a number of impressive real-world results telling us what makes them successful (or not).

As I previously mentioned, one notable series of studies, I first came across when I was teaching a course in Industrial/Organizational Psychology in the mid 1980's. They form the basis of a book by Robert Levering A Great

Place to Work, What Makes Some Employers so good and most so bad. In contrast with most research in the field which examined organizations from the top down, this focused on employees' views. What did they like about the place where they worked? Their answer was not so much a program of employee benefits. What mattered, rather, was the quality of relationships in the workplace. These relationships were not, merely a nice incidental add-on, but a key component in an organization's performance. The book provided a useful perspective and, since then, its message has spread.

A great workplace possesses many features that make it a positive experience for workers and managers at every level, and for the entire organization.

Does the place where you work provide them? Let's take a look.

Focus. A great work environment provides clear direction for employees at all levels. Everyone knows their responsibilities and how their job influences success of the whole company.

Enthusiasm. If we believe we are doing something worthwhile, we become enthusiastic about our jobs. Knowing that our work is valued and valuable means a great deal to all of us.

Teamwork. In order to maximize productivity, teamwork is a top priority of any great workplace. Members collaborate and celebrate their achievements. Every type of group benefits from teamwork. In fact, a 2018 special issue of American Psychologist (Vol 73, No. 4) reveals the status of ongoing scientific research on teamwork in such diverse areas as health care, the military, aviation, space exploration and business.

Fairness. We all want to feel recognized and reinforced for our efforts and know that our concerns will be heard and addressed. Innovation. The workplace is open to positive change and encourages new ideas. Employees in doing their jobs are in a natural position to notice how improvements can be made. Innovation percolates up from the bottom if encouraged. In contrast, I have heard workers say, "I don't get paid to think!" What they mean is, "My ideas are not welcome".

Leadership. As we have said, the adage that leaders should be fair and firm, really means they should know employees and treat them with respect, and that they should be clear in communicating their responsibilities and listening to their concerns. Then too, good leaders serve as positive role models by their commitment and their positive relationships with colleagues.

Friendliness. One of the things I treasure about my "record-breaking" tenure at La Salle University (70 years) was that it was such a congenial place. Most of my best friends I met there, and students, faculty, staff and administrators liked and respected one another. I also appreciated the unbounded humor of so many colleagues, adding enjoyment to the work.

One outcome of this research recommending these seven conditions, was the founding of the Great Place to Work Institute. It stimulates businesses around the world to conduct additional studies and use their results to improve workplaces. In turn, better workplaces make for a better society.

Most major newspapers regularly publish ratings of businesses based on employee opinions.

National development. We move next from research in organizations, to studies of nations. In which countries do you think residents are happiest? We have had general impressions to go by over the past. Now, in recent years, a growing body of empirical study has gone into answering this question.

Bhutan, a small Asian nation by the Himalayas, took the initiative in this. They decided that rather than focusing mainly on the gross national product, a measure of economic growth, they should study national happiness, a measure of psychological well-being. Beginning there in the 1970s, the movement gradually spread throughout the world. Several organizations, including the Gallup poll, began sampling people and publishing results.

In 2015, UN Secretary-General Ban Ki-moon, stressing that social progress is as important as economic and political progress, said "happiness for the entire human family is one of the main goals of the United Nations."

Because of this rising interest in happiness research, many governments, and organizations are now using these results in developing policies that support better lives.

As you can imagine, the sampling process is far from ideal and results subject to controversy. For example, what do people think if you ask them how happy they have been recently? Are we asking about joie de vivre or contentment?

An additional concern is that past studies have concentrated on average well-being. Inequality of well-being is even more important- just as inequality of income is more important than average income. Consequently, researchers have now turned to studying this inequality. So far, unfortunately, they find it increasing in most countries and in the world as a whole.

You may be interested in highlights of the 2020 report.

Scandinavian countries scored highest along with Australia, Ireland and Switzerland. The United States came out well above average.

Many of the least happy countries bordered on Russia. Fear of Russian domination, and controversy within the counties over how to relate to Russia seem to be at work here. Among such nations, Poland had the highest rank.

For many European countries, membership in the European Union produced a sharp increase in satisfaction.

Countries in Sub-Saharan Africa have moved up on the scale as fighting within and between countries has markedly decreased. Leaders such as Nelson Mandela and Desmond Tutu deserve considerable credit for this. One related outcome is that tourism has become a growth industry in Africa.

It is no surprise that armed conflicts make people unhappy, and peaceful agreements raise happiness scores.

Governance. The Founding Fathers of our country envisioned much more than simply freedom from English rule. They sought a new type of government, one "of the people, by the people and for the people" as Lincoln described it fourscore and seven years later. A country where people had the right to the pursuit of happiness. In their planning, they drew on ideas of philosophers and scientists of that period, known as the Age of Reason or The Enlightenment. It questioned the traditional authority of the monarchy and the Church and incorporated the notion that humanity could be improved through rational change utilizing empirical evidence as exemplified by science. It stood for freedom of speech, freedom of press, and religious tolerance.

Franklin was a prolific participant in all of this. Both his official position as an ambassador, and his informal relationships with international scientific and intellectual societies provided him with a broad perspective. Our new nation would not exist in isolation. We would be a participant in the politics, economics, and culture of the rest of the world.

Looking back on the painstaking process of constructing a constitution for this new country, I would like to revisit two issues that turned out to be crucial. Ben Franklin played a significant role in each. The first asked should future generations be able to modify the constitution, or should it be immutable? Franklin, imagining major changes that might take place in science and in society, urged that a process for amending it be included. On this, the delegates agreed. Without these provisions African Americans might still be enslaved and women still disenfranchised.

The second issue: should slavery be prohibited in the new country? Although for a time he himself had slaves, by the time of the Constitutional Convention Franklin had become an active abolitionist and President of the Pennsylvania Society for Promoting the Abolition of Slavery. On this issue, he did not prevail. Delegates were divided. Representatives from states where plantations depended on slave labor called it a "necessary evil." Eventually, delegates settled for an ill-fated compromise in which the decision was relegated to the states. Imagine the difference in our nation today if Franklin had been able to carry the day!

International Relations

Nations of the world, large and small, weak, and powerful, with their people living under different kinds of governance and a wide variety of living conditions face the difficulty of sharing resources and competing for them. In the process, competition often leads to conflict, including war. Efforts to prevent and resolve conflicts and to live in harmony have a long history and are ongoing. Sometimes one nation reaches out to aid another in time of need. People remember it. A recent news story (June 2020) caught my attention. It tells of a time in 1847 when the Choctaw Nation, themselves impoverished after their long trek known as the Trail of Tears, that forcibly moved Native Americans west, raised $170 for Irish peasants starving during the potato famine. In 2020, Irish families have now raised $2.7 million to assist Native Americans hit hard by the Covid-19. They remembered!

Some efforts at harmony involve permanent organizations set up for that purpose. You are no doubt familiar with a number of them, but a sample of these is worth revisiting and their goals worthy of support.

The United Nations (UN) is "an intergovernmental organization that aims to maintain international peace and security, foster friendly relations among nations, achieve international cooperation, and be a center for harmonizing the actions of nations.".

In 1946, shortly after its formation, I had the opportunity to participate in a mock UN assembly of college students during spring break held at Lafayette College in Easton, Pennsylvania. Each college represented a country. We supported and opposed various proposals, formed coalitions and in general experienced the way the UN functioned. One incident stands out in my mind. A delegation representing one of the Soviet Republics managed to get a committee to agree that the United States should share secrets of atomic weapons with other countries. We rallied delegates against it and were confident of defeating it in the General Assembly. The resolution, however, was never submitted for a vote. Instead, it was released to the media. So, newspapers the following day featured headlines proclaiming "College Students Say U.S. Should Share Atomic Secrets With USSR." In the process, I learned a few lessons, including the importance of checking the story behind the story to get at the truth.

The International Peace Bureau, founded in France in1891, is considered the world's oldest. It was awarded the Nobel Peace Prize in 1910, and Henri La Fontaine who headed the organization received one in 1912. Several other Nobel Peace Prize laureates have been members of the IPB.

The Nobel Peace Prize is the best known and most prestigious recognition for contributions to peace. Since its inaugural year in 1901 until 2019, it has been awarded to 27 organizations and107 individuals. The International Committee of the Red Cross has been so honored three times and the Office of the United Nations High Commissioner for Refugees twice

Over the course of time it has recognized a wide variety of efforts to foster peace, as we can see from this sample of the 27 organizations that were recipients: Doctors Without Borders, The European Union, The Quakers' Friends Service Committee, The International Labor Organization, The U.N. Children's Fund (UNICF) and The International Atomic Energy Commission. And here are a few from the 127 individuals: Theodore

Roosevelt, Albert Schweitzer, Linus Pauling (who also received a Nobel in chemistry), Martin Luther King, General George Marshall, Mother Teresa, Lech Walesa (Poland), The Dalai Lama, Kim-Day-Jung (S. Korea), Maureen Corrigan (Ireland) and Barack Obama. Psychologist Carl Rogers was a nominee for his work in Northern Ireland and South Africa the year Mother Teresa was the recipient. Mahatma Gandhi, nominated three times, never received the award.

Other organizations besides the Nobel offer awards for work that benefits humanity. Recently, The National Institute of Health, awarded the 2020 $1.3 million Templeton prize to Francis Collins, Director of the National Institute of Health for his "integration of faith and reason." He supervised the Human Genome Project, intending to decipher the genetic code of life and wrote the 2006 best-seller The Language of God: A scientist presents evidence for belief.

And let us not forget our world's religions. They have great potential for improving our societies if they can cooperate in promulgating their basic message of love for one another and incorporate psychological findings in accomplishing this.

In addition to organizations awarded a Nobel Prize, numerous others are active worldwide endeavoring to improve societies. The following are a few of the larger ones:

United Way is a worldwide organization helping people enhance their lives through education, income and health.

The Salvation Army provides food, clothing and other necessities of life to people throughout the world.

Feed the Children delivers food, medicine and clothing to needy children around the globe.

Gifts in Kind partners with companies to encourage them to donate their products, rather than cash. They then use these products where most needed.

Americares delivers medicine, medical supplies and aid wherever there is a natural disaster anywhere in the world.

Catholic Charities has its primary focus on reducing poverty worldwide. The Peace Corps. A U.S. Government Agency formed during the Kennedy administration. Since its inception, more than 235,000 American volunteers have served with it in 140 countries, working to assist their development and advance international relationships, Currently due to the coronavirus pandemic all volunteers have been withdrawn from these countries.

Other Organizations. And that's just a small sampling! I know quite a few people who have worked with other organizations that benefit humanity. One of my long-time friends and colleagues in our psychology department was active in Rotary International a global network of over a million members. When he retired, he joined in their fight to wipe polio off the face of the earth. I recall his description of his experience administering drops of vaccine to children in Madagascar. Such voluntary actions managed to reduce polio cases by more than 99.9 percent. One last push is still needed to eliminate it entirely.

Two other close friends from La Salle fill me in about the actions of Habitat for Humanity which employs volunteers to construct or rehabilitate homes in communities in the USA and abroad. The sister of one, at one time, joined a team in Northern Ireland where they alternated between building a home for a Protestant family and a Catholic one. My other friend has a son who volunteers with this organization as needed. When a hurricane hits Puerto Rica or the Texas coastline, or when some other community needs help, they call, and he goes.

The most prominent volunteer with Habitat has been former U.S. president and Nobel Peace Prize laureate Jimmy Carter. For years, he and his wife, Rosalynn, joined by thousands, have donated one week of the year to building homes for Habitat.

And let's not forget The International Positive Psychology Association. As we mentioned, its mission is, to "further the science of positive psychology across the globe…". It has several thousand members from 80 countries.

With all the effort nations and organizations are putting into moving our world toward a better one, you may ask, what should we aim for? What should an ideal society look like? Since antiquity, this question has captured the imagination of thinking people and spawned fantasies of fictional utopias.

The word "utopia" was first employed by Thomas More for his 1516 book. but going back at least as far as Plato's The Republic, philosophers and other writers have offered their ideas on the topic. Prominent among them are:

A Modern Utopia (1905) by H. G. Wells – A worldwide social order in which social relationships and technology are in continuous improvement, physical labor minimized, and freedom guaranteed.

Lost Horizon is a 1933 novel by James Hilton which was turned into a film in 1937 by director Frank Capra. It depicts a utopian community called Shangri-La, hidden in the mountains of Tibet.

Walden II (1948), in which psychologist B.F. Skinner, a leading proponent of using reinforcement to foster positive behavior, applies these insights to form a fictional utopian society. It is organized in such a way that people are reinforced for actions enhancing the common good.

Far more writers have been concerned that attempts to manipulate society "for the common good," may create a monster in which life is akin to that under the Nazis and the Holocaust (or other hellish regimes). They have provided us with a wealth of dystopian literature. A sampling of these include:
   Brave New World (1932) by Aldous Huxley
   It Can't Happen Here (1935) by Sinclair Lewis
   Anthem (1938) by Ayn Rand
   The Moon Is Down (1942) by John Steinbeck
   Animal Farm (1945) and
   Nineteen Eighty-Four (1949) by George Orwell
   The Hunger Games Series (2017) Suzanne Collins

Understanding the change process, as we have seen in this chapter, enables you to become a more effective participant in supporting positive change in your community

.

Chapter 19.
Summary and Conclusions

We have spent considerable time together discussing how Ben Franklin met the challenges of his day, lived a remarkable and successful life, and contributed mightily to the progress of our society at a crucial time in our history. I hope this has stimulated your thinking about your own life and our current place in history.

Starting with yourself and your values, psychology reminds us that people are happier when working in concert with others to accomplish projects of value and contributing to the common good. To be effective in doing so, it helps to become a successful and influential person who knows how to work well with others.

Unfortunately, as psychological research and clinical practice makes clear, people are flawed, some seriously so. You have no doubt come across people who seek satisfaction in accumulating power and prestige by besting others by any means possible. Benjamin Franklin encountered despots whose intransigence convinced him that the Colonies only recourse was to oppose them forcefully. In a similar manner he exposed charlatans such as Mesmer who duped followers into believing he possessed extraordinary powers.

Ben had an insatiable intellectual curiosity. He read widely in philosophy, religion and the classics, but he leaned more heavily on research in empirical science, even when it disagreed with traditional beliefs.

Currently, when faced with the Corona Virus Pandemic, we see the tragic outcome from ignoring or denying recommendations of science.

And this current pandemic is a wakeup call to the need to work together to address societal problems. The wide gap in cases of the virus between Blacks and Whites, for example, is attributed to differences in general health care, more crowded neighborhoods and the need to work, even under conditions of high exposure to the virus. Improvement in any of those conditions would not only help Blacks. It would help all of us. We are all interconnected. So, discrepancies between agencies in our society that impact the two groups alert us that something more general is wrong. Police abuse, a more serious and more obvious problem for Blacks, is an outgrowth of a more general culture of abuse in the process of controlling behavior; improved education for Blacks adds more talent to meet national needs and helps reduce the number of unemployed and underemployed people. Every step of the life cycle, from prenatal health and childcare to retirement communities and nursing homes requires our attention in order to build a better community for all of us.

Psychology and other behavioral sciences are also a valuable source of progress for each of us and for our society. Here, even more people discount empirical findings and depend on ideas passed from generation to generation and modified by their own limited, often biased, experience. They know a lot of psychology; some useful; some partially right, and some completely at odds with the evidence.

Behavioral scientists find that careful analysis of past behavior reveals what to expect in the future. For example, if a person suffering from bipolar disorder is extremely hyperactive, unable to sit still, stop rambling or concentrate on anything, we can predict that a period of serious depression will soon follow.

And, if a person is afflicted with a major depression, we know that suicide is a very real danger. Similarly, the pattern of behavior Trump has exhibited throughout his life, would hardly lead us to expect him to retire to a relaxing life of leisure in Florida, playing golf and downing diet cokes. Since he first arrived on the political scene, large numbers of mental health professionals have concluded that he is seriously flawed psychologically.

It is not necessary for them to see him as a patient in their office to recognize him as a "high-functioning sociopath"- bright and charismatic, but devoid of a moral compass. He craves power and adulation, he manipulates people (using flattery, patriotism, theater, threats, punishments) to get more and more for himself without concern for others, or for what it does to the country. He will not change. Unfortunately, many people admire his unbridled self-confidence, his quick decision making and his disdain for tradition. They get caught up in his world of fake news, conspiracy theories and disdain for reality.

How can this happen to otherwise intelligent people? For a compelling case study, read Tara Westover's 2018 best-selling memoir, *Educated*.

Born to survivalists in the remote mountains of Idaho, there was no official record of her existence. Her family was isolated from mainstream society and wanted it that way. No birth certificate, no vaccinations and no enrollment in school (anything of value would be learned in the family and in their variant of the Mormon religion. In particular, no contact with the federal government, the enemy of the people, against whom they are stockpiling arms and ammunition for a final battle to come.

When she manages to enroll in college, including study at Harvard and obtaining a Ph.D. from Cambridge

University she becomes "educated" and rejects the beliefs of her dysfunctional family. Or can she? For rejecting their beliefs means rejecting them, and she still craves their love and affection. Perhaps their truth is a better one after all!

The family is not the only group with which we identify. Loyalty to other groups, including political parties, fringe groups and their charismatic leaders, also affects our belief **system. No matter how far-fetched a view might be, if leaders in our political party extol it, we believe it must be true.**